AUTHOR

Miroslav Krleža was born in 1893 in Zagreb, then a city in the Austro-Hungarian Empire, and died there in 1981, after it had become part of socialist Yugoslavia. He was educated in military academies that served the Habsburg monarchy. However, after fighting on the Eastern Front during the First World War, he was sickened by the War's lethal nationalism and became a fervent anti-militarist. Krleža joined the Communist Party of Yugoslavia in 1918, but his opposition to Stalin's artistic dictum of socialist realism, as well as his refusal to support Stalin's purges, led to his expulsion from the Party in 1939. He nevertheless helped found several literary and political journals, and became a driving force in Yugoslavia's literature.

TRANSLATOR

Željko Cipriš was born in Zagreb, Croatia (former Yugoslavia), and obtained a doctorate in East Asian Languages and Cultures from the Graduate School of Arts and Sciences at Columbia University. He is professor of Modern Languages and Literature at the University of the Pacific, and translator of several classic Japanese leftist novels.

In this solitary period, I hope you find the Balkans' revolutionary and satirical write-up entertaining.

HARBORS RICH IN SHIPS

THE SELECTED REVOLUTIONARY
WRITINGS OF MIROSLAV KRLEŽA,
RADICAL LUMINARY OF MODERN
WORLD LITERATURE

Translated and with an Introduction by Željko Cipriš

MONTHLY REVIEW PRESS
New York

Copyright (English translation) © 2017 by Željko Cipriš
All Rights Reserved

Library of Congress, Cataloging-in-Publication Data
Names: Krleža, Miroslav, 1893–1981, author. | Cipriš, Željko, translator.
Title: Harbors rich in ships : the selected revolutionary writings of
   Miroslav Krleža, radical luminary of modern world literature / translated
   and with an introduction by Željko Cipriš.
Description: New York : Monthly Review Press, 2017. | Includes
   bibliographical references.
Identifiers: LCCN 2017009914 (print) | LCCN 2017010024 (ebook)|
ISBN 9781583676486 (pbk.) | ISBN 9781583676493 (hardcover) |
ISBN 9781583676509 (trade) | ISBN 9781583676516 (insitutional)
Classification: LCC PG1618.K69 A2 2017 (print) | LCC PG1618.K69
(ebook) | DDC
   891.8/235—dc23

MONTHLY REVIEW PRESS, NEW YORK
monthlyreview.org

Typeset in Arno Pro and Amarelinha

5 4 3 2 1

Contents

Preface | 7

Introduction | 9

※

The Battle at Bistrica Lesna | 17

Barrack 5B | 43

Guardsman Jambrek | 59

National Guardsmen Gebeš and Benčina
Talk about Lenin | 89

Finale: Attempt at a Five-Thousand-Year Synthesis | 95

Death of Prostitute Maria | 105

The Glembays | 111

※

Glossary | 217

Bibliography | 229

*To revolutionary dissidents around the globe,
and to the creation of a better world, free from the muck of ages.*

"Jesus Christ was innocent too," said Švejk, "and all the same they crucified him. No one anywhere has ever worried about a man being innocent."
—JAROSLAV HAŠEK
THE GOOD SOLDIER ŠVEJK, 1923

When it comes to marching many do not know
That their enemy is marching at their head.
The voice which gives them their orders
Is their enemy's voice and
The man who speaks of the enemy
Is the enemy himself.
—BERTOLT BRECHT, *WAR PRIMER*, 1955

Hope, I thought to myself, cannot be said to exist or not to exist. It is like a path across the land: when many people go the same way, it comes into being.
—LU XUN, "HOMETOWN," 1921

Preface

> Our heads are full of dreams like a harbor rich in ships.
> —MIROSLAV KRLEŽA

HUMANKIND IN THE EARLY DECADES of the twenty-first century is going through a momentous transformation of consciousness: a growing realization that we have outgrown the dominant socioeconomic system and ought to move beyond it. The "vegetarian tiger" theory of capitalism—the notion that the system is not intrinsically predatory but can be tamed into benevolence—is becoming less convincing by the day as the voracious beast blithely continues to devour lives throughout the world. Although the overarching tragedy of economic polarization, overwork, exploitation, malnutrition, and countless humiliations that afflict hundreds of millions across the globe may lead to cynicism or despair, it can also be conducive to vigorous thought and collective action.

Art plays a tremendously important role in our efforts to emancipate ourselves from a stultifying status quo and to envision and engender a happier future. Artists who are no longer physically with us often prove to be at least as adroit as our own contemporaries at deepening our insights, invigorating and encouraging us in our search for a way out of the plutocratic labyrinth. Such artists form a sort of transnational and trans-temporal community of liberators, men and women whose caliber of intellectual and aesthetic accomplishments transforms them into neo-abolitionists. They are powerful and exhilarating allies in our long struggle *against* a new, incomparably more productive and sophisticated—yet no less pernicious—form of subjugation; and *for* a world of generosity, cooperation, leisure, intellectual growth, and happiness.

Miroslav Krleža produced much of his most powerful and iconoclastic work before age forty. This book presents for the first time a selection from it in English. It is my hope that I've done justice to this outstanding writer.

I wish to thank my sons Ljubomir Ryu and Shane Satori for reading through these translations and for their numerous and most helpful suggestions and corrections. This book is dedicated to them, and to a brighter future for us all.

Introduction

MIROSLAV KRLEŽA, A PRODIGIOUS AND PROLIFIC modernist writer, was born in Agram (Zagreb), Croatia, on July 7, 1893. Croatia at the time formed a subaltern province in the sprawling and gradually disintegrating Austro-Hungarian Empire, ruled from Vienna by the Habsburg monarchy. Krleža attended elementary school in Zagreb, a preparatory military school in Pécs (modern Hungary), and the Ludovika Military Academy in Budapest. Inspired by Slavic anti-colonialism, Krleža in 1912 broke off his studies to travel to Serbia, a Slavic kingdom outside Austria's imperial orbit, and to volunteer for the Serbian army. Failing once, he tried again in 1913. The Serb authorities, suspecting him of being an Austrian spy, deported him to Austria-Hungary where he was arrested and stripped of his officer's rank.

In the summer of 1914 Europe exploded into a catastrophic war that would destroy over ten million young lives and leave behind more than twenty million wounded. In 1915, at the height of this horrific collision of empires, Krleža was mobilized as a private and sent to Galicia on the eastern front where German and Austro-Hungarian armies—the latter heavily reinforced by Czech, Slovak, Croat, Slovene, and other national-minority conscripts—fought against Russian imperial troops. In the spring of 1916 the tsar's general, Aleksei Brusilov, launched a massive offensive that continued throughout the summer and escalated into one of the deadliest battles in human history, with the Austro-Hungarian troops suffering the brunt of its more than two million casualties. Although Krleža lived unhurt through the Brusilov offensive, his health broke down and he spent most of the remainder of the war in military hospitals and spas. About forty of his friends from the military academy were killed in the war.

Like millions of people across the world, Krleža responded to the Russian Revolution of 1917 with tremendous enthusiasm, regarding it as a promising first step in liberating humanity from the intolerable violence of plutocratic tyranny. In 1918, after the collapse of Austria-Hungary and the formation of the Kingdom of Serbs, Croats, and Slovenes—Yugoslavia—Krleža joined the Yugoslav Communist Party. Together with writer August Cesarec, a fellow war veteran of the Austro-Hungarian army, he founded a left-wing journal called *Plamen* (Flame), and over the coming decades also published several other literary and political reviews. Krleža's artistic production, which had already commenced before the war, now grew at a stupendous pace, making him by the late 1920s one of Yugoslavia's leading literary and cultural personalities. The Yugoslav monarchist government, strongly antagonistic to Krleža's politics, occasionally banned his work, even shutting down his 1920 play *Galicia* an hour before its first performance.

In the 1930s, as the Soviet Revolution degenerated into Stalinism, Krleža's forceful opposition to Stalinist terror and restrictions against literary and artistic freedoms made him many enemies on the official left as well. After the 1939 publication of his polemical essay "A Dialectical Anti-Barbarian" (Dialektički antibarbarus), Krleža was expelled from the Communist Party. Nonetheless, he remained friends with a prominent Yugoslav Communist whose nom de guerre was Tito. Almost totally isolated, Krleža barely managed to survive the Second World War. His friend August Cesarec, with whom he had edited *Plamen*, was shot in 1941 by Croatia's Nazi puppet regime. Krleža himself was arrested three times and on one occasion informed that he would be shot, only to be unaccountably released (possibly thanks to the intervention of government minister and novelist Mile Budak). After the 1945 Communist victory over the monarchists and the Nazis, Krleža's position improved markedly though he continued to experience considerable hostility from the Stalinist left. He founded a new periodical in 1945 and was elected vice president of the Academy of Science and Art in 1947. Once the new Yugoslav leader—and Krleža's friend—Josip Broz Tito broke with Stalin in 1948 and took Yugoslavia out of the Eastern bloc, Krleža became able to live and work in relative freedom. In 1950 he helped found a national lexicographic institute where he served as longtime director and contributed to the compilation of numerous encyclopedias. Over the coming decades Krleža consistently strove to enrich Yugoslav cultural life and to expand the liberties of his fellow writers. Krleža's scathing critique of "socialist realism"—a

Stalinist literary decree that promoted anti-modernist realism, beaming optimism, and idealized depictions of the working class—was warmly endorsed by Yugoslav writers and won official acceptance. Throughout the remaining years of his long life Krleža continued energetically to work, speak, and write, publishing in 1969 a monumental novel, *Zastave* (Banners), dubbed by some critics "Croatia's *War and Peace*." He won various literary awards, including the Herder Prize, and saw his work translated into numerous languages. Krleža died in Zagreb on December 29, 1981, at the age of eighty-eight.

WORK

Krleža's opus is vast: it comprises over fifty volumes of poetry, plays, essays, novels, short stories, memoirs, and diaries. The literary sources that he draws on and develops reflect the extraordinarily wide range of his reading and include Erasmus, Góngora, Schopenhauer, Nietzsche, Marx, Whitman, Verhaeren, Dostoyevsky, Ibsen, Strindberg, Proust, Baudelaire, Rilke, Karl Kraus, Robert Musil, and Antun Gustav Matoš (a Croatian modernist writer). Krleža's writing is characterized by a powerful intelligence and erudition, vigorously inventive diction, idiosyncratic modernism, and incisive commentary on people and events. His politics permeates and unobtrusively reinforces his oeuvre. Implicit in Krleža's work is a conviction that humanity cannot be free from the miseries of poverty and war so long as it remains split in two: a powerful minority that owns and controls society's productive resources—landed estates, factories, mines, and the like—and a vast majority whose essentially dispossessed status forces it to do the lifelong bidding of the powerful few. The solution is to create a rational and humane society, a cooperative commonwealth whose productive resources are owned and controlled by all. Only thus can a genuine human history begin, and each individual become free to grow to his or her fullest human potential. For the present, alas, a sort of barbarism continues to hold sway, a dark age whose ironies, hypocrisies, indignities, and tragedies Krleža's work chronicles with tremendous passion, artistry, depth, and compassion.

CROATIAN GOD MARS

One of the early works instrumental in consolidating Krleža's growing literary renown was a book of short stories—*Hrvatski bog Mars* (Croatian God Mars)—whose first edition he published in 1922, at the age of twenty-nine. A major text in the history of antiwar literature, the collection forms a centerpiece in Krleža's literary response to the cataclysmic bloodbath of the world war and to the forces that brought it about. Its intensely readable stories, steeped in an atmosphere of bitter humor, sorrow, and outrage, abound in vividly drawn characters: apathetic bureaucrats, vainglorious officers, absurd reactionaries, impotent or sold-out intellectuals, miserable aristocrats, thuggish noncoms, and—unhappiest of all—hapless young conscripts, most of them peasants torn away from their families in poor provincial villages and plunged into colossal orgies of human sacrifice orchestrated by the corrupt elites of dying empires.

Though the stories are heartrending, the author's narrative skill, ferocious satire, sharpness of vision, and sympathy for the innocent victims, enables them to transcend pessimistic gloom and to convey a powerful impression that such horrendous suffering is ultimately gratuitous, that it can and must be overcome. Abolishing the organized savagery of contemporary war will certainly not be easy: it will require nothing less than a revolutionary transformation. Krleža's anti-militarism is indissolubly linked to anti-capitalism. A lifelong Marxist—indelibly radicalized, like Jaroslav Hašek, Bertolt Brecht, and so many others, by the crucible of the First World War—Krleža views militarism and war as integral components of the dominant socioeconomic system. Consequently, to oppose modern wars while embracing capitalism would be as absurd as to denounce feudal wars while championing feudalism. In fact, Krleža finds that feudalism partly survives in the social formation that grew out of it. Amid the enormous changes that mark the transition from feudalism to capitalism, Krleža also perceives a profound continuity—and even intensification—of exploitation, oppression, and degradation of ordinary people by the profit-driven new system. Rebels and liberators past and present are Krleža's heroes, be they intellectuals—like Galileo or Darwin—or plebeians. His admiration for Lenin, leader of the Russian Revolution that would eventually be mangled by Stalinist terror, parallels his admiration for the Croatian peasant revolutionary Matija Gubec, legendary leader of a great popular uprising of 1573, which was ultimately crushed by an alliance of domestic and foreign aristocrats.

Hrvatski bog Mars (Croatian God Mars) in its standard edition of about 400 pages is composed of seven stories of widely varying lengths, from 22 to 136 pages, and an extensive glossary of military terms and foreign words. The stories are "The Battle at Bistrica Lesna" ("Bitka kod Bistrice Lesne"), "A Royal Hungarian Guardsmen Novella" ("Kraljevska ugarska domobranska novella"), "Three Guardsmen" ("Tri domobrana"), "Barrack 5B" ("Baraka pet be"), "Guardsman Jambrek" ("Domobran Jambrek"), "The Death of Franjo Kadaver" ("Smrt Franje Kadavera"), and "A Croatian Rhapsody" ("Hrvatska rapsodija"). The first, fourth, and fifth stories translated here are probably the most widely admired and republished narratives in the collection. They were written in 1921 ("Barrack 5B" and "Guardsman Jambrek") and in 1923 ("The Battle at Bistrica Lesna"). The present volume also includes a sketch titled "National Guardsmen Gebeš and Benčina Talk about Lenin" ("Domobrani Gebeš i Benčina govore o Lenjinu"), a revealing autobiographical episode from late 1917 that Krleža published in the journal *Književna republika* (Literary Republic) in 1925, and reprinted in the glossary section of Croatian God Mars. In addition, this translation presents a mordantly satiric dramatic fragment titled "Finale: Attempt at a 5,000-Year Synthesis" ("Finale: Pokušaj pedesetvjekovne sinteze"), the concluding self-contained portion of Krleža's 1924 essay "Ten Bloody Years: Pacifist Reflections from 1914 to 1924" ("Deset krvavih godina: Pacifističke refleksije između 1914–1924").

THOUSAND AND ONE DEATHS AND THE GLEMBAYS

This volume also includes the fifth story from a collection of ten titled *Hiljadu i jedna smrt* (Thousand and One Deaths) which was originally published in 1932 and soon banned. "Death of Prostitute Maria" ("Smrt bludnice Marije") was written in 1924.

Among more than a dozen major dramas that Krleža wrote during his long literary career, the best known and possibly the most emblematic are three mutually independent though loosely linked plays that make up the so-called Glembay Trilogy: *Gospoda Glembajevi* (The Glembays, 1928), *U agoniji* (In Agony, 1928), and *Leda* (1930). Krleža's earlier plays, dating back to 1915, tend to be expressionistic and experimental. The Glembays, however, represents its author's temporary reversion to a more traditional and more broadly accessible form of theater. This extraordinary, multilayered portrayal of a family of the haute bourgeoisie on the verge of calamitous change reads almost as though Krleža were collaborating with Aeschylus, Marx, Ibsen, and Freud to construct a potent allegory. The play exposes the barbarous core of a socioeconomic system that Krleža thoroughly understood and loathed. Structured somewhat like a symphony, it begins with a slow adagio and then gradually builds in tempo and intensity, with each of its three acts (or movements, as it were) culminating in a dramatic climax.

Decades after the fratricidal war that dismembered what was once Yugoslavia, The Glembays remains a "hit" across its former republics, judging by the large and enthusiastic audiences that have attended its recent performances in Serbia, Croatia, and Slovenia. In view of the current state of affairs at home and abroad, with so many Glembayesque oligarchs ensconced in power and lording it over everyone else, Krleža's play may be timelier now than at any other point in its history.

A CONTROVERSIAL FIGURE

Overall, Miroslav Krleža continues to be highly respected across the territory of former Yugoslavia. His work is still printed in new editions, studied, and read, and his plays are often staged. He does not, however, command unanimous acclaim: like China's iconic modern writer Lu Xun, or Germany's Bertolt Brecht, Krleža evokes widely divergent and often passionately expressed reactions. Some of his compatriots denounce him as opportunistic, arrogant, and overrated, while others consider him one of the greatest authors East Europe has ever produced. A 2005 poll conducted by Croatia's leading daily, *Vjesnik*, found him to be the most popular Croatian writer of all time. The lexicographic institute where Krleža worked for decades now bears his name. Anniversaries of his birth and death are scrupulously commemorated; the house in Zagreb where he lived for some thirty years with his actress wife Bela is now a museum; and his statue stands in a nearby park—a similar one stands in a Budapest park too, not far from the former military academy (now a museum of natural history) where he once studied.

Krleža's political thought, though condemned or dismissed by some, lives on. A left-wing journal founded in late 2007 and written for readers throughout the former Yugoslavia is named *Novi Plamen* (New Flame), in honor of its illustrious predecessor that was published in 1919 by Krleža and his friend Cesarec. As global capitalism continues to lurch through its inexorable booms and slumps, economic and military agonies, and the melancholy business of exploitation as usual, something akin to Krleža's emancipationist Marxism may once again come to the fore both within and beyond the borders of his native land. In any event, the literary power and radical humanism of Krleža's work call for a much wider international audience than this remarkable author already enjoys. It is the translator's hope that this small volume will mark a modest contribution in that direction.

A NOTE ON TRANSLATION AND PRONUNCIATION

As a reflection of the fact that members of Zagreb's elite society on the eve of the world war were highly educated and multilingual, and spoke to one another in a sort of linguistic mélange, the text of *The Glembays* is shot through with words, phrases, and whole sentences in German, French, Latin, and other European languages. Modern performances of the play—such as the one by the Croatian National Theatre in Zagreb that I had the pleasure of watching in May of 2011—understandably tend to reduce the foreign expressions to a minimum. In translating Krleža's play, I have tried to do the same. When such expressions do remain, their translations can be found in the Glossary.

The Serbo-Croatian alphabet has thirty letters; a rough guide to how they sound is given below. If a letter does not appear, it means it is pronounced approximately as in English. Many words are accented on the first syllable, e.g., BIstrica LEsna, MAtija GUbec, JAMbrek, GEbeš, MIroslav KRleža.

A = like A in *America*
C = like TS in *lots*
Č = like CH in *charge*
Ć = like CH in *chips*
DŽ = like G in *giant*
Đ = like J in *jilt*
E = like E in *let*
G = like G in *game*
H = like H in *home*
I = like I in *Indian*

J = like Y in *yes*
LJ = like GLI in *Modigliani* or *imbroglio*
NJ = like Spanish **Ñ**, or like GN in *lasagna*
O = like AWE in *awesome*
R = trilled, as in Spanish
Š = like SH in *shell*
U = like OO in *soon*
Ž = like S in *pleasure*

The translation is based on several editions. "The Battle at Bistrica Lesna," "Barrack 5B," "Guardsman Jambrek," and "National Guardsmen Gebeš and Benčina Talk About Lenin" draw on Miroslav Krleža, *Hrvatski bog Mars* (Zagreb: Izdavačko Poduzeće Zora, 1965). "Finale" is taken from Miroslav Krleža, *Deset krvavih godina i drugi politički eseji* (Sarajevo: Oslobođenje, 1973), and "Death of Prostitute Maria" from Miroslav Krleža, *Hiljadu i jedna smrt* (Zagreb: Knjižara Ljevak, 2011). "The Glembays" relies on Miroslav Krleža, *Gospoda Glembajevi* (Zagreb: SysPrint, 1997).

THE BATTLE AT BISTRICA LESNA

THIS HISTORY OF A DETAIL OF THE BATTLE at Bistrica Lesna has been written in honor of the late Staff Sergeant Mato Pesek and six dead National Guardsmen of the second battalion of the second company, namely Vid Trdak, Franjo Blažek, Štef Loborec, Štef Lovrek, Imbro Pecak, and Matija Križ, who all fell during a heroic assault against Hill 313, thus shedding their royal Hungarian Guardsmen blood for the glory of the thousand-year kingdom of Saint István, in the spirit of the Hungaro-Croatian Agreement of the year 1868. May they rest in peace!

Reserve Staff Sergeant Mato Pesek and the six heroes of our chronicle at first all lived the quiet and bitter life lived by millions of our people who have for centuries suffered in our mud, ploughing it every spring and autumn to extract from it a fistful or two of grain, in order to eat a slice of wheat-cake at Easter and Christmas, the two bright days when a person does not feel the everyday burden on one's back, and only feeds the animals in the stable, and smokes and spits through teeth before the church all forenoon. In the interminable fog of oppression and toil, serfdom and beatings, in that feudal fog which in the year 1914 under the rule of Franz Josef the First still wound over our village like a mournful veil, all of our heroes felt this life of theirs as something created long ago by Lord God. Their grandfathers and great-grandfathers (no blame to them) had lived that way, so what was there to think about, what was there that could be done?

Lord God Himself (praise and glory to Him) created everything as it exists, and men are indeed wretches, when Lord God Himself created them as wretches, and so it is written down in the rectory and in the land registry, in the district paragraphs and in the laws at court, where Lord God Himself placed their Lordships to watch over the wretched men so that they properly carry out the Lord's Ten Commandments, pay taxes and surtaxes and excise taxes and serve as soldiers, and when it pleases Him, by God, that they also go to war.

And so our seven National Guardsmen fed and watered their Cvetan, and their Lisak, and their sick consumptive Rosy, morning, noon, and night, every God-given day in summer and winter, in rain and in snow, for thirty years already. They dug and ploughed, sowed wheat and barley, rye and buckwheat, turnips and corn, delved in the vineyard, mowed hay, cut the second growth and the third (if the autumn was happy and warm), and always did so from morning till night, so that their backs stabbed with pain, because our land is barren and limp, and must be ploughed deeply and fertilized painstakingly if it is not to betray and fail.

And all that was hard. For ploughing is hard. Stepping across wet furrows while sowing and harrowing is hard. Foddering the animals is hard. An ox is an ox, a pig is a pig, and they need everything prepared for them: straw and hay and grass and clover! They need the muck scraped off from under them and fresh matting laid out, they need to be groomed, and all that must be done, it must, because if a single day is missed the next already yawns as a disaster, so it must be done! And it is all devilishly difficult, and one must do everything alone! The fruit must be picked, the vinegar pressed, the hemp beaten, the linen spun, because everything factory-made is expensive, so one must strain with all one's might not to drop dead barefoot and naked. A person drills a well (one cannot do without a well), and that swallows up thousands in cash. Whitewashing a house tears off more cash, a storage shed must be roofed with thatch and then the young beasts eat a tenth of it, and if a man wants to clothe self and family, he must empty out the stable. And what about obligations, old debts, mortgages, lawyers? Never an end to worries! The peddler carries off baskets full of eggs and beans in exchange for two or three dishes, a glass cylinder, and ribbons; the shoemaker at the market flays one alive for those damned shoes; taxes grow, excise taxes pull in one direction, bankers and gendarmes in the other, foresters, notaries, officials, chaplains, teachers, they all carry off and steal: eggs and poultry, brandy and wine, bacon and walnuts (like skunks and martens), and all beat up on the man as though he were a beast. And the man sees that he is somehow at the very bottom and that they have piled up loads and loads upon him, but even when he sees what he sees, what good does it do him that all is clear to him?

Bureaucrats and gendarmes, barracks and jurisdictions, districts, documents, offices—it all seemed to our heroes like a machinery invented by their lordships only so that they could locate the vein of their wretched life and take a count of the peasants' sacks and pigs and mares. Yet that entire lordly, doctorly, Triune-Kingdomly regal machinery, and all those royal decrees of that bureaucratic apparatus, underestimated the mighty and invincible life in them, and when our heroes thought about themselves and about their life, it looked roughly like this: "Here is my cottage, whose roof is steep, and the rainwater flows left and right and so it doesn't pour onto my head. That's a good invention, not having the water pour onto my head; it's what my late grandfather gave me to inherit, that sooty warm roof of mine, and I will leave it to my son, because that is a wise thing: a roof overhead. (A man would be like a poor beast without it.) I sit under this mushroom of mine watching the smoke as it billows, while heavenly water flows and saturates the field. And that is good. My wife is spinning yarn like a spider, potatoes are rolling about inside the pot, and a juicy rib or two could also be found in the smoke of the attic. That is all. In fact, I don't need more. It is good to live! A man lights up a pipe at twilight and watches a cat's yellow eyes shining like fireflies within the vapor of the ox's stable. It is good to live!"

All those miserable villages and hamlets of Zagorje, Prigorje, and Kalnik, scattered across forests and ravines, experienced in their past many, many catastrophes, and that final Habsburg war, which rode into the village one early evening when wheat was being threshed and winnowed, and all the village threshing grounds echoed with the dull pounding, that dismal war was for these people neither the first nor the last disaster. They had been burned to the ground several times, perished from plague and cholera, from famine, and aristocratic beatings. When the Turks flattened the fortresses of Karlovac and Podravina, they burned down the entire region, and the Austrian harquebusiers from Parma, Piacenza, and Spezia, and the Spanish and Swiss condottieri, under Austrian and papal banners, plundered all they could to the last sausage in the smokehouse and the last thread in a weaver's home after the catastrophic Stubica uprising of the year 1573. Hungarian gendarmes shot at these people in the spirit of the Agreement of the year 1868, Forty-Eighters and deserters from Custozza and Solferino raped their women and girls, and women when giving birth continued with their own hands to cut their newborns' umbilical cords with a sickle, and rose on the third day after delivery, and the dead had wine poured over them as in old pagan times. On the shores of European seas countless empires rose and crumbled, new lands were discovered, life changed from its foundations—yet all that mattered nothing to the life here. True, churches and penitentiaries were constructed in the valleys: stone buildings with banners and Roman crosses, with lightning rods and organs, iron bars and paragraphs. But all those penitentiaries and offices and churches had not existed yesterday, and it was quite possible that those churches and documents and paragraphs will not exist tomorrow either, and Jezuševo and Saint Jalžabet and Saint Ivan will once again be called Lisjak and Vučja Jama as before, and that will be that! Glory to God!

Observing matters and measuring events by this elevated and experienced criterion, our people of course were not greatly perturbed by that so-called war.

"Huh! War indeed!"

"Eh, my God! War! What can you do? Their lordships must know what they want when they're pushing this war!"

"That's their lordly affair, this war of theirs!"

It happened and the news broke that the war had bitten a leg off this man or that, and by God a head as well. Women started to reek of iodine, and it was heard that some men had fled up into the forests to join the Green Cadre of deserters (but that shears the wealthy more than it does the serfs, that Green Cadre, so let that turn out as it will).

"There was a time when there was no war, so a time will come again when there won't be any!"

"Women have gone rotten, God's truth, but men in the barracks and hospitals are no better!"

"To each his own. Who lives through it, sees what comes of it! Everything has its season. Every dog will have his day!"

It all began idyllically. To the tillers and cowherds who had all their lives slept in stables and jostled with horned animals, to them being in an asphalted city (where, when it rains, pavements glisten like mirrors) seemed at first easier than that desperate and dark drudgery, and so they felt as if they had surfaced from their unbearable, hard, convict-like existence—for a minute. They had heard talk about the wonderful land of Schlaraffe, where roasted ducks and chicks fly into people's mouths, spitted pigs and piglets graze in the meadows, and silver watches and chains dangle from trees, and the urban life appeared to them during their first days in the city as just such a Schlaraffe. Nothing but shops with cured meat products! Rumps and ribs and red bacon of fat pigs, the deadly wounds neatly sealed with oily black soot, nails thrust through bloody holes, swollen intestines hanging, overripe sausages dripping, while cracklings exhale their aroma in porcelain dishes, wound with wire lest they fall apart. Nothing but cured meat! A city filled with cured meat! Hams hanging like flags! And in butcher shops, severed heads of white piglets, cloven calves around the church, white sheets in the wind all nicely doused with fragrant fresh blood, butchers' bloody hands imprinted on sheets, nothing but fine barbershops redolent of the finest soap, where barbers' dishes hang squeaking and squealing sweetly in the wind. And the countless famous inns and restaurants painted in ultra-fine colors, nothing but black tomcats and cannoneers, cannons, then white tomcats and skinned chicks with broken joints, stabbed through with five-pronged forks, then large glasses of foamy beer, and in the windows oily pancakes and fritters and pies and pastries, all of that fragrant, all of it singing. How magnificent it must be here on a Sunday afternoon, when a man's pocket packs an entire bundle, and he sips a drop of plum brandy and mead, sweetens his mouth with a crimson heart-shaped honey cake and washes it all down with wine and mineral water, and there are girls and tambouras and accordion, dancing rattles the inn, and female breasts are warm, so that you bite them and on the burning roof of your mouth feel the salty sweat and fluid of the female body, the nakedness, and you dance like a bloody masquerader, beautifully drunk, nothing but girls, serving maids, starched underskirts, red ribbons, bare black muddy knees and thighs, dancing, tambouras, bagpipes, *du du, du du, digu gigu dun knee*, granny loves her bunny, *yoo hoo hoo, yoo yoo, ee yoo hoo hoo.*

Reserve Staff Sergeant Mato Pesek and Guardsmen Vid Trdak, Franjo Blažek, Štef Loborec, Štef Lovrek, Imbro Pecak, and Matija Križ began this affair of warfare in such an idyllic manner too, with dance on a Sunday afternoon, but later on, by God, the affair grew huge and inflamed like a wound, and our heroes did indeed travel hundreds and hundreds of miles by train and on foot and did much moaning in hospitals and prisons and learned many truths before that Sunday morning when they were fated to fall one after the other at Bistrica Lesna, during assault on Hill 313.

On the morning that the battle was expected to take place, Guardsman Vid Trdak was the saddest of all. He had dreamed about his children, and then he recalled the void, that horrible void into which he had peered fewer than five days ago, and something tightened in his throat so that he could not even drink his black coffee, but poured it into the mud. Just before his departure for the city, for the barracks, he had buried his wife, leaving at home two children, the elder a boy of seven, and the younger four years old. He had quarreled with his own relatives and with those of his wife, and until the arrival of the telegram notifying him to go, spent many and many a night groaning on a stinking straw mattress, wondering how he could take care of the children. On the last night, he hit upon the idea of going to the resplendent royal Croatian-Slavonian-Dalmatian government, up at Marko's Square, to the illustrious Viceroy himself, and complaining to the Viceroy: What will happen to his children when he departs for the front? Let the illustrious Viceroy do something about this.

And so our Vid Trdak trudged through many doors on Marko's Square, and knocked on many in vain. He did not know whether to leave the cap on his head and salute like a proper soldier, or to bow, cap in hand, like a proper peasant and serf when he begs for his right. And so in some places he saluted bareheaded, and was laughed at, while at others he was thrown out for being an insolent swine and entering office chambers with his head covered: "Surely the lice on your head are not about to catch a cold!" Thus did he, on his Way of the Cross along the endless corridors and rooms of the royal government, happen upon a little man with expressionless eyes over whose head burned a yellow gaslight flickering loudly; the room was half dark.

Vid Trdak sang his sad song to the man, and the little old man with the expressionless glass eyes listened to him, gazed into the air above him, filled *Riz-Abadie* papers with medium-quality B-H tobacco, and placed the cigarettes side by side in a box that was nearly full.

"Yes! All right, my good man! I have heard all that already, my dear man! Yes! But where should I place your child? We have no space here for your children! We can put your case on record. That's it, my dear good man!"

"Oh sure! Please, doctor sir, your honor. What can I do with a record? I don't know what to do with the kids!"

"How much land do you have?"

"Two acres!"

"And a house?"

"A house too!"

"Well, then! Why shouldn't the children stay at home?"

"Sure, doctor sir! God help them! But the elder is seven years old! How can he stay by himself?"

"Look, my good man, you receive a monthly subsidy! Give the subsidy to someone in the village!"

"That lousy subsidy? Nobody'll do nothing for that!"

"Give it to your relatives, then! You have relatives, do you not?"

"I have 'em, I have 'em, and I wish I didn't have 'em. What the hell kind of relatives are they? May God wash 'em away in a flood! If they had things their way, there'd be grass growing over me five times already! They ploughed over my ridges, wrecked my house—what'll my kids do with relatives like that?"

"Well, what can we do, my good man? We will not, on principle, take children into the city! Because if we take them, your children will grow degenerate. They will become proletarianized. They will turn into paupers, you understand?"

"Sure, doctor sir, but ain't I a pauper? We're all paupers!"

"Have your children stay home on the land! Look, my good man, our people are degenerating as it is! And what will happen with us if we neglect our land, if we become proletarianized! Your children, my good man, will turn into urban riffraff!"

"But what'll I do with them? Then I gotta wring their necks so they don't die by theirselves! What can I do so my kids don't get to be riffraff? Your honor, I'm all riffed myself, God help them!"

"Dear man! Give them to good people somewhere!"

"Ah, but I ask you sir, where in the world are these good people?"

"Believe me, my good man, in the interest of your children it makes no sense to drag them into the city! It is in your children's interest that they stay on the land!"

"But where, where, by the five wounds of Christ? Stay where?" Vid Trdak desperately cried out in a stinking room on Marko's Square, and wanted to cry, so hard did his chest constrict. By the merciful God! He is setting off for the front tomorrow! How can this "doctor" not understand that he is setting off for the front tomorrow?

"Something will be found, my good man! We are going to write a nice memo to the borough administration!"

"The notary is a thief and a crook!"

"We'll write to the priest!"

"Ah, please sir! Our reverend." Vid Trdak waved his arm.

"We will write to them all! To all, my good man! To the district and to the county! We will urge that your subsidy be raised. Subsidies will now be raised in any case. There! Now we shall nicely draw up a record with you, my good man, and all will be well!"

As he signed that record up there at the royal government, there occurred to Vid Trdak the unpleasant thought that the record is a lie and that there is in fact no royal earthly government, no illustrious Viceroy, but merely one shortsighted man filling rolled cigarette papers and placing them next to each other in a little box. He had thought many times already that these records, offices, and documents were a fraud and a lie deceiving the peasants and the poor, but it had never all been as conclusively and irrefutably clear to him until that moment. It is all a void and there is no one anywhere, only in one half-lit, dark, dim room sits a man with glass eyes filling *Riz-Abadie* cigarettes with medium-quality B-H tobacco.

Marching next to Vid Trdak in second column's double file was National Guardsman Štef Loborec, an old campaigner, whose wound on his right shoulder burned under the straps of the knapsack and the Mannlicher. In vain did he shift the rifle from the right shoulder to the left, the cut hewed and pained him all the same with every step.

Guardsman Štef Loborec had chased about trenches and taken part in assaults here and there; been felled with a hit to the hip, and having healed in a hospital he was thrown at the front once more where he fell ill with typhus; lay dying a long time and didn't die, but was thrown into the recovery ward; had already been allotted a six-week leave when some special commission dropped into the hospital and threw him and thirty-seven others into the battalion barracks. Štef Loborec had not been married even two months when they tore him away from his wife, and he felt those six weeks of leave as "his sacred right," which no one was entitled to rob him of, and yet they had robbed him of his "sacred right." Thus embittered, he fell into a quiet apathy, and did not give a damn about anything. Before this he had gladly polished noncoms' shoes, and when sent to the canteen used to run there and back, but now he grumbled offended by everything and had to be smacked on the head or kicked in the rump to make him run in response to an order.

He was standing sentry when the company was being equipped for the front, and the next day there were no shoes left for him. The noncoms talked about some trunk in the main depot that supposedly had not arrived, and later they laughed at him. "Let him go in torn shoes! A gentleman who is chasing girls when the company's equipping—"

"I was standing guard!"

"Shut up! Get out! Insolent ox!"

He reported his case, had it written down, and did not get his shoes so he headed to the battalion to accuse his company, to get his "right": why should he make a gift of his shoes to the thieves at the depot?

But they drove him out of the battalion HQ with a kick, called him a convict, dog, ox, swine, and a crook! "Better take care you don't get hanged before the morning!"

Stumbling down the battalion stairs, he skinned himself against the banister, and deeply depressed, turned toward the depot; the depot warehouses were fastened shut with heavy iron bars and locked with padlocks. Everything before him was fastened shut and locked with a padlock, and he wanted nothing more than his "sacred right!"

An old campaigner's sense of right needs to be understood! At a time before departure, when the eight pouches packed with sharp lead cartridges squeeze midriffs, when bayonets are honed in the battalion metal shops so that files and naked steel squeal all day, then the campaigners feel within themselves certain primeval, wolfish forces awakening in their depths. That bloody and savage feeling gradually fades in the mud of the battlefield and the sufferings of camp life, but in the barracks, where everything is still operatic, where swords glisten, trumpets blare, and troops march keeping time, there the campaigners feel like heroes. And measuring themselves against the battalion clerical staff, these poor people appear to their own eyes as giants and colossi, who are off to great exploits, into carnage, blood, and fire, instead of remaining under a warm roof like these thieves, clerks, swindlers, brigands, crooks, and lazy gray baker pigs and contractors. "These battalion hedgehogs have it good! They won't freeze for seven long nights in cattle wagons, the damned lousy nits, but scribble black fleas on paper in a warm room, gobble up chow, and guzzle liquor. Why shouldn't they too get a whiff of those chirping shots?" There awakens in the campaigners the hatred of a hungry wolf that has caught scent of a warm stable, and that is why it is not good to tangle with the campaigners, so the experienced and peaceable clerks in these final days avoid campaigners like lepers.

Sad and with bowed head, Štef Loborec was returning from the depot, already aware that he will now be forced to travel into the mud of Galicia with old torn shoes and that his feet will be wet from the first rain onward, when, absorbed in such thoughts, he nearly collided with fat Sergeant Šmit, the head of all depots, and so resolved to try his luck once more and to complain to this supreme commander of all stored shoes and nails about his predicament and the dishonest and swinish treatment he had received.

He halted in front of Šmit and clicked his heels neatly, to make the best possible impression, but Šmit irritably scowled.

"Go to the devil! Leave me in peace!"

"But sergeant sir, humbly report, my shoes …"

Sir Sergeant, whose blood they had been sucking all day at the divisional headquarters over the matter of twenty-seven crowns and sixteen fillérs of some counterclaim, was in the midst of calculating batches of goods and problematic sums and searching after forgotten expenses, so when Loborec muddled up all his computations, he flared up.

"Get lost, you peasant crook! You're all crooks!"

"I'm no crook, it's you who stole my right!"

Šmit had not in fact heard what this character wanted or what he was talking about, but the unheard-of insolence of being stopped by a common Guardsman and being accused of theft infuriated him, all the more so since the Hungarian swindlers at the divisional HQ had been playing him the same tune all morning.

And so he slapped Štef Loborec, loudly, with all his might, to rid himself of the whole damned thing.

Just at that moment cooks carrying a large cauldron of hot black coffee were crossing the yard, and Loborec, maddened with fury, his campaigner's honor outraged that here in the rear a warehouseman, "a peddler crook," had slapped him who tomorrow would travel for the third time to the front, leapt upon the sergeant, hoisted him, and pitched him into the cauldron of black coffee. Bathed in boiling coffee, Šmit drew his saber, struck at Loborec's right shoulder, and cut deeply into his flesh so that there in the half-darkness, among torn chestnut trees, beside a cauldron of spilled black coffee, disarmed by guards and cooks, Guardsman Štef Loborec perceived that all this that had happened was not good.

Wounded, bleeding, beaten up, frightened by wartime clauses and threats of being shot, he agreed that same night to a compromise, only agreed to travel to the front wounded as he was to avoid complications and getting court-martialed and shot, because he had drawn a bayonet against a superior. And so the following day he did indeed set out feverish with a drunken transport that growled like a menagerie of wild beasts and cursed Lord God and all the heavenly saints from the commander to that miserable guard at the rear of the train who was shivering sleepless in the caboose with his red signal flag.

It was a time when the war was ripening and when these journeys of transports to the front gave off a sense that chains somewhere had already burst; there were no more flags nor music nor flowers—cauldrons of goulash were being overturned instead, because this wasn't goulash but stinking urine, not beef but boiled cats; rolls of hard stale bread were being thrown at the windows of waiting rooms, waiters were being thrashed in train station restaurants, light bulbs smashed; and when someone threw a cigarette butt into the stacks of pressed hay that stood piled two-stories high at a Hungarian station, and when the transport pulled out illuminated by the crimson glow of the conflagration, everyone loudly laughed.

Somewhere in the Carpathian Mountains, where the letters on train stations were written in the Cyrillic script and where directly in back of the stations tall black slopes strewn with evergreens rose steeply, a Hungarian unit got into a machine-gun fight with Tyroleans. Štef Loborec had heard that a Hungarian allegedly didn't like his ration of black coffee and that the Hungarians brought a muddy latrine drum into the station's waiting room, at which the station commander shot one of the lads. In short: the soldiers got into a fight. In those swarming lines lying across the tracks, in the rattle of machine guns, telephoning, shouting, and shooting, Loborec sensed a need that he too get involved in that battle because another man had no doubt been robbed of his sacred right.

When he conveyed that idea to his freight car, people shrugged, nodded their heads, spit and stretched out again on the straw, tired and hungry, yawning loudly, all with faces bitten and pricked by the sharp stalks that covered the carriage floor.

And that idea gnawed and burrowed within Štef Loborec during the entire trip. Why is he traveling to the front again when that is not just? He has been out in the trench already, lying outside for a full seventeen months. They didn't give him his leave, which belonged to him according to all the regulations; they stole his shoes and bloodied his shoulder and threw him outside thus bloodied once again, into the fog, into mud, into blood, into death.

The Battle at Bistrica Lesna

It was a quiet Sunday morning and layers of fog rose in smoke to the east, lit here and there by the barely perceptible speckles of dawn. The unit marched through a forest, in mud and rain, and nothing was heard, only the clanking of weapons, shovels, and lamps. A huge mass of forest was perceptible to the left and right of the path, and within Štef Loborec one and the same thought kept drilling: If only he had crept into a stable down in the village where they had spent the night, and buried himself in the manure and stayed put till the night, he would have gotten rid of everything and could have gone back. He's wounded, and bleeding, they would have taken him into a hospital somewhere. He would have saved himself from everything and not have had to agonize like a beast.

∞

The unit halted in a clearing, in semi-darkness; while officers awaited telephone orders, people were allowed to rest.

The people scented a battle. Cannons had been audible for two days already, and someone up ahead in the front lines was saying in a sharp, squeaky voice that he could not recall the face of the Russian whose living flesh he had stabbed the last time he was out here. That donkey had hidden under a beech, but he had dug him out of the fallen leaves with his bayonet and the Russian had bit him during the struggle, here, on his left forefinger, even now a trace of the bite deep into the bone could be seen.

The air smelled of wet fir boards from which the divisional telephone men had knocked together their hut there in the clearing, and smoke was rising; a telephone man was washing cauldrons and telling people that two days ago a spy had been hanged here, from this very telephone pole. He had wanted plums and bread, to fill his stomach before dying, so they gave him plums, to eat his fill of those plums. But he couldn't bite; he was so scared that the plums leaked and he looked like he was bleeding from his mouth. And it wasn't blood, but plums!

"Hee-hee!"

"He couldn't bite the bread either, so he crumbled it up with his palms and scattered it in the mud, to leave it for the birds!"

"And what's our Rucner doing? Hee-hee!"

"Ah! He's better off than we are!"

"He almost is better off!"

"He was a good fellow; it's a pity what happened."

It was evident from the words "our Rucner" that he had most likely been favored with sincere sympathy by the company, and that people had liked and respected him. He had been a clerk in civilian life and had long led a malnourished life in provincial boroughs, and then he had scored success and crept into a stinking chamber of the royal Croatian-Slavonian-Dalmatian terrestrial government on Marko's Square and there drew register lines with a ruler, and filled crosswords with ciphers and letters.

"Our Rucner" had read several books in his life about the fact that God did not exist and that democracy would unconditionally and undoubtedly save the world, and all that had gotten mixed up in his mind; he racked his brains a great deal over the subject of God and democracy. Rucner's nerves had long been in a rather devastated state, and his kidneys were as spent as a ripped sieve. He had christened the issue of his nerves "nervous disorganization," and of his kidneys he always spoke as about something that possesses its own destructive tendency and "that is it!" By the phrase "that is it," Rucner thought himself to be solving the very innermost secret of life. He felt his own teeth rotting and falling out, and his glands (some greasy poisonous glands deep within him) were not functioning as they should. Everything within him had fallen apart. His heart quivered helplessly amid a mass of events and he sensed the quivering of his rotten heart, sensed his nails, too, growing of their own accord like those of a corpse; thinking thus about the fact of "that is it," he had lived sadly and haplessly before they allocated him to the battalions and got him shot twice. As a civilian, he had most liked to stroll along the embankment of a stinking canal at the end of the city, in which rolled the mud and stench of the entire city and rats as huge as rabbits jumped about. Rucner had at that time constructed for himself a final and very sad view of the world, which consisted of the fundamental idea that the entire city actually exists only for the sake of that stinking canal. People slaughter each other and agonize, ingest calories and travel, write books on the theme that "there is no God and democracy will save the world"— all so that ultimately, from all the suffering and conceptualizing, there flows out one such black and muddy canal. This pessimism only hardened within Rucner after his experiences at the front; moreover, he began to have doubts about democracy and no longer wished to think even about that. It was all the same! Democracy or no democracy! Everything was ultimately bound to end up in a muddy canal!

In the village of Bistrica, where they spent the night, Rucner hooked up with a blacksmith's wife whom he had gotten to know two years earlier when he had passed this way. A fertile woman whose man they had shot, she had been left a widow with five children. That night Rucner

The Battle at Bistrica Lesna | 29

stayed with the woman, and there was nothing remarkable about that. A warm bed, a mass of feather bedding striped red and white, strong sweaty female hips atop the feathers and somewhere far off a mumbling of cannons. A rider with a lamp was gingerly stepping across a muddy road, and the sound could be heard of the horse laboriously extracting its hooves from the mud. A fog drizzled. Rucner remembered that he had left his pipe on the table in the kitchen (floored with red brick), and in that moment the space through which the rider was stepping struck him as extraordinarily profound. A child in the room began to cry, and he stood there, stupid, sick, abandoned.

They found him the next morning in the hayloft, hanging from a thick beam. He was holding his pipe in his left hand and he left an extraordinary impact on Vid Trdak. They had been paired together, and whenever they were ordered "squad right," Vid Trdak had spun around Rucner like a forward around a goalpost and always jumped into double file with him; thus they talked together much in the line and in the train carriage and in the barracks. Rucner knew Trdak's worries, but he never consoled him.

"You will die and your children will die and I will die, and no one will be bothered over it! I ask you: Do you think I don't know Marko's Square? You think that that old shortsighted clerk sits there rolling *Riz-Abadie* cigarettes, right? Hee-hee. And you think he is a doctor? There is no one there! No old doctor, no Viceroy, no government! All is empty! All that is off to the black canal!"

"There you have it! He was here, yesterday he was still marching here in double file, and now he is no longer in the line! He simply stepped out of it!"

The men behind Vid Trdak were making fun of the battalion bricklayer Viktor who had received leave from the major only on the condition that he go home and shoot his wife like a bitch because she had deceived him most foully with an old miller (while he was bleeding at the front the wife left the house and moved into the mill), and yet Viktor is back without the result!

"Listen to me, Viktor," the battalion commander had told him before the departure on leave. "I am releasing you from the front! All right! But give me your word of honor that you will shoot that bitch of yours no matter what!"

"I will, major sir. My word of honor! I will shoot her like a bitch!"

And the bricklayer traveled off from the front and did not shoot the wife! Whatever happened to your word of honor, Viktor? Viktor!

Officers (all in gum and rubber) emerged from the telephone hut, mounted their horses, orders spread out over the massive body of the battalion, and everything began to move once more, heavily and wearily.

The man who decided the fate of our heroes in the battle at Bistrica Lesna was called Rikard Weisersheimb, Ritter von Reichlin-Meldegg und Hochenthurm, and possessed the rank of lieutenant colonel in the general headquarters and was the operational chief of that military aggregate in which our second company from Zagorje was lost as a barely visible stroke drawn with a red pencil on a gray scribbled map with the ratio of one to seventy-five thousand.

On the lieutenant colonel's map it could not be seen that the entire region was torn up by artillery shells (as if the earth had been ravaged by rabid wild boars), and those thousands who that morning moved invisible and silent along the valleys and ravines of the terrain did not look like heaps of wounded and pus-covered flesh, but rather were red arrows aiming their points at the wavy blue lines of the Russian positions. On Hill 313 stood a little brick chapel with a crucified Christ made of tin, all furrowed and peeled by deep bullet gashes. A German command had nailed to the wall a black tablet bearing the names of twenty-nine men they had buried in a grenadiers' mass grave three months back. These were the grenadiers from an assault column that had been pushing east across Hill 313 when the front collapsed twice at that spot and the Russians overran the chapel before starting to abandon it in the reverse shifting and swaying. This piddling hillock, overgrown with brambles, dominated the entire surroundings and opened a vista far into the distance across brooks and fields, furrows and poplars, to the village where "our Rucner" had hanged himself after midnight, and farther to the expanse of forest where with a good pair of binoculars one could make out a destroyed and burned-out train station and where the first units from Zagorje were dug in.

That Hill 313 was of great importance to the general development of battlefront relations, a sort of angular pivot around which moved all the combinations of Herr Rikard Weisersheimb and of Baron von Frederiks, his double on the Russian side, a gentleman with silver spurs, a Boyar title since the time of Peter the Great, and high decorations. This Baron von Frederiks was, according to Weisersheimb's deepest expert opinion, a "dunderhead," a "dilettante," an "ignoramus," and a "bungler."

"Idiot! If he had taken that Kazan brigade, which bled here yesterday, and thrown it into line twenty-four hours earlier, everything would have turned out the opposite. But now! We'll show that 'bungler' who and what we are!"

And so Rikard Weisersheimb Ritter von Reichlin-Meldegg und Hochenthurm, as though he were playing chess with Baron von Frederiks, his opponent from the other side of the front, crossed out Hill 313 and drew across it a line of his combinations, and for the brigade of our martyrs (which, freshly ironed and still sprinkled with camphor from the depot, had pitched camp behind the foggy woods) this meant that they would wade into the blood already on the following morning, on God's very Sunday itself.

Among the people depression grew from step to step and all felt as though a stone had lodged in their innards, forcing them to stop and urinate abundantly; every minute someone fell out of line to step into a ditch, then broke into a run to reach his place, and from this nervous trotting the equipment on the men jangled as a hammered yoke does on heavy packhorses.

They passed the destroyed munitions wagons, beside which lay a barefoot corpse covered with tent canvas, the soles of his feet were dirty and waterlogged; a single jackdaw perching on his hip did not fly high up but alighted in the mud squawking loudly.

The forest grew steadily thinner and the sweepingly shaped terrain sloped downward toward a brook that wound about, etched deeply into the mud, as though someone had thrust a supernatural long-nailed thumb into that soggy grayish-red clay and ripped the soil so that it leaked pus and dirt like an old wound. The wind was rustling the dry leaves when the first shot fell.

It had been preceded by a sinister silence, such as always announces that something is about to happen. Patrols that had been sent out far ahead of the unit returned with the news that the Russian positions are at the forest's edge, and the shot echoed far across the meadows and fields. The men who had not yet had a whiff of gunpowder sighed deeply and did not think it all so terrible! That cracked as if somewhere far away one board fell on top of another! That's nothing!

Then the second shot fell.

Two more.

Then a hush.

People were stepping across a leafy toppled tree trunk, their faces all dirty and smeared so that the pallor of their cheeks looked supernatural.

All treaded timidly, making the voice of Staff Sergeant Pesek sound doubly rough and stern within this solemn silence (when everyone felt his heart in his throat).

"What the hell? You ain't a bunch of ballerinas! Damned donkeys! Run!"

They all ran down into the bed of the brook, flooded with water to the ankles, and lined up there; some foreign and unknown soldiers were making their way across the ploughed fields, sometimes hopping and sometimes crawling. It all looked comical and incomprehensible at the same time. Štef Lovrek gazed at these unknown foreign soldiers moving along the furrows like distant ploughmen (though not ploughmen, and with rifles instead of ploughs), and he gazed at the wet and heavy devastated earth and bent down to feel with his hand the quality of this earth, because it seemed to him that it was ploughed deeply and properly and that the earth could be good. In that moment, as Štef Lovrek bent down and scooped up a handful of earth, a sparrow chirped, and Vid Trdak, his comrade from double file's seventh row, leaned against him as though he were sick at the stomach.

Within the silent treacherous hush a machine gun started to rattle somewhere far off on the right wing, the crashing racket pouring across the dales and rolling in waves further and further, and in that broad undulation of its echo a cannon announced itself. The cannon thundered as if it stood five paces away, deafeningly and deeply like a gun in front of a church at Easter. At the same moment cannons from somewhere far ahead rang out like voices of an organ and something flew across the ditch and the brook and over the people like a bird.

"Too high," someone shouted in amazement.

"Shut up!"

Lovrek had heard the cannons and had tensed up curious to know if they would fire again, when Vid Trdak clutched at him convulsively as if drowning. Lovrek only felt that Vid Trdak was soft and crawling earthward, with blood welling up at the mouth and pouring onto his hands.

"Vid, Vid, by the five wounds of Christ, Vid!"

Vid Trdak did not respond with so much as a word. The whites of his eyes shone with a bluish glow and bloody foam drained through his teeth; he was swallowing hard and smacking his jaws as though masticating. Trdak had heard the sparrow, and had heard the shout, that it was too high, then it grew foggy and he remembered that he had forgotten to ask that doctor at Marko's Square to act urgently, and finally that he had not forgotten, rather that the doctor had no time, the doctor was filling

Riz-Abadie cigarettes—and Rucner had said that nothing exists—nothing exists, no Government, no Viceroy, no doctor, nothing...

Štef Lovrek bent down to Vid Trdak wanting to lift him up and to do something that would be wise and fitting and proper, but somehow he could not recall where his bandages were, where had those damned things got lost, in his bag or in his knapsack? Once again a shell whined musically over the ravine and that too was too high; and immediately afterward three more, all three high. People began to run like cows before a wildfire, nothing could be made out, only crazed shouting and whistling, so that Lovrek grew utterly confused and did not know what to do. To run after the people, to shout, to leave Vid Trdak there in the mud—what, what?

"Damn your mad mother! I'll shoot you like a dog! Move it!"

Lovrek jolted as if startled out of a dream. Staff Sergeant Pesek stood before him menacing him with a revolver and shouting and swearing at the top of his voice; there was no one anywhere, all the people had vanished someplace beneath the earth, only he stood there, and Staff Sergeant Pesek with the revolver. Obedient as a puppy, Lovrek ran off as far as a tree stump, and he wasn't three steps away from that stump when a shell struck somewhere nearby and a blast of earth flung him into the brook. He had barely jerked away from Trdak and fallen into the water when a vertical black pillar of water and mud flew up to the right and immediately a similar black pillar of earth to the left, and thus the earth began to leap like drops against puddles in a storm: Here one and there another, then more and more, and faster and faster. Lovrek felt the wet clothes and underclothes sticking to his skin, his eyes were spattered with a mass of rotten greenish slimy moss and his hands were bloody with Trdak's blood. His elbow burned like fire, he had skinned it, and his knee (that's nothing, a little scratch); *whiz, whiz, whiz,* sharp threads whistled through the air, like on a shooting range when they set up planks in a shelter, and a fat slice of the slope broke off above him, greasy and heavy, like dough cut off with a knife. Watery blisters were heard bubbling within the mud: *cluck, cluck.*

Whistles shrieked and there was firing somewhere up ahead among the rosehips and blackberries. A bugler ran along the ditch on all fours rapidly like a monkey, and Lovrek wanted to call after him, to ask where the second company is, but not a word could be heard within the uproar that reverberated above the whizzing, only the shells droned like bagpipes. The booming grew ever more intense, and a shot zipped past Lovrek's ear with a ping like a needle. In the same instant another stabbed the earth before him and ripped it, and the earth moaned dully and deeply, as defeated beings moan. In the forest a tree was audibly splitting from the foliage to the roots. Lovrek lay on his back in the curve of the brook, where cattle come to drink leaving their footprints and stinking cowpats all around. He wanted to turn, to crawl under a felled log (it would be warmer), but he could not stir from some inexpressible fatigue, such as he had not felt even when threshing wheat within the most blazing heat of August. He felt such a weight within his legs as though his body were a waterlogged bag of cement, and his eyes were closing; he still kept his eyes just barely open so that the faint horizontal line of light poured into his pupils, and the drops of rain gliding from leaf to leaf along strands of spider-web were visible through an oily shroud as if through tears. Štef Lovrek clearly remembered Trdak clutching his belt and growing quite limp, starting to vomit blood, and Pesek barking at him revolver in hand, and now all these images were contracting into something soft like the feelers of a crushed snail and all appeared so slobbery and soggy and cold. It struck Lovrek as strange that Staff Sergeant Pesek had shouted at him so vehemently and even threatened him with a revolver, and now he lies here by his feet, green, deaf, inert, while white cloudlets of shrapnel fly over his head, like snowballs. The earth is pouring as though someone were tossing it with a shovel, and all that smoke and that mud, everything is so mute and deaf and quiet.

Štef Loborec was deeply preoccupied with his idea of crawling into a manure heap in a village somewhere when the first artillery fire fell; he remained lying in a ditch like an old and experienced veteran who knows that the first principle of successful and wise warfare is to remain lying with head thrust into the mud and eyes shut, the longer the better. He stayed thus immobile and stiff and when he moved, he didn't know whether it had been only an instant or terribly long, he had lost the sense of time and it seemed to him that he had awakened from a dream; there were Hungarians all around him cursing in Hungarian and advancing, and a huge Hungarian giant halted above him and aimed a kick at his backside, so he rose and ran after the Hungarians.

The Hungarians go, he goes too! Doesn't matter! Hungarian clowns! To hell with them. Nothing to be done! The Hungarian swine might shoot him like a dog yet! He stayed as long as he could. Doesn't matter now!

The Russian double of Herr Lieutenant Colonel Rikard Weisersheimb, Baron von Frederiks, the "dilettante" and "idiot," who yesterday

The Battle at Bistrica Lesna | 35

had wasted his Kazan brigade in such a harebrained manner—downright heedlessly, did not permit them to snatch away Hill 313 by any sort of counterattacks. He had accurately foreseen such an attack and therefore the previous night had reinforced the entire position with doubled artillery reserves and with a red pencil on a map had drawn close several Kyrgyz transports, which had been traveling three weeks already along muddy Russian train stations, and so he issued the order to hold the front until these transports arrived.

Black fountains of earth rose from the artillery shells left and right. Štef Loborec scurried like a lost ant in a dark colonnade of sooty pillars of smoke and holes, and sweaty, overheated, breathless, threw himself into the fire stunned, as though someone had punched him in the nose with a fist. It was a clod of earth.

Greasy black clouds of smoke kept on rising while splinters of shattered tree trunks, thorny brambles, and muddy earth all shot over human heads. Loborec felt something warm spatter his face, and when he drew his hand across it to see what it was his finger was bloody, as though he had crushed an insect. The sky was drizzling blood.

People were shouting left and right, but not a single word could be made out, while the thunder and the needle-sharp threads of rifle bullets and machine-gun rounds and the fire, smoke, the moaning of the wounded, the heavy and intoxicating stench of gunpowder, all that crept into eyes and ears, into pores and nerves, so that Loborec, driven by a weighty need to conceal himself somewhere, plunged his face into the earth like an insect and breathed with difficulty. Steam rose from him as from a horse. Someone moaned to his right and the moaning filled Loborec with a fateful anxiety. His body flushed with a scarlet fire, and he started scratching at his shaggy chest, hips, knee, like a man stricken with pruritus, wanting to strip, stand up, flee, scratch the sole of his foot that itched so fiendishly, to shout, to howl, but at that moment a shot buried itself just in front of him and whizzed over him. At that instant Loborec was gripped by the feeling that the bullet had pierced his eye, and began to touch his eyeball and marveled that it remained in place intact. His eyelids flickered nervously from the incessant bursting of explosives, and within that rain of bullets that poured like grain, his membranes swelled so that everything thundered within him as though someone were banging his skull against a wall.

In the intense heat that licked at him out of his insides from the unusually powerful pressure of the explosions, in the absolute momentary darkness, Loborec pressed his hand against his eyes and stiffened with an effort to bury himself yet deeper in the earth, then everything blazed up and hoisted by a fireworks of green sparks he felt himself flung outward, somersaulting several times, bareheaded and glued with mud that crawled down his neck, doused with a heavy and suffocating phosphoric resin that tickled his nostrils and windpipe so he wanted to sneeze. He would have sneezed, but he dared not even twitch and merely listened to the rifles that rattled like vineyard rattles in a fast wind; here comes Saint Mihal . . .

He stayed motionless for a long time, then he took courage and slowly started to touch his body, was he still alive? He dug himself out of the earth, and next to him lay someone's head. It was a head from the assault column, tied with a strap like a postal parcel. "Double file, right!" Farewell! Charge! God rest his soul! A shattered rifle butt hummed high up in the smoke, while white fumes dragged along the ridges and all reeked of burning and of the raw iron that endlessly hissed and extinguished itself in puddles, like horseshoes in a smithy.

As it occurred to Loborec that it would be good to deepen that hole of his, into which he may have been tossed by Saint Roch himself, he began with great difficulty to grope for his spade, which had crept down his back, and when he finally extracted it, something clanged, and the spade flew out of his hand in a high arc.

"Gone to hell," thought he, curling into a ball in the hole, when the next instant something zipped and scorched his head. His flesh burned, the scratch bled, and he, bloodied and filthy, tapped his head and switched back and forth between stupidly staring at his bloody fingers and stroking his head, while his heart pounded animatedly and loudly. Before him in a pile of soil lay someone's raincoat; a bullet tore off its button so that the button squealed as piglets squeal when swineherds chase them in the meadow. "A ricochet, devil take its mother, and another one."

"Someone's shooting at me on purpose, damn his bloody mother," thought Loborec and reached for his rifle. His rifle was nowhere to be found, it had remained behind in the ditch while he, sheltered by somebody's corpse, lay without a rifle, still thinking that it would have been much cleverer to have stayed in a manure pile in Bistrica than to let himself be butchered here in a ploughfield on God's own Sunday. Until that moment he had still been a man who dimly felt he had been wronged, and that it would be more honest to turn against those bums and bastards, sons of bitches and swindlers, to take a rifle and begin to shoot all those crooks in the rear from the general to the battalion shoemaker. Like a tame calf he had feared that fire, but now, sticking his nose under the green raincoat of an unknown Hungarian corpse, bloodied and provoked by a deep conviction that someone was deliberately shooting at him, he snatched up a rifle and commenced to fire into the fog, into the mud, into blackberries, into nothing!

What harm had he done to anyone? They robbed him of his six weeks of leave, and drove his own wife away from him with a rifle butt at the barracks fence! They tormented him, dragged him through hospitals, stole his shoes, and now on top of everything they're shooting at him? Who is that swine who is shooting at him! Just watch if Štef Loborec will put up long with everyone beating up on him!

Thus raged Štef Loborec and the rifle thundered like a motor, the barrel smoked and the wood began to burn and the casings flew searing from the magazine as if from a sawmill, while white burn blisters fumed on Štef's hands. He was traveling full speed aboard the steam engine of battle.

In the public elementary school of Bistrica Lesna, divisional coroner Palčić (in civilian life a student and a nervous wreck in whom the least of life's trifles causes a constriction of the throat and whose eyes sparkle with inexpressible sorrow) was counting the previous day's dead from Hill 313. The first battalion of the Zagorje regiment, which had been on the left wing, had suffered the worst casualties: Seventy-two death certificates from the first battalion lay on the table of the coroner student Palčić, who peeled these death papers from their yellow metal covers and transferred the material into the files and records of divisional losses. Within the second battalion, the second and third companies had suffered the most. In the second platoon of the second company, seven men lay fallen, namely Staff Sergeant Mato Pesek and six National Guardsmen.

The first in order was Guardsman Matija Križ. Born, vaccinated, killed, leaving behind in the addendum: two letters, twenty-four crowns, a penknife, a mirror.

The first letter to Matija Križ, written in a heavy, fieldworker's hand, was from Katica Rodeš, and it read as follows:

> If I had little wings to fly Id fly to yore dreemy brest if I had eye of hawke Id peek in yore brawd boosem if I had flowers round my neck Id put em on yore heart jus to make you more byutiful an sweet an dear. There thats how much I love you an if needbe Id give my life too for you. An yet from yore letter I see you blame

me an say Im not feithful dont you worry bout me my dear I can be blest and satisfyd only thru you an that I cant describe I will take out my heart an put it before you so you see yore face init an see how much I love you.

Yapping tongs cant keep quyet so they slandre me too tho Im innosent an didnt do nuthin. Thats my stepfathers fawlt cause he wants me to be his till my Pepo come home from Idaly. Dont you believe noneovit. Its sad when yore mother curses me cause I sleep at stepfathers but where can I if not at his when I cant with you, cause what will Pepo say if he comes home cause Štefek Francetić was in Idaly with Pepo an Pepo is alive an well. Thank Jezus an Mary goodbye Katica Rodeš.

The second letter to Matija Križ was not from Katica Rodeš but from Ljubica Jankić, evidently a young woman not yet married.

Here is a sweet and loving greeting from Ljubica Jankić. Jesus and Mary be praised Dear Mato my Treasure I let you know that I received your postcard on the third in the evening and my heart was happy when I received your postcard. Now I write you this letter because my heart wont give me peace dear mato my love my heart my treasure like brite moonlite in the sky my love for you will never die My sweet I pick up a pencil to write you a letter cause we love each other yet cant be Together. Shining star of this heart of mine I love you more than God divine Fair sun rises from the Eest, sweetheart greets you who are missed.

My sweet write to me after that letter you got on Feast of Our Ladys I beg you write to me are you really sick poisonous like Blaž Kovačev told me cause I'm writing for third time so I'm afraid that your in the city in love with others. Receive sweet and gentle greeting from Ljubica Jankić.

Divisional coroner student Palčić grew thoughtful over the letter of Katica Rodeš which by arriving thus at his coroner's table came to mark the end of a love affair.

Katica Rodeš had no doubt spit into the dry and dusty inkwell and stirred it with the pointed end of a penholder as though stirring sauce in a pot, and had then spent all Sunday forenoon copying some Harambašić-Badalićesque phrases, in order to weave into all that sugary patchwork a single small truth, bitter as wormwood.

The Battle at Bistrica Lesna | 39

Student Palčić was familiar with that style of correspondence and had read thousands upon thousands of such letters, glued with seminude pink cherubs and bleeding hearts, written always in the same hand with the letters aslant from the upper left corner into the lower right; student Palčić could accurately predict when that certain shift from the sweet to the bitter would come, and it all seemed to him boring and sad.

To sit here in an empty schoolroom and read all night about Eva Katančec sending three doves to the late Guardsman Blažek: "The first brings you love, the second a little letter, and the third a little rose I knew all about what you done up there in the vineyard with Janica Goričan and why you don't write me farewell." And he knew about Jaga Pecak writing to the Croatian king that "the reverently undersigned takes the liberty, with the view to having the supreme paternal mercy bestowed upon her, to submit humbly the present lowly petition to judgment."

The present lowly petition of Jaga Pecak was officially referred by the royal domain to the appropriate military authority for its relevant recommendation, and the appropriate authority having dealt with it summarily by way of submission returned the petition to the petitioner (respectively her husband, Guardsman Pecak) with a note that His Highness the Croatian King "did not condescend to be lenient nor did he kindly deign to extend and bestow his supreme paternal mercy" and consequently Guardsman Imbro Pecak would not be returning home to his land, as Jaga had petitioned and fervently hoped, and to which end she had presented the municipal scribe with a fat goose and twenty-seven eggs.

All of it fell through! The goose and the twenty-seven eggs and Jaga's hope and Imbro Pecak! All of that is inside those metal covers enclosing the death certificates that the coroner student Palčić is peeling, where it is written in black on white that Imbro Pecak fell, that he was vaccinated against cholera and typhus, born and married in the village of Trnje Jezušovo in the municipality of Saint Jana. The silver watch belonging to Staff Sergeant Mato Pesek is here too and under its lid a clipping from the calendar "Šoštar" where it is printed that Mr. Mato Pesek won that silver watch as a prize from the editorial board for having solved puzzles published in the calendar "Šoštar" whose solutions read "He who's up before dawn, falls into a hole," and "He who digs a hole under another, doubles his luck." Student Palčić has peeled all too many death certificates, read all too many petitions and clearly sees Blažek's Marica on her deathbed with godparents lighting her last candle: Children are crying, she is dying from consumption, and her Franjo is lying here on the desk of a public school in Galicia's Bistrica Lesna, along with three loving doves from Eva Katančec. The first brings you love, the second a little letter, and the third a little rose! And if Štef Loborec had returned to his young wife, he would have found her lost to drink. Cow, pigs, chickens, half an acre of meadow—Loborec's wife drank them all up in a mad notion that Štef is dead and will never return. Wardrobe and pillows and sheets—she drank them all up, at four crowns per sheet. At the home of Štef Loborec everything has fallen apart, so that if he had by some chance returned, he would have found his wife drunk, lying unconscious in a ditch, with the village brats pelting her with stones. No doubt he would have beaten her bloody, so it is better that he never did return at all. And the father of Guardsman Blažek, who has passed seventy and is weak and ill and has no one to wash him and cook something warm for him: His horses are blind, the pigs have died, hail has destroyed everything, so he writes to his son, his right hand, to return to the land, to write a petition, to stop, to apply that they let him go home, because this can no longer be endured.

Death certificates are falling like rain onto the table of the divisional coroner, and along with the death certificates rain the letters and petitions of the late Guardsmen, and all of this student Palčić reads, registers, and it is all finished and to all of it there is no longer any medical or legal remedy, or recourse, or appeal.

It isn't only Vid Trdak with his six companions from the second platoon of the second company, with his petition in which he forgot to write that he requests urgent action; brigades and divisions of corpses have strolled through these files and march on into infinity, mute, bent, miserable, condemned innocent to death.

They advance four abreast, in the deaf footfall of endless nocturnal columns, their equipment jangles, the Mannlicher rifles, spades, knives; they audibly extract their army shoes from the mud, causing the divisional coroner to pause momentarily in his counting, prick up his ears like a dog and hold his breath with a terrifying sense of clarity.

The miners of Zagorje are marching outside, those who all their lives swallowed soot and stench and poisonous fumes; they have risen from one grave, lit their oil lamps and are quietly going in lines of two into another hole and into a realm of no return. The vineyard workers of Podravina, the fieldworkers of Stubica, grandsons of Matija Gubec, all of them are marching outside in the darkness and all of them will return here to his coroner's table. And he will read their love letters, and petitions, gaze at those terrible barbaric photographs, leaf through the documents, and there will never be an end to it.

BARRACK 5B

COUNT MAXIMILIAN AXELRODE, COMMANDER of the Sovereign Order of Malta, became in his fourteenth year a *chevalier de justice* of Saint John in full regalia with a silver cross. Instead of sixteen noble and knightly ancestors in the lineage of his lord father and lady mother, a highborn princess, that are required for the rank of a high dignitary in the exalted Order of Malta, Count Maximilian Axelrode's family tree boasted twenty-eight plumes and helmets under which already coursed blue blood, so when the Grand Priory of the Sovereign Order of Malta sent to His Noble Highness's cabinet office priceless scrolls bearing the golden seals of the high and highest "Imprimatur" it was a grand event, such as rarely takes place on the terrestrial globe.

Count Maximilian Axelrode had all his life entertained only one idea, to unsheathe his sword for his lofty Maltese motto—*Pro Fide*—drape himself with his black cape which hangs in heavy folds, and plunge into death with a bright and valiant brow. As when he traveled for the first time to Jerusalem, bursting into bitter tears over Santa Maria Latina's marble ruins out of grief that he had not been granted the great happiness to sow his noble bones here eight hundred years ago, with the great Gottfried of Bouillon, or if not that, that he had at least been born three hundred summers later, when cannons thundered on Rhodes and on Malta. But no! He fell onto this globe in a pathetic and stupid age, when the noble Villiers de l'Isle-Adams have become some sort of socialist agitators and incite the rabble on May First, and when the greatest military event is an occasional maneuver, during which soldiers fire blindly, and barely even that, because some minister of finance and some "silly" parliaments shout that armed forces are costly. Devil take this idiotic age of steam locomotives, when everything is tied up with tracks and so-called social (in fact socialist) democracy, and when noble Maltese knights meet in hotels wearing bowler hats like shopkeepers, and even duels are abolished by law.

Count Maximilian Axelrode had thus been grieving in vain for a full sixty-three years when he awoke one morning and thought he must be dreaming. A lackey handed him a telegram from the priorate of the exalted Order, informing him that mobilization had been declared, and that the Sovereign Order of Malta, in accordance with its exalted tradition, will plant its banner in the name of the great motto *Pro Fide* and that it will pitch tents on an imperial base out somewhere and organize hospital service. Thus Count Maximilian Axelrode became the chief of a large Maltese hospital, which comprises forty-two large wooden barracks, its own electric generator, entire companies of Red Cross nurses, et cetera, et cetera. As troops shift sixty miles east, then a hundred and twenty miles west, then once again east, from season to martial season, so the war goes on, and so Count Axelrode has been traveling with his Maltese circus from east to west from Stanislavov to Cracow and back again for two full years, and now it is August of the year '16, the sun sears at one hundred and twenty degrees Fahrenheit and the situation is tense and grave.

The hospital is filled to capacity with one thousand five hundred soldierly bodies and it seems that the Russians are about to cut the railway lines left and right, and that his lordship the count, the grand Maltese master, will in two weeks be in Moscow. At noon a telegram arrives saying that the Russians did indeed cross the northern line between two stations, but that the hospital should stay put, because a counterattack is in progress. That the Russians cut the line in the north means that all the transports on that line began to move south, and this naturally led to a pileup (seventy-two dead, countless wounded) and to the trains running out of provisions, so without food and water the wounded are screaming for the fifth day, and they are feeding them anti-worms peppermints (oh, don't laugh, it's true!), and all the stations along the line have lost their heads, and so Count Axelrode has been forced to receive five hundred additional patients into his already packed hospital. That very day was the hottest day of the whole summer, as the sun virtually crushed the earth with its fiery mass, and it seemed as though someone had thrown a blazing millstone onto the white wooden barracks, making everything burn. Boards warped and snapped with the drought, lime on the walls cracked like aged skin, while the green convolvulus and the tulips along the round decorative flowerbeds all grew withered, rotted, decayed, and were trampled.

Among the group of five hundred new wounded that Count Axelrode had to receive on top of his full hospital lay Vidović, a student, shot through the lungs and bleeding. Truly, nowhere can a man get as muddy as at the front, but when they carried Vidović into the large steam bath—he who was as streaked with filth as patients will get in the month of August in cattle wagons of a transport of wounded—he was still capable of feeling disgust.

If you bring a pitiful nervous figure, like Vidović, out of a certain European lifestyle into this bath, it is highly likely that such a Vidović will convulse and begin to vomit. But after everything that had happened to him yesterday and today, after that fire last night at the train station, when cans of gasoline were exploding one after another, after those anti-worms peppermints, when one thousand two hundred throats were crying for water, and there was no water, after that swinish train carriage, Vidović did not vomit in the steam of the bath, but even so it all disgusted him.

Stinking yellow water splashes back and forth in the concrete pool, grayish-green soapsuds foam, and bloody bandages and cotton float about, cotton saturated with pus. The water smokes reeking of mud and clay, steam showers stream in jets, and black shadows flicker within the dense steam, running to and fro in the fog, and all the human faces are swollen and bloody, the dynamo of the generator is rumbling somewhere, and it is noon in August. Here atop a glass table a man is dying under the shower, there another is moaning, ventilators hum like invisible insects, while Russians in khaki shirts carry new wounded material like sacks, and the nurses and the wounded and the physicians are all shouting, all running, all have lost their heads.

They bathed Vidović in the bloody and muddy hell, and carried him into Barrack 5B, which looked like the belly of a big barge. Sixty beds, each with a body in it, stand precisely arranged with cruel Protestant pedantry; a chart hangs over each body to make it known how it stands with the body. The barge is divided into three groups. First group: broken bones. (Bones protrude like wooden slivers. During the day people lie voiceless. Only at night do the wounded call out, as if from Golgotha, in smothered voices.) Second group: amputations. (An arm or a leg, or an arm and a leg. The wounds are not bandaged but are drying under tulle, like cured meat.) Third group, left of entrance: adjuncts. This category is merely transiting through 5B. It is traveling from the bath to the morgue. And when someone is placed into the third group, then Barrack 5B already knows how the matter stands, a new candidate for death, an adjunct!

When they carried the wounded Vidović into the barrack and laid him down on bed number eight, a Hungarian, a hulking giant from group number one (broken bones), spit scornfully and drew a cross in the air with his finger:

"*No hát, Istenem.* They could have taken this one directly into the morgue. *Szerbusz!*"

"A new number eight is here! Children!"

"Number eight! Number eight!"

The voices poured across the barrack, and many a head lifted to see the new number eight. True, they had all been thoroughly torn apart and bloodied by life. But still, even if a man has no leg, at least he isn't number eight! He is number twenty-one! Or number fifteen!

My arm is gone! True! And my bone is broken! True! But I'm alive! Lord God, I'm still alive! So when the Russians bring in a black coffin tomorrow and cram the new number eight into it, I'll cozily fill my pipe and gaze at flies squirming on flypaper, and drink milk! After all, it's a life! It isn't the fate of number eight!

Number eight has been changing its occupant four days in a row! Just this morning the Russian slaves carried out a compatriot of theirs. His intestines had been ripped apart and he had been hollering for two days and two nights. Before the Russian there had been a good fellow from Vienna, and now Vidović has arrived.

On number seven, left of Vidović, lies a Mongol, a Siberian, with a bullet in his head. He is shouting something, some sharp vowels, but no one understands it, and everyone thinks that he is already finished, when he begins anew to toss and twist, while a red ribbon of burning blood breaks through the bandage on his head. On number nine, to the right, a young Slovak is dying, shot through the throat. His windpipe is severed and he breathes through a glass tube so the gurgling of foamy saliva, pus, and blood inside the tube is clearly audible.

And so Barrack 5B began to take bets on Vidovic's head, that he wouldn't last till the morning.

"I know our doctor. When he doesn't go under the knife right away, then it's amen."

"Not true! He wouldn't leave him till tomorrow if that were so! He's still young!"

"That 'uncle' from Vienna was already eating rice and laughing! And we all went under the knife right away."

"Well then, what'll it be? Are you good for a bottle of red? Till the morning?"

"I'm good! A bottle of red!"

And so descended a night in August.

Big stars lit up, large and shining, and the immense blue dome covered the entire basin of Axelrode's Maltese hospital like crystal, thousands upon thousands of tons of heated gases leaned upon Barrack 5B, and not a trace of breeze anywhere to stir the air even for an instant. Flies in the barrack have now fallen asleep and stopped buzzing, while somewhere in the middle of that perverse boat loaded with human flesh burns a green light, and everything floats in semidarkness. Darkness, darkness, semi-darkness, and pain, inexpressible pain, lurking during the day but now breathing through all the pores and throbbing with every heartbeat. Now each tiny sliver and the smallest sawed-off bone makes itself felt, now a quake shakes nerves disgorging voices from human depths as a volcano disgorges lava. A man grits his teeth, chatters in a sweat, foams as he bites his tongue and lips, then suddenly his lower jaw expands, his face twists into a beastly grimace, and a voice roars from the pit of his insides like from the hole of a wellspring.

"*Mamma mia, mamma mia!*" cries someone in Italian down at the bottom.

"*Gospodi, Gospodi, Gospodi!*" moans a Russian with a bullet in his intestines, and then it is silent once more, a green silence, semi-darkness.

Exhausted from loss of blood, Vidović slept the entire afternoon, and now he has woken up and doesn't know where he is or what has happened, or how he got here. He hears human voices moaning, that seething in his wounds has subsided, his fever seems to have died down, and the tormented Vidović after prolonged searching finally locates a seemingly cooler spot on his pillow. His parched eyelids are once more stickily lowering, a deaf and heavy silence pours over him, thirst has evaporated somewhere, and the barrack has already started to melt and dissipate into a pleasant blackness, when a beastly cry of incarnated pain tears through the barrack once again, that howl instantly shattering the entire edifice of sleep so painfully constructed on the cooler edge of the pillow, so that it all crumbles in a flash.

And so it goes on throughout the night, always anew.

"Oh! Only five minutes! Only a minute of sleep!"

The night must already be far advanced, because a clear light pours in through the green tulle that covers the windows. Guards shout outside, and the convolvulus, climbing up the twine, seems to tremble in a morning breeze. Small butterflies circle the nightlight, fluttering their wings.

"What time is it?"

There is no time! There is nothing! Only pain.

"*Mamma mia! Mamma mia! Gospodi! Gospodi!*"

"Ah, if I could fall asleep for only a minute! For only a second!"

"*Gospodi!*"

The following morning, the situation began to seriously change. Early at daybreak the Russians penetrated south to cut the last imperial and royal railway link, so trains began to turn back, engineers were issued the order, and locomotives flew into the air like toys. Everything hit the rocks. Artillery, the wounded, transports, big divisional stoves with sooty chimneys, pontoons, horses—a deluge; only the detonations of blowing up locomotives thundered dully in the distance. Troops were marching throughout the morning, so the patients of the Maltese hospital from barracks A, C, and D (the lightly wounded, those who don't travel on stretchers but move on their own) happily watched through barbed wire the horror outside, where the retreat is on, and where people today will be collapsing from sunstroke along the roads, whereas they themselves, lo and behold, are more or less faring well. Here they stand, under the Red Cross, and no one will chase them anywhere, and if the Russians come, they will again be transported somewhere far away, into Russian hospitals and camps, where there will be no war, and they will remain alive and so the war will, most likely, end for them already this morning. And that, to have the war end as soon as possible, is the only thought in the heads of the wounded.

Count Maximilian Axelrode, chief of the Maltese hospital, has sent off by automobiles the distinguished female personnel (two or three baronesses and a general's wife), and resolved to remain to the last with his Maltese flag here amid danger. The bell rings at the morgue while Count Axelrode in his black robe with the Maltese cross walks through the barracks as he does every morning and gazes upon yellow naked corpses, which the Russians are carrying in coffins; the Russians carry the dead yet greet the count, lowering their caps to the ground before him.

"Hard to believe how lax things have gotten in the entire hospital over the last twelve hours."

Yes, indeed! Yesterday was an extraordinarily nerve-wracking day. The damned sun heated up everyone's brains, while the alarmist news, telegrams, and mined locomotives all affected the mood! And then that new transport, which entirely disrupted the hospital's domestic order, in the kitchens and in the medical wings! Indeed! That transport! But today, when units are passing outside and when all is seen as on a chessboard, when the falling chess pieces are visible, today it's all the more conspicuous and it all looks more destructive. As recently as yesterday, that medic corporal would never have dared to drink cognac from a big bottle in His Excellency's presence! But here, he noticed the Count's arrival, and yet goes on drinking calmly as though it had nothing to do with him. And why are nearly all the patients grinning so mockingly? And what are the Russians singing for? (The Russian slaves are singing at a service of theirs in the barracks, because today is a Russian Orthodox holiday.) No one is watering the flowerbeds today even though that is specifically stressed in the hospital decree! And there is no one anywhere! He is utterly alone in this mob!

Thus the Count stands by himself like a shadow, all shaken, and lacks the energy to restore matters to their proper order, and doesn't know what to do. He cannot get a connection to the supreme command, doesn't know what the dispositions are, and the divisional generals sped by in automobiles several minutes ago without stopping! And so the Count calls a meeting of section chiefs to decide what to do.

Some favor keeping fifty percent of the personnel and sending the other fifty percent away; others are against that, and the third group favors neither one nor the other but rather something third, and the tugging goes on back and forth until in the end nothing is resolved, "until further notice."

That "further notice," however, arrives around five o'clock in the afternoon when it becomes unquestionably clear that the hospital will most likely find itself in no-man's-land that very night; because the Russians, it appears, maintain no contact with our troops in this sector of the front. And if the planned counterattack on a major scale, announced twenty-four hours ago, does not succeed (as is very probable), then by this time tomorrow the person making decisions concerning the Maltese hospital will in all likelihood be a medical officer of some Russian division.

And so it is resolved after all that Count Axelrode, together with the surgeons, the highest-priced equipment, and fifty percent of the personnel withdraw for the night to a landed estate some ten miles west, to establish contact with some larger group and to produce a written complaint that he and his hospital have been forgotten, as though he were a needle, when he is not a needle but rather a Maltese hospital with one thousand five hundred wounded bodies.

The last of the larger infantry units were falling back, and cannons were heard close up. By then the patients had already broken up the barbed wire fence and were sitting along roadside ditches talking with the men who were arriving from battle, about "Him." And "He" was Brusilov, "He" was the Russian.

Where is "He"? Is "He" here? What is "He" up to? When will "He" get here?

"He" is on his way, by God. "He" won't stop till Vienna. "He" is on the move.

The troops were worn out and thirsty, and each said something different, and no one knew anything except that "He" was definitely coming.

Evening arrived and searchlights began to wave across the sky, cannons thundered in the distance, last units passed by, but of "Him" there was no sign. "He" had stopped for unknown reasons, as strangely as a suspended breath, stopped and stood still.

Two miles in front of the hospital a muddy swollen water flowed among willows, bridges were burning there, and this was clearly visible, but on the other bank it was peaceful and there seemed to be no one there. At this mysterious time, when nothing was known, neither where "He" is nor what "He" is doing, the entire Maltese hospital felt itself hanging in the air between Vienna and Moscow, and most likely closer to Moscow than to Vienna—so someone had the wit to steal the first bottle of cognac from the warehouse, for who knows what will happen tomorrow? Russian supply officers are even more pedantic than the Austrian.

The warehouse contained cognac and red burgundy and Hungarian Villány wines and champagne, and an hour later the entire Maltese hospital was drunk as a skunk, and the wine flowed through the barracks, and full bottles of beer were smashed because who wanted to drink beer! Russian slaves intoxicated by the bright illusion that now, already tomorrow, they will go back to their villages in the Urals, along the Volga, began to dance across all the barracks, and when a Hungarian doctor fired his revolver at the corpsmen to try to conquer alcohol with gunpowder, a full-fledged minor battle broke out, with sporadic gunfire, until the Hungarian doctor withdrew defeated before the elements, and vanished with the nurses into the darkness. Two German women, Sister Frieda and Sister Marianna (whose fiancé fell at Verdun and who was always reading Ullstein) were seized while still in their rooms and raped, and after that everything burst, and the crowd began to drink freedom all the more forcefully and deeply, guzzling that illusion to the point of madness, and everything became like a drunken dream. Every flare, rising from time to time from the other side out of the forests was greeted with wild ululating and whistling by these drunken wounded, in shirts, bottles in hand, and all lost their heads as at a folk carnival.

They brought wine by the tubful into Barrack 5B to those pitiful wounded wretches, and those broken bones, and those cut-off legs, drying under the tulle like cured meat, by God, they all got drunk, and some Hungarians started to play "Einz" on Vidović's bed.

"Dealer, hit! Hit, dealer!" fall the calls, and cards are mixed, and liquor is drunk, and the faces all look like Chinese pirate masks, twisted and grinning, studded with broken teeth, as they cheerfully grimace: "Hit, one!" Some devil has climbed into the barrack's attic and started to dance making the plaster crumble and it seemed the attic would break and everything fall through. From Barrack C an accordion is heard and an ocarina and a one-string fiddle, men from Srijem are there, and everything is booming with the song "Mama Too Papa Too," its mischievous and unrestrained scherzo vibrating and clearly audible here in Barrack 5B where the riddled, desperate Vidović lies, with a single thought coursing through his head: "Will they operate on me? If they had taken it all out today, I wouldn't be bleeding! Where are they? Why don't they operate on me? What's happening here?"

"Hit! One! Hit! Dealer!"

"*Mert arról én nem tehetek, hogy nagyon nagyon szeretlek*, taralala lalalala"—one of the amputees sings a Budapest couplet; and having put the organzine cover for his amputated leg on his head as a hat, he is coquettishly bowing left and right. An Italian is singing a song of the irredenta, his tenor sobbing with emotion, "*Amore, amore, amore!*" There is singing, drinking, pouring brandy; scabies patients have started chasing one another through the barracks with brooms, yelling, and all are growling like a menagerie, and it looks as if all these barracks, like maimed dirty and blind chickens, will converge and start to hop on a single solitary severed and bandaged leg hither and thither to the rhythm of the music of cannons thundering from the train station, ever more violently, ever louder.

"*Hande waschen vor dem Essen / Nach dem Stuhlgang nicht vergessen . . .*"

Tyroleans have begun to yodel in a chorus, to lyrics from tablets written in the three so-called state languages that hang in hospitals. Hungarians will not be outdone, so next they too sing their Hungarian stanza:

"*Egyél, igyál se mindig elöbb mosdjál!*"

And the third stanza:

"Wash hands always before food you taste / And after cleansing body of its waste . . . "

Among Croatian Guardsmen no one sings that third stanza, they only mock it as something African. A shortsighted Styrian "*Kaiserjäger*" (the lenses of whose glasses magnify his eyes so that they bulge green like glass marbles), an "imperial hunter" from some elite alpine unit, is bursting with laughter. Coughing roils and rasps within him, he is all red and about to choke, breaking his tongue trying to read that glorious Croatian poem: "*Peri ruke svagda prije jela, peri poslije izpražnjenja tijela.*"

"Ha-ha! *Ist das aber wirklich dumm! Ist das dumm dieses* 'peri'*! Was ist das, du, dieses*—peri?"

"Vasistas! Vazistas! Stupid moron. Niks! Niks! Štef, you tell him what he wants to know! You were in Graz! Bro! Bro! Schnapps!"

They are drinking and roaring with toothy laughter, hauling at each other, singing, howling: a great Babylon! Someone learned in an Italian POW camp to say: "*Porca Madonna io parlo Italiano!*" and is now yelling it to the Italians and waving to them. "*Porca Madonna, porca, porca, porca,*" and someone is mocking the Romanians with a quote from typhus-epidemiological hospitals: "*Nu este permis a ščipi per podele!* Ha-ha! Šči rumunješči!"

"Dear brothers! Please! Quiet! It hurts! It hurts me terribly!" shouts Vidović, but his voice is faint, rattling, and blood is welling up to his teeth.

"*Te! Mi az?* Hurts? *Mindig ez a* hurts? *Mi az* hurts?"

"That's when you're hurt, my dear," a shot-riddled man from Bunj explains to the Hungarian. "You know, when you get wounded, it hurts! Or when you hit yourself! Then it also hurts!"

"*Micsoda? Hit yosef?* Hurts! Ha-ha! Hurts! Ha-ha!"

"Mama too papa too . . ."

And the cannons grow ever louder, as though someone were chopping wood under the barracks.

That major counterattack announced a full forty-eight hours earlier actually succeeded, and at dawn the Russians were thrown far back in a single push, with a strike from both wings. Some fifteen infantry battalions and several artillery batteries were captured, so Count Axelrode, accompanied by Baroness Lichtenstein, had already arrived at the hospital by automobile at nine thirty.

Before all else, there was a major inquiry into the rapes of the German women (who were sexually used by Hungarians) around twelve-thirty; seven Russians were shot, having first dug their own graves; and some three hundred and fifty malingerers (cases of trachoma, scabies, venereal disease, lighter flesh wounds, and all inmates of barracks A 2, 3, 4, and 5 except temperatures above 100.4°F) were thrown into combat, and by ten thirty the sober Johannine Maltese order reigned over the hospital once more.

In order to reestablish the authority of the imperial flag and discipline, which had seemed so compromised during that night, Count Axelrode issued an order to the hospital that the great victory of the previous night be celebrated with a torchlight parade. All patients (with no distinction) were to file past the black and yellow banner, those who were immobilized would be carried on stretchers, but everyone would file past. And so it was done.

All the barracks have arranged themselves into units and everybody has been handed a burning lantern; the procession is led by a supply officer who has never in his life sat on a horse, but is jangling his spurs and arranging the crowd like a film director. The procession of several hundred heads in gray bloody caps has assembled, everyone's hand is holding a green or red lantern, the strong colors are vividly burning in the blue-gray liquid of twilight, and it all looks like a spectral vision.

Grandsons of the dead who fell at Viennese barricades in '48, children of Garibaldi's standard-bearers, Hussites, God's warriors, Jelačić's frontier guards, Kossuth's *honvéds*, all of them limbless, lame, disfigured, bandaged, amputated, on crutches, in wheelchairs, on stretchers, jostling each other, carrying and pushing; and there stands the great black and yellow flag, and under it Count Axelrode in black with his Maltese cross, and behind him nurses with red crosses and doctors, all singing in a chorus: *Gott erhalte*! People are treading quietly, with bowed heads, as though ashamed, still dazed from the night before, carrying yellow lanterns like candles at a funeral, while a bugler has climbed to the roof and is trumpeting "*général de charge.*"

When they brought Vidović back to Barrack 5B from that shameful parade, he was blazing with high fever.

The previous night everything had gone bad, and the whole barrack, fired up with alcohol, now feels its wounds most intensely. The Siberian at number seven got drunk and was already dead by morning; they carried him out of the barrack only in the afternoon, and everything smelled awful, because that mass of blood had gotten inflamed. The Slovak with the tube at number nine is still suffering, his labored breathing audible. And somewhere down among the Hungarians, a Russian is screaming horribly. Last night he wanted to dance, and now he is screaming like mad.

"*Az atya úr istennét, ennek a Ruszkinak! Ruszki!*"

"Shut up! You Russky! What're you yelling for?"

"I'm hurting too, and I'm quiet!"

"Russky, shut up!"

"Shh! Quiet! Shh! Shh!"

Vidović lies and listens to the barrack as it quarrels and senses the end.

"What was I really born for, what purpose did it have? To be born in such a silly pseudo-civilization, that lacks even sadness and where everything is an operetta. How shameful my death is! How deeply shameful! I wanted to live, to live it up! And what happened? Hospitals and nothing but hospitals! What words on this earthly planet can make sense out of this hospital? Nothing but hospitals! For two years now I've been traveling through nothing but hospitals! Decorative city hospitals with highborn whores! Convents where consumptives are dying! They squirt serum into them, and no one believes in that serum. Barracks! Dirty, stinking, lousy wooden barracks like these! Ah, how sad and disgusting it all is!"

And out of a need for some action, to budge, to jump, to sprint, to shout with all his might, Vidović wants to sit up, but he can't. It squeezes him. The pain conquers the uproar of his nerves, and he loses his way in the fog and begins to groan loudly.

"Shh! Shh!" the barrack protests and hisses from the darkness.

And pain has begun tightening the screws ever harder on countless bloody and shredded limbs scattered throughout Barrack 5B. Pain has begun to take supernatural forms, and people have begun calling on God. Lord God Himself is appealed to as the last resort, as petitions are written to the court chancellery, when all else has failed.

Some Hungarian is summoning his *Išten*! To help him! To have his Lord come in his big horse-groom's pantaloons, drink up two or three bottles of red oxblood, play some devilish tune on the fiddle, so that one can at last either die or be resurrected. It can't go on like this any longer! "*Gospodi, Gospodi! Gospodi!*" shouts a Russian, transparent and pale as a Byzantine icon, praying to the Russian Lord God in boyar's furs who sits on his golden throne in Kremlin town, and the Russian man shouts, shouting so hard his voice carries all the way to Little Mother Moscow, shouting so hard, and clasping his hands, and crying like a newborn: "*Gospodi! Gospodi!*"

And Vidović starts, and it seems to him that *Išten* has come to the Hungarian, and sat on his bed and is letting him drink from a round flask, and the Hungarian drinks more and more vigorously, he drinks and the fiddles squeal, ah, it's good to drink out of someone's hand to the squeal of fiddles! It's good! That puts one to sleep! And the Russian Imperial Lord God, he too walks through the barrack with his opulent retinue, and icons blaze and bells of the Holy Little Mother ring, and that old Lord with a white beard and silken furs is digging through Russian guts and extracting that bloody bullet from the Russian man, and it's better, ah, it's better, thank you, Lord, it's better!

"Look! Each one of them has his God! Each one of them has his God!

"That one from Fiume too (*'Mamma mia! Mamma mia!'*) he too has his cardinals and popes and Roman flags, and the Russian and the Hungarian, they too have their Lord Gods, and whom do I have? I'm hurting too! I've been shot just like they! And I don't have anyone!"

And Vidović is gripped with such pain that he raises his arms and stretches them out after someone, and his arms stay in the air, and he feels a terrible emptiness, and his throat tightens, and he begins to weep aloud.

"Oh, yes! I saw Christ hanging in front of our inns! That was a real Croatian Christ, all of his thirty-three ribs broken, his tits run through, and bleeding from countless wounds! And I never believed in him! A wooden Christ like that on a muddy road soaked with animal piss; no drunk passes him by without cursing him; a wooden Croatian God, naked, pitiful, with a missing left leg, oh, a God with a soldier's cap, he, he— To pray to him, so he helps me..."

"*Lieb' Vaterland, magst ruhig sein,—Wir wollen alle Mütter sein, Treu steht und fest die Wacht am Rhein.*"

"What is that? Am I mad? Who is this I'm praying to? It hurts! I'm praying! What kind of voices are these?"

From the outside, through the green tulle above Vidović's head, a yellow light pours in and female voices in a minor key are heard, quietly crooning the lyrics. And the clinking of crystal glass is audible! It rings quietly, and the voices are quiet, but clear: "*Lieb' Vaterland, magst ruhig sein...*"

Adjacent to Barrack 5B is a bower in which doctors and Templar ladies of the Red Cross regularly dine. And tonight Count Axelrode is in special attendance at that solemn supper, to celebrate the victory with the personnel.

Exhilarated by the magnificent phenomenon of victory, when it had already seemed that the die had fallen wrong, and then it all turned out so beautifully after all, and lulled by the patriotic melody of his Germanic ladies, who are ready to conceive in the interest of war and warfare, Count Maximilian Axelrode, commander of the Maltese Order, arises and raises his glass, to toast victory. He speaks passionately about His Majesty's victories, alongside which the Maltese banner also waves, undefeated and supreme.

"My ladies! *Luogotenente* Fra Giovanni Battista Ceschi a Santa Croce, who with his own eyes witnessed the Jacobin assault on this our sacred Maltese cross, which I have the honor to represent here, that noble knight inscribed in his chronicles as follows, my ladies: When His Divine Being shall be separating good from evil over an extinguished sun, the black Maltese capes shall stand as a guard in God's shadow..."

Vidović hears the clinking of glasses in the bower and recognizes the voice of the Count commander and recalls his mask of a face at tonight's torchlight parade.

"I've gone insane! I was about to start praying! Oh! And those out there are singing! Indeed! They're celebrating victory! And that Maltese knight is saying..."

"What's with number nine? He tore the tube from his throat! He's bleeding! Nurse!"

"Shh! Shh!"

"But number nine is bleeding! Nurse!"

"There's no one anywhere! Where's the nurse? Number nine..."

Out in the bower, on the other side of the whitewashed board, glasses are clinking, and here number nine has torn out the tube in his agony, and blood is pouring out. Number nine is breathing with difficulty, he is gurgling, as a slaughtered pig gurgles, and then more and more quietly...

Vidović wants to shout, but he cannot find his voice. It is clear to him that a candle should be lit for number nine.

"A candle should be lit! So his soul can rest in peace!" He keeps repeating this, his eyes locked on the puddle of black blood of number nine. He wants to roar out with all his might, but it only whistles within him as in a sieve.

"Shut up! By the mother of God!"

"*Az apád istennét! Csönd!*"

"Shut up!"

"Number nine has died! Number nine has died! And these cavaliers outside are singing and clinking glasses! Fra Giovanni Battista a Santa Croce! Let me see him! Let me see the Cavalier from Malta..."

And in a transport of final effort, which is really already a death struggle, Vidović arises like a specter and tears apart the tulle above his head! There is a bright square out there and within the bright-green light among the leaves of the bower, white ladies with red crosses are visible, half-drunk, laughing, loud, future mothers of future vampires.

"Damn you," Vidović wants to shout, and a bright thought flashes through his head that he ought to fling his porcelain pot with its muck onto that white tablecloth and befoul it all—befoul it, so that a great terrible stain remains on that white tablecloth, and that everyone cries out: A stain, a stain.

In the realization of that final pitiful thought Vidović reaches down for his pot, and feels, even while falling, his hands slither into a terrible matter—and everything drowns in blood, which gushes out in a torrent...

GUARDSMAN JAMBREK

IT WAS RAINING WHEN JAMBREK ARRIVED drunk at the battalion with a whole horde of recruits. Adorned with tricolors, the boys strode down the middle of the street with arms around each other like a phalanx, crossing the entire city, and it all looked festive and victorious. Carriages and wet umbrellas along the asphalt seemed to give way left and right before this youthful mob from Zagorje, going to the battalion and singing.

"Shut up! Damn your drunken peasant mothers! Shut up! Shut those stinking snouts!"

"You'll holler, all right, you will! Just you wait! Damn your recruit mothers!"

Thus the battalion's non-commissioned officers greeted them, and there was in the non-com voices much sarcastic, downright butcherly malice with which calves are struck across muzzles in slaughterhouses, when they bleat. And they shoved the hundred of them into a small basement room where everything was battened with steel bars, and the glass panes gray and filthy so that nothing of the outside could be seen.

Stinking straw mats rose in stacks to the ceiling, and there were so many straw mats and recruits that no one could sit down. Drunks vomited and spouted obscenities and gibberish; an epileptic fell to the ground and, foaming, began to kick about. This affected another epileptic who also collapsed and began to bite himself till he bled; and thus they waited a long time, and it was already late afternoon when they shoved them out into the corridor where they remained standing while a barber sheared off their hair to the scalp, like convicts.

Then they herded them into the supply depot and gave them reeking, bloody and tattered old blouses (that was the uniform), and thus Jambrek became a National Guardsman.

It was raining, and in a second-floor room flutists were fingering over the notes of *Die Meistersinger*. Down at the barrack courtyard, in dreary emptiness reminiscent of an execution ground, there in the rain they were "suspending" Ignac Sovec, a Guardsman from an infantry company who had "slapped back" a staff sergeant. At that time recruits did not yet know what discipline meant, and this "Sovec incident" came in handy to the non-coms to show the recruits graphically what discipline really is and what it entails.

"There! That Guardsman 'slapped back' his superior! They could now hand him over to be court-martialed! Tie him up and hand him over to a court martial, and there they'd shoot him like a dog. But the company commander doesn't want that! The company commander is a good man! He'll let the swine live! Let him better himself! Give him a chance to lick up all he's done!"

"This is an exemplary lesson, that Guardsman! Take a good look at him, boys!" And the recruits, who have no idea about any of this yet, and know neither what a company is nor what discipline is, stand in a frightened huddle and gaze at Ignac Sovec as he hangs from the oak.

Ignac Sovec hangs like a torn coat, his hands have turned blue; he has fainted twice already but they always drench him with water to make him come to. Guardsman Sovec's body is twisted with pain, he is grunting like a pig, two yellow snails have emerged from his nostrils, and his eyes are jutting out like those of a crushed frog.

And thus they drive these "boys" like cattle, falling upon the Guardsmen from all directions, and now they will start to tame these peasant swine and cabbageheads, carcasses and yokels, fools and blockheads and hey-yous.

"Hey, you!"

"Hey, you carcass! Devil take your father and mother! Wipe 'em like a shot! Those boots ain't yours! That's army leather, damn you!"

"Hey, you! Damned swindler! Faking it again!"

"Hey, you! Lazy scum! Get me a glass of water!"

"Hey, you! Shine my shoes! If you don't shine them tips, you'll be licking mud off the soles with your peasant snout!"

"Hey, you! Damned crook! Pull in that gut of yours! Drawers in, chest out! Get it straight, you blockhead!"

Staff sergeants exit and enter slamming doors authoritatively, and the people have squeezed together timidly and sit on their black trunks taking out bread rolls, cheese, meat (depending on what each peasant has), and crouch silent and scared. That is how it looks in the lowest third-class decks of transoceanic giants when the peasant material of Zagorje is transported in bulk to the infernal steel mills and mines over on the other shore in the free USA, and the entire Guardsman throng looks trapped in a terrible cabin of a strange Austrian ship of death, sailing slowly—with mathematical certainty—toward shipwreck.

In a corner's half shadow, Platoon Sergeant Repić is sipping the recruits' brandy and lecturing on theft. Every thief caught among the Guardsmen will have spikes driven under his fingernails and be shod barefoot to make his blood spurt, for that is military justice.

"Don't you steal, I'm telling you, damn your peasant mother! Because you'll be sorry when I catch you! You think I won't catch you? I'm a platoon sergeant! Your Lord God platoon sergeant! Understand?

"If you're a Guardsman thief, I'm your platoon sergeant super thief! Understand that, you ass of a recruit!

"Keep in mind that I am higher in rank than you, and my rank sees through your rank! I see through you because I'm a Lord and you're a serf! I can see through your guts! So if you steal, I see it all and know it all right away! Where you stole it and how you stole it—you got that? You can't hide nothing from me! Got that? And if you snatch a bill, even if you graduated from a thieves' college, you think I didn't? If you snatch a ten and knock off a five, then stick a five back with the ten, you think I'm so stupid I don't know that so-called trick? Ho-ho!

"Shut your faces, bastards! If you're a poacher, then I'm a super poacher! I'm always higher than you! I see everything! And I know everything! That's why when you report to me, you report hum-bly! Got that? Hum-bly!"

Thus the platoon sergeant drinks the recruits' brandy, explaining the principles of subordination, pointing out that he is a super crook.

Further off, Staff Sergeant Gradiški is feasting on fatty chicken and duck, washing it all down pleasantly with fragrant blood of the grape, and (to enhance appetite) holding forth on the cleanliness of latrines, insisting that cleanliness of the latrines is a barometer of company discipline and culture.

"We are now a cultivated people! Got that, boys? He who makes a stinking mess will gobble up his own stinking mess! By God he will, boys, gobble it up and devour it! Devil take my mother if he won't, boys! Got that?

"He'll be gobbling it up all around! When I tell you that you will, peasant swine, then you will, and devil take me if you won't. Piss-soaked hooligans, I'll teach you how to behave."

"Corporal Sir, please take this little bottle, kindly request. See how yellow it is, like a gold coin?"

"I've told you a hundred times I'm not a corporal, you ox! I'm a staff sergeant! Staff Sergeant, sir, humbly request! Hum-bly, not kindly! You hear? Stupid animal!"

These first days of the green recruits are a colonial delight for their lordships the Royal Hungarian non-coms. The new recruits, like cattle driven into a new stable, are afraid of everything, don't know what to do, and are careful not to arouse anyone's resentment, because recruits are as timid as cows.

At present the recruits are loaded with food (and stuffed with money), so the golden vein needs only to be located and a good method found, for during this early period recruits can be sucked dry. A recruit can be milked like a cow, merely by touching the udder.

Over there "staff sergeant of the day" is collecting money for lamps, petroleum, wicks, candles, cups, shoe polish, brushes—devil only knows all the things "staff sergeant of the day" is collecting money for. A man in the barracks needs a hundred trivial items, and though they all look superfluous at first, life in the barracks is impossible without them.

"You gotta have a stiff collar if you want them young ladies to give you the eye," shouts the experienced dandy, renowned Don Juan "staff sergeant of the day" whose blouse has been retailored officer-style, collar starched and hard, white rubber stars sharp and pointed. (Five for two crowns over at the "Happy Guardsman"!)

Recruits are paying out tax, duty, surtax, and Guardsman dues for all the articles that they could buy themselves at the canteen for half the price, but alas, recruits are stupid and don't know any better than to hand everything over. Like rams, they have surrendered to mercy and to cruelty, and now what will be will be. Can't get loose from that noose. A man twitches his ears like a donkey and sighs deeply. These are the first days of Guardsman University, and in the second or third semester these freshmen will sail off to Tobolsk, to Barnaul, to Semipalatinsk, just to be rid of this Guardsman plague!

Guardsman Jambrek got his Mannlicher rifle, learned double rows and quadruple rows left and right, and now he is a real Guardsman and marches to the drum as it is prescribed: left-right, one-two! Hay-straw, one-two. Guardsman Jambrek is the seventh man in Sergeant Repić's platoon, a platoon of the second company, and to the left and right of him stand none but chicken-snatchers and pickpockets from the Drava River region.

Platoon Sergeant Repić is a stern master who despises recruits on principle, an old warrior, an expert at drilling company troops.

"No tractor's been made that can drag Guardsman wisdom into a recruit's head. A recruit's like a calf! You gotta show him everything with a fist!"

Platoon Sergeant Repić hence operates in line with all the tested methods of solid Guardsman education and shows everything with a fist.

He is the one who discovered that the concept of a trajectory, and all ballistic principles, can most easily be explained to a recruit by spitting from a distance into his face. The reason the earth attracts a bullet, and the way it happens, is nicely seen in the parabola of urine, thus all Guardsmen must urinate on command, to get a vivid idea of that line, known to Guardsmen as trajectory, which a bullet describes when it flies from the barrel. "That's a para-bola—got that boys? And that's why a *levorver* is called a para-bolum!"

Sergeant Repić stands before the second platoon, legs spread in tyrannical challenge, arms behind his back, explaining to his platoon the meaning and the function of patrols in Guardsman life.

"Guardsman patrols are called 'recons.' Got that? Pay close attention, boys! What's it mean, for instance, when we say 'right recon'? And why do we have patrols, what we call 'recons,' and what are they? Eh? Who knows?"

Second platoon stands at attention, silent and staring, and no one has the slightest notion of what 'right recon' might actually mean.

Such stupidity infuriates the platoon leader, making the veins in his neck swell up like those of a bull, and now he will gore someone with his horns.

"You're stupid, and blind, and deaf, and lazy! It's hard to get anywhere with you! Jambrek! Come here! Hey! Come here when I tell you! Damn your mother! You hear me, Jambrek!"

Guardsman Jambrek steps out frightened, not knowing what will happen to him. Something will happen, and whatever happens will clearly not be pleasant!

Maybe he will be forced to urinate again, and that is difficult to do in front of everyone, because a man gets embarrassed and trembles, making it impossible to succeed, so Repić then wrings the water from him by slapping, and the entire platoon laughs at that.

Jambrek stands at attention while the scoundrels are already grinning at the platoon sergeant's latest prank, because they are veterans who have gone through all the Guardsman colleges and universities.

"Hey, come here! This way! You hear me? You dumb ox! Step on it!"

Guardsman Jambrek steps up to the platoon sergeant, from three paces to one, and stands there rigid as a pillar.

"Right! Shut your eyes! Hey! Shut your eyes, you damned dolt! There! Shut 'em tight!"

Guardsman Jambrek shuts his eyes as commanded. He stands tensely at attention with his eyes closed, awaiting his destiny as a rabbit on a medical table awaits the lancet. A pause.

"See anything?"

"Nothing, humbly report!"

"Right! Just stay the way you are! Now everybody pay close attention here! Dimwitted peasant donkeys!"

The platoon sergeant silently steals up to Guardsman Jambrek and swings his arm.

There is a slap. Forceful. Loud.

Guardsman Jambrek staggers from the slap, stunned as if startled out of sleep, while the platoon bursts into unrestrained, brutal laughter.

"Ha-ha-ha, hee-hee-hee!" laughs the platoon in a chorus, the voice of a circus arena laughing cruelly at a slapped clown.

"Shut up, you mules! Shut up!" Sergeant Repić bares his teeth at the platoon, putting on an act of being angry! He is not angry at all but only pretending, even enjoying his role and this whole comedy which vividly demonstrates the deeper significance of "right recon."

"Now, now, now! What are you laughing at, like split blood sausages? And what are you looking at me for, like a roasted cow! A cow! What are you looking at me for? What did I do to you? Eh? Don't you hear what I'm asking you? Jam-brek!"

"You slapped me, humbly report, Platoon Sergeant, sir!"

"That's right! I slapped you! And why did I slap you? Eh? Why?"

"I don't know, humbly report!"

"You don't know nothin'! You're stupid! You're a roasted cow! A cow! If you hadn't closed your eyes like a blind mouse, damn your blind God, if you'd been looking at me like you're looking at me now, what would you've done when you saw that I was gonna smack you? Eh?"

"I don't know, humbly report!"

"Go to the devil! You'd have raised your arm for sure! You'd have defended yourself! You wouldn't have let yourself get smacked! You wouldn't have, right? You'd have defended yourself with your arm! There! That's it! You'd have raised your arm! Right! Good! Scram back in the ranks! Now pay attention, boys! Look! A company, when it travels in the world, across a mountain, across a valley, up and down, left and right, when it travels, it don't see neither left nor right, nor up nor down, nor nowhere. Why don't the company see, when it travels in the world? Eh? Who knows?"

"It's got its eyes shut, so it don't see," calls out a chicken-snatcher from the left wing.

"The devil's mother's got her eyes shut, and not the company, you damned moron! The company don't have its eyes shut, the company *can't* see! It can't! Because a company is small! A company is small, mountains are tall! A company can't see what's over on the other side! A company is blind! A company is blind, like me now!"

Platoon Sergeant Repić closes his eyes and walks before the platoon with eyes squeezed shut, up and down, up and down, thus demonstrating clearly that a company is small and blind in the broad terrain across which it moves as it travels through the world like a caterpillar.

"There, you see! Now I'm the company! And any devil can smack me left and right, like I smacked Jambrek, 'cause I don't see nothin'! But a company ain't stupid like Jambrek! A company ain't no Jambrek! A company got more brains than Jambrek! A company don't let itself get smacked! That's why the company got its arm raised ahead of time, to defend itself, 'cause the company's smart! The company knows what it's doing! Like this! Take a good look this way! The company lifts up its left arm here on the left! And the right one too, the company lifts it up here on the right! Did you see that, ya dumb chicken-catchers, did you see what the company does? Eh? There! That's it! These two arms of mine, this one on the right and this one on the left, they're the right and left 'recons,' they're the company's right and left patrols . . . "

Repić mumbles all this like a bear, and raising both of his big hairy arms aloft he keeps on strolling before his second platoon with his eyes closed, like a living symbol of company patrols.

This problem of patrols will be explained even more profoundly through metaphors, that the company is an insect and the patrol a feeler, that the company is a blind man and the patrol a cane with which he feels the way, but for today it is enough for these rustic muttonheads and pumpkinheads to know that a patrol is a fist with which a company protects itself from getting smacked, because a company is not a stupid Guardsman pumpkinhead but a Royal Hungarian company!

"You got that, boys?"

"Yes!" laughs the second platoon in a chorus. "Yes!"

"There! That's it! All of that looks terribly hard and clever, but when you grab hold of it and look at it up close, to figure out what this patrol stuff is all about, you see that there's nothin' to it! Nothin' at all! It's all easy as marmalade!"

⚯

And so Guardsman Jambrek began to drill in mass firing formations and to shoot sharply, he washed latrines and corridors, offices and waterworks and shoe repair stores, and every seventh day, on Sunday, he went to church.

Amid the beatings and humiliations, amid that filthy torrent of obscenities and curses, Sunday stood out as a bright, decorative chord. Sunday is the day when the Guardsmen, accompanied by music, go to the city to attend Holy Mass. Fifes, trumpets, and drums resound, nickel sparkles on drawn sabers, and to the hungry company of serfs and beggars it fleetingly seems that this idiotic Royal Hungarian war is not sorrow and misery, but rather that it's all a joyful game of well-nourished and strong soldiers, who will truly dash into battle with supernatural vigor, and it seems to the men that they are dancing at a solemn, strange costumed ball. Up on the marble pulpit beneath the Holy Ghost appears an officer clothed in a rochet with a crucifix in hand, a cavalier with golden fringe and decorations, his spurs ringing, who courts the ladies like a seventeenth-century musketeer, one such masked cavalier appears beneath the canopy of the Holy Mother Church of Rome ("our benefactress, our protectress"), and he will now speak in the name of His Majesty the Emperor of Rome and the King of Jerusalem and in the name of Lord God, who is here with us on this side of the front, warring at this fateful time on the side of the Central Powers, on the side of the Hungarian crown in accordance with the Agreement of the Year 1868.

That cavalier, Christ's standard-bearer, blazes up with rhetorical fervor beneath the marble Holy Ghost, and this glorious figure who has three mistresses (because he looks elegant in a uniform), this fastidiously shaved knight in a rochet speaks of the Habsburg Dynasty and of blood and of death, which is especially glorious on the battlefield, where the wounded fall like Saint Sebastians. In order that not a single solitary word should fall past a Guardsman's ear, but that it should drop straight into the serf's heart, this cavalier speaks in the glorious dialect of Zagorje, filling the peasant's ear with mellifluous music like a cunning bandleader, because that is the way to handle the Twenty-Fifth Domestic.

And the man of Zagorje, beaten down all week with the torture dealt out to recruits, dazed now by the colors and music and incense, listens as the beloved sounds flow into his ear intoxicating him with an ancient Slavic Pannonian melody.

(Strange is this melody of the Austrian barracks and the Bible, capable of flinging a man into the depths and awakening within him a dead specter that treads over fires bloody and mad, and is a beast and not a man, and yet, if even that beastly depth is taken away from him, what then is left in this pitiful creature to whom no one has addressed a single word in all of eight hundred years?)

Thus Jambrek too is dazed every Sunday by the ornaments of the colorful church, when the organ so strangely thunders, and Jambrek sinks into bestial dreams as for a moment it becomes terribly clear to him that it is none other than our enemies of a different faith who are to blame for all evil, because "they are the ones who wanted to kill our Caesar!"

Jambrek listens to the word of the Lord, and blood pounds in his head from the great and fearsome Truth which is here announced to God's warriors, the National Guardsmen.

The Roman cavalier speaks of Ezekiel, prophet of the Lord, who once in a dream saw a mighty host of angels, immeasurable, fearsome, and enormous.

"A terrible army, a whole shining army of angels! As great an army of angels as you are, you who are a great army, my dear Guardsmen and brothers in Christ!

"And all the angels had swords in hand, burning swords, and they swung them like burning torches, and it was terrible to hear as these angelic legions hummed in the air like a tin windmill.

"And Ezekiel, prophet of the Lord, saw with his own eyes that army of angels flying, and heard it humming, and saw Our One and Only Lord God commanding over it like a general!

"And down below our Lord God was the burning hell, with all those stinking rabid Lucifers and Beelzebubs in that sulphur and stench of hell. And the Lord God smote his enemies with that angelic legion and destroyed them forever and ever!

"Dear Guardsmen and boys!

"God's angels, those same ones whom Christ, our heavenly king, saw in their legions in the Garden of Gethsemane, those angelic battalions and regiments stand around God's throne and defend Him, and with them Lord God thrashes all his Beelzebubs and Lucifers of hell.

"And as the angels are God's army, God's battalions and regiments, so you Guardsmen too are the imperial host, the army of the emperor and king, my dear Guardsmen! And as the angels defend God and blow their trumpets and thunder with their wings, so do you too defend the emperor and king and home, and that is why you are National Guardsmen! Our king defends himself with you, like God with angels.

"Just like Beelzebubs and Lucifers struck at God, our enemies struck at our good white-haired king with sulphur and fire of hell, because they don't believe in our church, the damned heretics!

"Boys and Guardsmen! The Lord's prophet Ezekiel saw the army of angels fly, and heard it hum shining and burning, and your regiments and battalions must smite like heavenly legions and fall like hail on the sulphur of hell, and your rifle and your saber must blaze in your hands like a burning sword—my dear Guardsmen and brothers in Christ!"

Guardsman Jambrek listens to all these exalted titles, from the Only God and king Jesus Christ to His Jerusalemite Majesty, generals and angels, sulphur and hell, and his Guardsman's head is getting all fogged up from the political and historical smoke and conflagration. Sixty trumpets of military fanfare strike up together with the organ, and the air in the church trembles as if heavy artillery were booming, the incense smokes, Haydn thunders, and the men of Zagorje kneel, and in their Guardsmen hearts a strange joy blazes up, that all this is after all a great thing, what is happening with them here, and that they are fortunate to be able to sacrifice themselves for the Austrian emperor and Hungarian and Croatian king.

Every seventh day Guardsman Jambrek thus cleanses himself of his shameful little hurts, which drag him somewhere toward the mountain in Sad Bistra, and when he marches through the city, he now raises his head boldly and proudly, and it is as if a radiance emanates from him which the prophet Ezekiel saw aglow over the burning angelic army! *Tra-ta-ra-ta, boom, boom, boom!*

Our miserable Guardsmen fired off the prescribed series of sharp bullets, put on the green nettles, confessed themselves and took Holy Communion, and now adorned in tricolors they wait to depart. All is finished; only the banners still need to unfold, cymbals and drums to sound, and the locomotive to whistle, and the unit will vanish as if it had never existed.

"So, we're going after all, eh, boys?" Commander of the Infantry Formation and Transport, Reserve Lieutenant Dr. Lulić, puts the question to his men next to the barrel of beer that is being tapped in the middle of the courtyard. The boys have already drunk two tubfuls and are now starting on the third, and the music strikes up with: "Not a man from Zagorje ever sold his wine yet."

"So we're off, we're going, eh?"

"Sure! We're off, by God, we're off, Lieutenant Sir!"

"Already now at noon?" asks an old man, small and homely, from somewhere behind the gangly fellows of the first platoon, his voice vibrating with anxiety, as though he is afraid it has already come to this, and it's time to depart.

"When if not now? Of course we're off! As soon as the double-baked bread is distributed, off we go, old man! And what's wrong with you? Not scared, are you?"

"His daughter said she'd come, but she's not here," calls out someone from the crowd for him, barrister-like, because the old man has grown embarrassed.

"So, men, are you happy? Eh? Are you sincerely glad that we're off?"

The men, packed in a tight cordon around the commander, make faces and remain stupidly silent as they sip and slurp the beer, as though reluctant both to travel off and to reply to stupid questions from their stupid intelligentsia, not a single word of whose they have believed for centuries.

"What's the dumb ass bothering us for? All of that's a load of empty straw!"

There is a feeling that a whole string of stupid historical questions ought to be answered, but what to say? How to say it? Is the Guardsman called upon to say something?

Silence. Someone has brought a fiddle, and the company Gypsy has begun to play a Syrmian kolo, which has drawn many of the curious away from this group, while here and there men fired up with brandy have started to dance.

"Old Franz Josef bought some gasoline..."

Doctor Lulić (professor of Latin and Greek at a provincial academy) senses the sound of the violin, and feels like talking with his men, telling them something, so that all is not left so disproportionately tattered and stupid at such a historical moment.

"All this is nothing! At least it's all over now! No more drills or drill-grounds! Now we'll go nicely up to the front, to show what we know! War, boys, is an exam! There we get to show how much we learned in the rear! So if you've been industrious, you'll get a reward! But you won't show anything, nor will you get anything! Because you know nothing!"

"We do know, we know," voices call back, here and there.

"You know! You know! Only you're lazy! But all will be well! It must be well! All right, children, to your health, God grant you long life!

"Isn't it true that you're happy to go into battle? Eh?"

Pause. Silence. Quiet.

"Well, by your Guardsman mothers, what is war? Haven't we been to war already? For hundreds and hundreds of years we stand in war and we're alive all the same! Didn't your pa and grandpa go to war?"

"Sure! By God they did! They went to Italy! And to this day we keep the silver dollar that Pop earned in Italy!"

"And my grandpa was with Jelačić, whipping the Hungarians!"

(Dead wars, like the dear departed, are spoken of with sentimental piety. Dead wars are spoken of as if those wars had been idyllic excursions into romantic regions of naïve adventures that the childish human heart chronically hankers for as recreation, so that we shouldn't be so hopelessly bored on this gray and miserable planet. These ancient dead wars were indeed provincial operettas compared to the present industrialized slaughter, so when they are spoken of, these dead wars are draped with a consecrated veil of gilded memory, and stories devoid of truth are told about them with a historical accent, as though it all happened as in fact it did not.)

"There, you see! How your fathers and grandfathers got through all that! So what! We're all alive and healthy! And we too have already been to the front! We know what a front is! Raise your hands, those who haven't yet been out there!"

Many green sleeves rise up.

"Right! There's quite a few of you! You'll twitch your ears, when they shower you with shrapnel. You'll squeeze your gut, and leak a little water! But that's nothing! And even if someone bites the dust, so what! It's stupid to live anyway, when they don't let you live! At least you'll have fallen for the homeland and for our honest king!"

"Is it true, Lieutenant Sir, that Franz Josef rides a white horse?"

"He rides a black one too! He's got thousands and thousands of horses!"

"A-a-a-ah!" The Guardsmen marvel greatly at this, and nod their heads over the opulence of their Croatian king.

"Well, what do you expect? Would His Majesty be able to defeat so many enemies if he weren't so rich? Tell me, men, who is it we're fighting? From whom are we defending ourselves?"

That is a problematic question for the people of Zagorje. Until the war, and during the war itself, their orientation was much more logical and precise than the overall orientation of our intelligentsia. They understood the state as fundamentally imperial, and recognized none of the phrases about some Constitution. The Emperor is the state, the Emperor is the government, and a man from Zagorje was a serf both before and after 1848; he was always a serf. The war started because those damned eastern heathens (who butcher their kings once every ten years) wanted to butcher our emperor and king, and they did butcher some prince somewhere. Then the emperor called his faithful Croats (because he doesn't trust Hungarians and Germans, the damned curs) and so the Croats moved to defend the Emperor and King, who is a Croatian king, but the Hungarians won't let him be that.

After the debacle in Serbia, right at the war's outset between August and December of 1914, men of Zagorje felt defeat with their own flesh, and the question began to be asked around the barracks: Why doesn't the Emperor sue for peace? The main source of confusion for the people of Zagorje from the very outset was the war with Russia.

"The Serbs whipped us! They whipped us, by God! They're better soldiers than the Hungarians and the Krauts! If only Croats had been at the Drina, they wouldn't have whipped us! What the devil are we doing in Russia? What did the Russians do to us? Where is Zagorje? Plus we can't do nothin' to those Russians! For every one of us, a thousand Russians!"

And now there is a void in the Zagorje brain, and the man senses that it's all windmills toward which he is being shoved. Windmills, he senses it. And also senses that the rations are worthless, that the Guardsmen are in tatters, that what they clothed them in is paper, and the army shoes are paper, and it's all nettles and it will all get waterlogged and fall apart. He senses it, that paper, those stinking cabbages and nettles. How, then, to respond to all this!?

Thus the men grow thoughtful at the question of who it is they are preparing to fight today, and fall silent.

"Well? What are you quiet for? By a hundred devils, surely you know what we are fighting for."

"Because they killed our Caesar!"

"Who? They killed who? Caesar?"

"Yeah!"

"You stupid ass! That wasn't Caesar! That wasn't him," call out voices, feeling this is a mistaken outlook on events.

"That wasn't Caesar! That was that other one! That other one! They killed that one!"

"Franz Josef wanted to conquer Bosnia to take it away from Mohammed!"

"Blockhead! Turks are our allies! We're fighting against Russians and the English!"

(That is something that the Zagorje head cannot take in, that the Turks are our allies. There is still to this day fear in Zagorje from that time when Turkish hooves clattered around Toplice and Konjščina.)

Lieutenant Lulić senses himself surrounded by doubting Thomases and wants to say something about the Englishman who smokes his little pipe having bribed the Russian Tsar who needs the pounds; the Doctor wants to sketch in a few geopolitical hypotheses, to orient "his" company, when the band breaks off "La Machicha" mid-beat to strike up the roll, and the battalion trumpets announce themselves. There is a stir among the officers around a speakers' platform draped with tricolors, because the colonel with his retinue has appeared at the battalion entrance.

"Infantry company! Fall in!" shouts Doctor Lulić drawing his saber, as the Guardsmen begin to run around the stacked pyramids of rifles, and the company forms into eight meaty walls, gazing shyly and absentmindedly at the priest who, crucifix in hand, flanked by the red white and blue banners, climbs the speakers' platform to bless the imperial legions.

At the place where Jambrek alighted from the train carriage stood a factory, whitewashed a pure white, with a hundred blind windows, destroyed, only the walls jutting up raggedly, broken and charred. There were graves with Byzantine crosses here and there, and ravens flapped low over the muddy ploughed fields.

Jambrek passed with his unit through small wooden cities and towns, and watched gray-bearded pitiful Jews selling brandy and honey cakes. Seven-branched lights burned in synagogue windows; women were perpetually crying; nights were long with those bare rows of poplars lining the flat endless roads, nothing audible but the wind in dry leaves, and the unit tramped through the mud, and the tin lamps clanked at the head of each platoon emitting stinking smoke like funeral lights. That is how Jambrek arrived at the front, and grew accustomed to all there was at and around the front, as did so many before him.

For, what else can be done, other than get accustomed to it?

A Guardsman accustoms himself to it according to regulations, cleans his shoes and rifle, digs a hole, builds a loophole, and waits for rations and death. Between rations and death there exists one other possibility, a third variation: namely, to be wounded.

It is a great fortune if a Guardsman is well wounded, but if he is not and he meets with disaster, well, then that is that!

The gray tedium of the barracks has here been transferred into a hole, less than two meters wide and already dug in the shape of a grave, so a Guardsman need do nothing more than calmly lie down, and all is done. A quiet Guardsman death has taken place. They simply extract the death certificate from a man's pocket to transfer the Guardsman from fighting status to that of deceased, and the matter is once again in order. The Guardsman has fulfilled his Guardsman duty.

And so Jambrek lived for a time burying his companions, and then one day the white cloud of "Guardsman duty" fell upon him, in the higher bloody sense of that concept.

This was at the time before the great spring offensive, when the Russians were launching major-style assaults to feel out a weak side of the Zagorje positions. An entire infantry battalion charged Lieutenant Lulić's position, but he broke the attack by fire and on his own initiative moved into a counterattack that unexpectedly succeeded. Jambrek was struck down during that counterattack, and lost consciousness. The same evening Lieutenant Professor Doctor Lulić wrote the following letter to his Madame:

My dear and only Katica!
Last time I wrote to You from Munkacs in Hungary. Did you receive that letter? Take care to write down my new address correctly. It is no longer 364 but rather F. P. 371. We traveled around through Hungary again and have now shifted positions.

All is very well with me. I have a carpenter in my company, he built me a beautiful underground shelter, and there Your picture now hangs. Meals are much better than at home, meat twice a day. We often drink champagne too. Especially before a patrol. But don't worry in the least, dear Katica. There's a bit of shooting, that's all. Last night one of my boys captured eight enemy personnel. His name is Franjo Sabliček. I proposed him for the great silver decoration. Truly, I keep my company in beautiful order. You should see how beautifully brushed and shaved they are. One can hardly believe it. The men are humble and good, and like me very much, and when I tell them to, they would wade through fire and through water. After all, you remember my Seven-B class? There you have it!

My darling Katica! I must praise myself before you in a big way. In short: I have been proposed for a *Verdienstkreuz*, and they telephoned from the division just half an hour ago to say that I will certainly get it, and that I was proposed at the *Armee-Kommando* for an extraordinary promotion. I cannot tell you anything else for now, only that my men performed a miracle. A miracle, my dear Katica. There are quite a few wounded, and seven have fallen, whom we have nicely buried. Heroes! Our people are truly beautiful! And how bright!

My dear Katica! Just now they are telling me from the regiment that they're asking there for my photograph, they will send it to the *Illustrated*, to have it printed there, and the battalion commander congratulated me personally five minutes ago! Today has been a great day!

I hope to go on vacation soon. And if I come home as *oberleutnant*, Ljubičić will have to be the first to greet me. Haha! That swine will hate that! Then off we'll go to Zagreb for two or three days, to celebrate my victory, *Madame Oberleutnant!*

How are things at home? What is sweet Milan doing? I dream about the little scamp nearly every night. Is he playing with the *luftgewehr*? That thing is expensive! You take care of it too, dear Katica, so that it doesn't break! Kiss him a hundred times for Papa. Give my best to Mama and Godmother and Lajček and let me hear from you soon. I have no more time today, so I'm scribbling all this in haste.

Kissing every one of you, Your eternally loving and faithful hubby.

The "miracle" that the Lieutenant Professor Lulić underlined in his letter was the counterattack in which Jambrek was struck down. His entire sad history is alluded to in the Doctor's phrase that there are "quite a few wounded," and all the positive results of Jambrek's catastrophe are

74 | HARBORS RICH IN SHIPS

reduced to this that a certain Professor Ljubičić in the provinces (presumably a colleague of the Lieutenant Professor) will have to be the first to greet the victor of Hill 257 "who on his own initiative not only broke enemy dominance, but by his courageous act also greatly contributed to a clearing up of the situation," as it was lithographed in the divisional order of the following day.

When Guardsman Jambrek regained consciousness for the first time, it was noon.

He is lying in an enormous freight car of the Red Cross, and countless automobiles are rolling in the mud before him, engines roaring. Steel chains rattle as if somebody fettered in irons were walking there, and the car rolls along the tracks and holes like an enormous boat, while the wounded moan and cry.

A pale sun that has broken through the clouds and ignited the spring mists is lapping at the mire of muddy ditches where gray rags of snow are oozing.

Jambrek gazes at all this and listens to the moans of the wounded and remembers how he stepped out of the trench, and still sees in front of him those stakes with stretched wire and sees only a white cloud with flickering yellowish orange tongues, and is so beaten down, exhausted, and tormented that he simply cannot build a bridge between these automobiles and that trench and those stakes with the spiked wire.

"What does it all mean, what's it all about?"

Automobiles! He is riding in an automobile. And look, here next to the automobile rides a black horseman. How strangely that black horse is running!

The horse's slender ankle bends as if about to break, soaring over the soil in a flattened arc, and the hoof folds up from the mud so supply that Jambrek wracks his brain struggling to understand whether that horseman is flying or merely riding. That black horse is flying! It's flying! The sun is radiating warmth as pleasantly as a stove, and Jambrek feels no trace of pain anywhere, only thirst.

Guardsman Jambrek lies in a tin trough (the tin cools his sweaty fingers as he touches about), and he feels that he is all tied up, and he would like to know why he is tied up and why these men around him are moaning and crying, and he briefly tries to sit up, but at that instant something cuts him through the middle, across his entire body, and a blackness descends again over Jambrek's eyes, painless and deaf.

The second time he regained consciousness was in a train carriage.

Jambrek lies in bed, a night lamp flickering over his head, and hears the snores of sleeping men, all assorted like coffins within the black innards of the carriage.

The train travels on and on, rolling along the tracks, and the big wheels beat against the steel of the tracks the same way as the train in Zagorje. It's the same rhythm!

A rather strong opening beat, distant and deep, with two reflexive weaker ones, as if echoing the first, which once again booms distantly and deeply, and thus the beats pursue and hunt each other, and the carriage shakes like a watermill and mills its way beneath it.

The deep noise thunders, *dum-dum-dum, dum-dum-dum,* and two hammers skip over it like mallets against a cymbal, *ta-ta, ta-ta, ta-ta,* and it all plays in one long and terrible melody of the provincial railways: *dum-tata, dum-tata . . .*

How many times did Jambrek listen to this tedious song of Zagorje, and it seems to him now that he is riding the Zagorje train, as he listens tensely, quite dazed by the beat yet careful not to fall asleep, to hear, when the train stops, whether it is Zlatar-Bistrica or already Budinščina.

The train has flown across a railroad switch, the noise grown quiet, and everything stopped, while vague and alien voices resound outside.

Some people are walking along the carriage, quite a few of them, making the gravel strewn between the sleepers and tracks slide away, and they can be heard staggering as if carrying something heavy, and someone is yelling loudly, then a trumpet blares, horses snort and the beating of horses' hooves is heard against the wooden floors of the carriages.

"What sort of signal is that? That trumpet is a cavalry signal."

Jambrek is a Guardsman in the infantry, and cannot for the life of him puzzle out what the signal might be. "It isn't assembly; it isn't attention! What is it?"

The train remains motionless for a long time; outside they carry lights whose yellow beams fall into this black carriage, flow across its dark hollow from corner to corner, then vanish again; hoof-beats are heard and a sharp clanking of chains; later a strange bird calls from somewhere with a harsh and sour cry, and then all reverts to silence.

Locomotives whistle and pant, and the carriage slowly and voicelessly jerks into motion again, starting to rush somewhere and now it is flowing again, all of it just flowing: *dum-tata, dum-tata!*

The carriage sways right and left, this roughly hewn box shakes on steel axles, and the yellow rays of a little oil lamp burning feebly somewhere high above have begun to dance over the boards and the large white faces.

Someone snores in a corner, and from Jambrek emanates heat, he is all sweaty. He has flung away the blanket and the fresh air pouring in through a gap by the door pleases him, so he breathes in deeply to suck up a lungful of the cold night air.

"*Umiráju, umiráju, gospodi, umiráju,*" groans someone behind Jambrek, directly behind his head, and though Jambrek hears that voice he is quite unable to see who it is.

Wanting to rise, a trifle nervously and forcefully, to see who is groaning, and what is really happening to him, he makes a sudden move attempting to get up, when the pain announces itself to him for the first time.

Wounded, bestially mortally wounded, comprehending that pain Jambrek roars out in a voice that echoes across twenty-two carriages of the entire transport, and even the engineer hears him and thinks that one of the wounded has probably fallen under the wheels.

Something unspeakably turbid and violent appears to Jambrek, and everything is hurled into a dark whirlpool, and he feels something dragging him deeper and deeper, into a horrible dying that will never end.

―

They cut off Jambrek's left leg above the knee inside the Templar train, and cut off his right exactly at the hip in the private sanatorium of Her Highness Maria Annunziata Valeria Constanza.

It happened quite by accident that Jambrek landed in Her Highness's Belvedere.

That ordinary military Red Cross train composed of freight carriages distributed all of its material along one of the Trans-Carpathian lines in accordance with a telegraphed order from the A. K. (*Armee-Kommando*), and returned at the speed of fifty miles for new material, because there had again been blood. It just so happened that there was no more space at that small provincial Polish station on the line (the hospital was full), so the heavily wounded waited in the waiting room for more than twenty-four hours for the headquarters-bound Templar train, and there in the Templar train of the Red Cross they amputated his left leg and handed him over to the specialists in Belvedere, because there was very little hope that he would survive.

Belvedere was a baroque castle of Her Highness Maria Annunziata who had had it refurbished at her own expense to receive heavily wounded ordinary soldiers, and there she herself attended them and cared for them.

That lofty Samaritan gesture of Her Highness was a certain twist in the final phase of so-called spiritual crises that the exalted lady had deigned to undergo on this terrestrial globe.

That is to say, Her Highness Maria Annunziata had completed the final spiral of her internal victories with an ascent to traditional Catholicism, which her grandfathers and great-grandfathers, who once walked about in armor and lace, had served with sword and banner, and in that pursuit of their earthly transcendental mission slaughtered quite a multitude of people.

As befits an anemic and hysterical lady from the highest circles, she, barren as she had been all her life, opened herself to the Host in her fourth decade, knelt before the mystery of the Mother Church and bent her head.

After numerous Nadásdy hussars in blue embroidered jackets, barons who won at London Derbies and elsewhere, some diplomats with monocles and tails, et cetera, et cetera, she had finally encountered Holy Father Benedict who succeeded in opening her eyes to the seraphic music of the thirty-third Neo-Thomistic sphere.

(This Holy Father Benedict had of course been a baron and cavalier in his time, and he too had discovered the meaninglessness of helmet and sword. A Vatican career and a cardinal's hat came to seem to this baron and cavalier much more valuable than a military regulations manual and a riding pavilion, so he converted one night while riding not to Damascus but to Rava Volczyna, his Galician garrison, and took off his dragoon's jacket, to wind a rope about his waist.)

Be that as it may, all this is ultimately peripheral to our present history which chronicles the sad adventures of our compatriot Guardsman Jambrek on his Way of the Cross from Galicia to Belvedere.

What is important is only that it was Holy Father Benedict himself who personally persuaded Her Highness to sacrifice Belvedere (her smallest estate of some thirty thousand acres) for charitable purposes, precisely in the interest of this imperial and royal enterprise that has resolved to penetrate as far as Salonika to enable the princesses of the High Court to collect seventy percent interest on their investments.

She yielded with a sad heart and at first discovered a singular sensation in the nursing vocation, especially now when it is so boring in Europe and a person can neither go to Egypt nor to the Riviera. There had been all sorts of things in her life. There had been music and champagne and moonlight and duels, and all of that had evaporated, and there remained like a shadow only the death mask of *Oberleutnant* Freiherr von Brausewitz, an exalted youth, who had barely kissed her knee when he got into a fight with His Highness the artillery general and fell in a duel. Since that time there have always been thirty-three rooms between her and His Highness the artillery general, as the family tradition does not permit breaking the bonds of the holy sacrament, and since that time the shadow of the dead Freiherr has pursued her about, with a hole through the skull, and Her Highness fears darkness and twilight. Hence from time to time Her Highness comes to Belvedere, there to attend "her" poor patients, and that often lasts a full seven days. The mere act of Her Highness attending "her" wounded signifies about a hundred liveried retainers, ten cars filled with baronesses and surgical specialists, adjutants and nuns, and thus it happened that Maria Annunziata appeared at Belvedere just on the third day, when they cut off Jambrek's other leg at the hip.

"What pale child is this?" The lofty lady stopped over Jambrek's bed surrounded by a retinue of baronesses, surgeons, and specialists, having immediately on the first day undertaken a tour of the rooms of the castle.

"That's some Croatian boy, Your Highness," explained the head physician in a servile tone, summarizing Jambrek's condition: that both his legs have been cut off, that a shell had showered him breaking his bones, and that it was a miracle he had survived the catastrophe.

"And will he live? Poor child! He's white as paper, *um Gottes Willen!*"

The head physician shrugged skeptically, and all became silent. Her Highness grew thoughtful for a moment (a whisper of "*Ihre kaiserliche Hoheit denkt nach*" spread through the circle of Her Highness's retinue), and then Her Highness quietly said that "this pale child" should be immediately taken upstairs, to her, under her lofty protection.

Upstairs meant the chambers of the second floor, adjacent to those of Her Highness, comprising a special wing for those fortunates whom the Highness had selected out of a mass of wounded in order to snatch them away from the elements through her own personal care.

Such a patient was simply not allowed to die, because Her Highness considered such patients her metaphysical good cards, which she would play at the Last Judgment when her soul was weighed over green flannel to determine whether it was ripe for the left or the right side of the universe. And if it happened that such a patient of Her Highness should despite everything die, then it usually led to hysterical outbursts and scandals, and the following day all those automobiles with boxes and baronesses and hats departed from Belvedere in a rage like Furies.

⁓

Her Imperial Highness stepped up to Guardsman Jambrek and stroked his hair with much maternal tenderness, and a moment later they transferred this "white paper child" upstairs to the second floor into the lofty protection of the good Christian lady Maria Annunziata, Austrian princess and general's wife, for whom her husband had slaughtered in this war more than thirty thousand enemies.

⁓

Jambrek was born on Saint Sylvester's, the very last day of the year, and if he had arrived only a few hours later, he would not have been called up for the present stint but a whole year later, and his life would most likely have taken off in an entirely different direction.

But it so happened that he became a Guardsman while still a beardless boy and thus set out on his thorny path to the stars, as many generally do at a time when the stars are stars on a military uniform.

Jambrek had been breathtakingly beautiful, and if one saw him back at the time when he still walked vertically on two legs as a complete human being, one would have stopped in one's tracks to admire that magnificent appearance. And if he had also been dressed in some elegant European garments, no one alive would ever have guessed that this aristocrat had been born in Zagorje's Sad Bistra, and that he was a rustic peasant such as the old men of Bistra remember for a full four hundred years.

It is certainly true that at the time when Jambrek's late mother still dug the soil in nobility's vineyards, the count of Slavetica often appeared in orchards and lingered outdoors, but though all the other women of Bistra constituted potential conquests, Jambrek's mother, who was renowned throughout the village as a virtuous beauty, did not. All that will at any rate remain forever draped with the veil of a secret, but the fact is that Jambrek's shining eyes and bold high forehead dominated an unusually clear-cut face, and his slender Velázquez-like fingers resembled a finely woven fabric within which pulsated blue blood. Jambrek's muscles were shaped with remarkable suppleness, his thighs symmetrically molded as though of marble, and so that wretched shell did indeed demolish a masterpiece of nature.

At the very first when Her Highness noticed Jambrek, his curly hair and his still childlike face, dusted with the first pollen of instinct, reminded her of a certain bronze Narcissus whom she had once seen in some museum somewhere, long ago. That Narcissus had held grapes in his hand, and his curly hair had been tied with a ribbon, so Her Highness instantly thought that a dark-blue silk ribbon would so beautifully color these curls, and she had this Narcissus—"this unfortunate beautiful child"—brought to her right away, upstairs to the blue salon on the second floor. At first there was a great crisis, and everything hung on a single thread, while gentlemen doctors with smooth-shaved chins and pince-nez stood with rolled-up sleeves in pure snowy white, watching this solitary problematic thread on which was hanging the fate of Narcissus.

But Jambrek overcame it all and remained alive.

While the bone could still be felt at the hip, protruding from the bloody flesh, and while the wound was still wet, not covered with filmy tissue but burning and stinging, then Jambrek cried like a child who is dreaming a painful dream.

He did not awaken during his entire time at Belvedere, and that golden furniture and blue curtains and the princess all in white silk crying with him like a mother (he felt her fragrant face on his and her warm tears, flowing into his mouth, salty), oh, those bloody legs, Belvedere and the princess, all of this to Jambrek seemed to be a dream.

Jambrek had been an astonishing child.

His was the brightest head in class, and the teacher, a widower who read even the Cultural Institute's books with pencil in hand ("This is stupid!" "This is lovely!"), and who copied out extracts from Šenoa and Kozarac into a special notebook, such a teacher had wanted Jambrek to continue his schooling at all costs. But it did not work. With less than two acres of land it did not work, and so the child, who used to read Andersen in the pasture, set off one day for Graz, to the Hotel Esplanade, put on a red tailcoat with rosettes and became a bellboy at the Esplanade. There in Graz Jambrek began to read newspapers and go to the opera, and those kings and princesses singing in the yellow light whom he watched from the high gallery, understanding nothing, only listening to the music and dreaming, all of that appeared to Jambrek like a dream.

In the red uniform of the Hotel Esplanade he dreamed about kings and princesses, and now here he is in a golden castle in silk, and a real live princess is kissing his hands and crying over him and feeding him chocolates and cakes—what does it all mean? Hotel Esplanade, opera, garrison, front, Belvedere, princess, there is so much, so terribly much of it, that it's all boiling, seething, and overflowing as though someone had spilled a cup of many colors, and they all ignited and are now smoking and shining, all burning up strangely like fireworks. And though it was actually terrible to lie on one's back and be cut off, and to feel oneself cut off, yet when she came, the princess—and you know that she is a real live princess, and you feel her hand on your forehead and feel her gently caressing your hair, caressing you, fondling you, Her Highness the Princess—why, not only would a man let his legs be cut off, but his head too, and have his ribs smashed, and destroy himself, self-destruct!

At first Her Highness indeed felt a nuance of Samaritan compassion toward this pale boy. It was a feeling such as arises in the soul when we see a person who has fallen from the third story, or a bloodied dog on railway tracks. But later, after those long sleepless nights in the blue salon, when Her Highness knelt with bowed head on her purple kneeler, and then quietly on tiptoes approached the wounded boy to see whether he was sleeping and how he is (if she might pour some lemonade for him), later that Samaritan impulse began to acquire strange morbid forms. At first there were nuances of thought, and later concrete fantasies that give rise to unspeakable horror, so delightful to the exhausted nerves. Nerves in that riven aristocratic body of Her Highness were so constricted, so frayed into sickly strands, that such a horrible thought would course across that fragrant body, like a soft hand smoothing out all these asymmetries in the soul and nerves, as though we have lain down naked into otherworldly furs and are snuggling.

Jambrek breathes in half-sleep monotonously, his bare rib cage rising and falling, rising and falling, while Her Highness holds Jambrek's hand, feels his pulse and gazes at that white marble statue, upon which a pale bluish light has fallen, at those noble shadings and lines of that bloody form, and feels the presence of a body, a male body, a body that is not there.

Here lies a shattered nude figure whose legs have been severed. A torso of a marble Narcissus, who only needs to be unveiled. And a secret thought occurs to Her Highness to rip away the white tulle from this anatomic mystery, to sink her face somewhere, to disintegrate, to go insane, to snatch up this tulle-swathed torso, like a figure from a wax museum, a figure congealed with red blood, and together with this bloody grotesque body to spin round and round and hurl herself somewhere through a window into the depths.

And so night after night Her Highness descends into strange morbid abysses, only to start up with fright, so terrified by it all that she could scream insanely, alarming all of Belvedere, and thus she suffers till the morning; and the night lasts long, as though time has stopped.

Only toward daybreak, when bronze specks outside begin to shine over the forests and curtains rise from the borderland, then, worn out by her vigil, she hands her patient over to Sister Clementine and leaves as if drunk along those priceless carpets soundlessly and mutely like a specter.

And at night it is again the same. She prays for the hundredth time for the unhappy soul of Freiherr von Brausewitz, but she cannot bring her prayers to an end because a fiendish thought seizes her halfway through.

"What lies in that bed wrapped in white tulle under the baldachin is a child! That Narcissus is still an untouched child! Maria Annunziata! A child!"

Suppressing that thought she crosses herself and crosses herself again, then she rises nonetheless and approaches the child, removes the tulle and gazes at the child's bloody hams, gazes at them and is moved by the yearning to kiss them just one single time. To touch them with the edge of her lips. Nothing more! Just one single time!

And so, bending over the bloody tulle-wrapped nude she ascends within herself to spectral heights of tantalizing torment, to reach the apple, and Jambrek lies and feels the princess, feels her breath on his body; he is not asleep, he is only feigning sleep, and is actually awake and feeling the princess who is here with him, removing from him all that is bloody and horrible.

On Good Friday, Her Highness leapt up and rushed off by automobile to town and there confessed to the Benedictine father and cast away from herself all of that infernal weight. The Benedictine father suggested that she flee far from this fiendish temptation (as far as possible, to forget), and the Highness set off for the sea where fruit trees were already blossoming and spring was at its height.

When the princess vanished, to Jambrek it was like waking up. He did not wake up right away. He awoke the first day, and the second, and the third, and he felt dreadful but hoped that the princess would come back. But when she did not appear for an entire week, and then for two weeks, then a demonic fear grabbed hold of Jambrek, and only then did he begin to feel just what it was that had happened to him.

He broke into fevers, began to shout, tossed about, fell into seizures, burned like a fire; they tied him up lest he throw himself off the bed, but what is the use of thrashing about when the princess has vanished forever.

"Oh dear God! They cut off my legs! Mama! Mama! They cut off my legs! Both of my legs! Dear mama! My legs!"

And just because the Princess had hovered over his eyes like a veil so that he lay here at first as though dazed, now that the veil was suddenly ripped away and he actually saw what had happened to him, he flew into a rage at this highborn lady and began to rave that she had bitten off his legs, that she was a whore who bit off his legs!

"Damned swine! Make her give me back my legs! My legs! My own legs! Disgusting whore!"

Thus curses Jambrek, and his leg nerves have not yet quite withered so he feels that he could kick away this golden bedding, he only needs to raise his legs and strike, and struggling to raise a leg hurts, and he curses violently, and the nuns stand over him without understanding a single word, injecting him with sedatives and marveling at the source of such awesome strength in this child.

But that too passed. Jambrek's wounds healed, and he set off by car to the headquarters and there received artificial limbs, so that one day he found himself once again in his garrison city in the dirty and moldy barracks, like so many others who walk on springs and hop over sticks three or four feet high, thus training like dogs for a new life.

An incomprehensible and immense longing for life, for the great wonderful life of Belvedere, blazed through his nerves, and he began to torment himself brutally with all that blackness which yawns from every corner of the barracks. And so he lies throughout the days in this stinking barracks, where rats and mice jump over beds, and watches the huge black shadows of these people flow in the half-light across rotten and waterlogged stones.

He listens to the conversations of his comrades and to the bells in town somewhere far away, and feels as though he were dreaming.

Whatever happened to him? Is he really that Jambrek who carried the cross in the Mother of God procession, that bellboy of the Hotel Esplanade, who now lies here damned and bloody and reeking of carbolic acid? A Princess loved him! Her Highness the Princess! That was a woman! What are these here doing talking about a woman? That in Belvedere had been a real princess! They have no idea what a woman is!

Ah, he only dreamed all that! Now too he is only dreaming! Indeed! He is dreaming! Stones lie on his chest, forcing him to sigh every moment! There is a salty bitterness clogging his windpipe and throat, he feels nauseated, and it would be good to wake up. But he is not waking up! It is not a dream, all of this is really happening.

He lies on his bedbug-infested field cot listening to water dripping outside in the rain duct, and he has no legs, only artificial limbs, and that is the truth and it will remain so until death and nothing will ever happen.

If only the barracks would catch fire! If an earthquake were to shake the entire city, and everything were to collapse! If something were to happen, so that it doesn't go on like this, because this is horrible!

And for a moment it does seem that something will take place after all, but then a terrible doubt descends again into Jambrek's thoughts, heavy and dense like smoke swirling over a conflagration.

It becomes clear to Jambrek that he has indeed been abandoned by the Princess. And only that princely life makes sense. Golden Belvedere! That is life! Not sooty stinking huts in Bistra, or garrisons, trenches, barracks, artificial legs, accordions, and village church festivals.

And now when he listens as these people talk about women, something tightens in his throat again; he is aching for the princess. The princess is not a woman for him now! The princess is now something white and quite unreal, distant, something that once was and now no longer is. If he could again feel the princess as then in Belvedere, it seems to him that he would break into a dance on his artificial legs as though he were mad and drunk, he would dance and he would live.

If he were able to live that royal life for just one more instant, he would let his head be cut off on the spot!

What women! Waitresses! If they asked him, he could tell them what love is!

What are those people laughing at? They're smoking. Yelling. Yanking at each other, as they drink wine from a green bottle. What does that red woman want, the one who entered the room? She is carrying two baskets and yelling. Yelling loudly.

"Tobacco, boys! Tobacco! Here! Tobacco! Cigarettes! *Hum! Bosnia! Flor!* Tobacco, boys! Tobacco!"

Thus yells the woman with the baskets.

The woman comes into the barracks and yells, and in her red shawl and with her green, swollen, watery eyes she looks like someone who has drowned.

That woman is stripping the barracks, buying sheets and cups, shoes and raincoats, buying everything, for tobacco. It's bad when one is desperate with nothing to light up. At such a time a man would sell even God's mother off the altar, let alone his shoes.

The woman stands in the barracks shaking her tits, and instincts are awakening, beasts have already begun to growl. As the occasional long-nailed and greedy soldierly claw sinks into those soft female thighs, that overripe calf, the woman coquettishly squeals but does not run anywhere, and will even sit on some devil's lap and lie down awhile on a bed, because if the men won't give up a pair of old army shoes for a pack of *Flor*, they will surely give it for the *Flor* and a skirt. And so they tease each other and laugh, the men playing with the woman and buying tobacco and stuffing their pipes and drinking wine, while outside it rains for days on end.

Someone is saying that in their village on Ascension Day seven years ago they ripped open a young woman, raped her and cut her into pieces, butchered her entirely and thrust an umbrella into her eye.

Jambrek listens to those words and feels his artificial limbs.

They cut up a woman somewhere seven years ago! On Ascension Day! And raped her! And thrust an umbrella into her eye! And did they not tear him apart? And rape him? And cut him into pieces? They tore him apart and threw him out of Belvedere! And they got away with it!

"They raped all of us, and stuck an umbrella in the eye of every one of us!"

"What, what?"

"What? Nothing! They raped us! They butchered us! Well, didn't they? Didn't they throw us out on the street?"

"And who raped you, you ape?"

"The Princess raped me! At Belvedere! She bit off my legs!"

"Hee-hee! Wha-at? You? A princess?"

Jambrek senses that they are laughing at him, that no one believes him that the Princess bit off his legs. And so he stands among them as though he were lying. And he is not lying! It is all true! Only they are fools, so they don't believe him!

And once again he feels so very clearly this sad truth of his, and that he is alone and forsaken and cast out forever.

So he turns without a word and steps out into the rain, slowly, leaning on crutches lest his knee fold up and cause him to collapse.

And tapping thus, step by step, accompanied by the melancholy tin music of the springs, he drags himself through the wet and muddy streets.

It is raining at twilight and store windows have already been lit, their yellow gaslight flowing along the asphalt, and everything is so pitiful and desolate, and bells are ringing and dusk is pouring in foggy and gray and dragging beneath fences like a sick cat.

Jambrek advances, limping up to the corner, to the illuminated window of a beauty salon. In the window stands a lady made of wax who has the same reddish hair as the Princess had, and her teeth are so bright, and she is laughing and she resembles her, and her lips are burning, burning as terribly as the seals on court letters and sentences.

And Jambrek will stand there, staring through the glass into that rose-colored light, and thus, his eyelids half lowered, he will mutely dream about the laughing Princess. And dream, and dream.

NATIONAL GUARDSMEN GEBEŠ AND BENČINA TALK ABOUT LENIN

IT WAS A WARM, LATE AUTUMN. The windows of the sickroom (the *Marodezimmer* at the Imperial and Royal, and Royal Hungarian Regiments) were open and the moist smell of early evening fluttered in at intervals through the reinforced steel bars. The fields in front of the barracks were saturated with a gray slush, and since a blast of southern wind had brought on a thaw, rags of snow shone whitely among dry cornstalks as though someone had drawn them in asymmetrically here and there with soiled brushstrokes of Post-Impressionist technique. The clear acoustics within carried the clanging of carriages from the southern train station and the squealing of steam locomotives, and echoed an anvil from a nearby smithy. An adjutant was chopping wood in the corridor, and I was lying feverish on a hard straw mat, and in that mild and heavy autumnal twilight I was carried away by an inexpressible aching for broad and blue distances. I stared at those steel bars, listened to children shout joyfully in the twilight, and daydreamed womanishly about how good it would be if one were a bird and not rotting in these damp and dirty blankets, not sick, not a colonial soldier, not fighting mindlessly in a war, but flying high over fogged in willows, over a quietly flowing river, and over railway tracks glowing with signal lights.

Amid the heavy and stifling semi-darkness, amid helpless efforts to break out of leaden and repulsive spaces, amid a sickly yearning that all of our misery and filth be prised off by a solid and hard lever, there arose the voice of National Guardsman Gebeš of Stubica—returned days ago via Stockholm and Berlin from Russian captivity—like the voice of a knightly, heroic trumpet!

Mirko Gebeš, with pockmarked Guardsman features, pale tubercular cheeks, riddled with bullets several times, fell into Russian captivity during the insane Austrian charge at Dniester, tramped around Asian POW camps of Siberia, and returned to the barracks as one of the first harbingers of the Russian tempest. He had attended Russian revolutionary meetings—"went through that revolutionary apprenticeship"—and, as he told it, heard Lenin speak from atop barrels and trunks in some Petrograd warehouse, an event that will remain indelibly marked in his memory...

Gebeš presented Lenin to the sickroom's inmates as an ordinary Russian muzhik who speaks to peasant soldiers about peasant uprising, about barracks, about war, and about how it's a shame to hold a rifle in hand and bleed and shoot for the masters, and not at the masters!

Oh, how beautifully every simple word of the pockmarked and tubercular Gebeš coincided with my passive and sickly musing about exit, about breakout, and about rescue from that sickroom, from that fever, from those moral contradictions that appear to a man in a barracks, when he is warring for the interests of others and against his own conviction, and when nothing else is left to him but to daydream in a sickroom bed about twilight and about birds. What a devilish minimum the life of a contemporary human being is reduced to when his ideal is to become a sparrow and to chirp in the twilight above the civilization and barrack roofs. Within this personal misery of mine and that sad depression, the words of Guardsman Gebeš thundered in the filthy and stinking room like a mighty drumbeat. As though I had suddenly glimpsed in the semi-darkness of the foggy space the colossal outline of the Fiery Rebel Matija Gubec as he sets into motion and with a huge scythe in hand strides like a giant above the barracks and the city.

Fiery Matija has arisen, our glorious man from Stubica, and all Gebešes stand with him, from Krški to Sevnica, from Mokrice to Susjed; they have started to move through the smoke of fires and the ringing of church bells, to show that they too exist, to obliterate that stinking, Austrian, Habsburg, symbolic sickroom and to break all metal bars, all these frames, treaties, protocols, assembly speeches, majorities, minorities, paragraphs, phrases, lies, stupidity and sadness of our exitless impasse, to break out, to emerge from all that, to win.

I don't recall the details, but only remember that everything in the room dimmed, and that people in their beds quietly sighed in the dark and fateful silence. The dark weight of the stupidity of our life was palpable, and Gebeš's words rumbled in our souls like an explosion against the concrete parapets of that entire fortress-bound and military life that presented for us our deadly reality, the reality of an Austrian, Habsburg war, the reality of hideous senseless death for the sake of that manifest stupidity.

"Lenin stood on a barrel in a warehouse and said clearly and loudly so that all of us heard him, that the real war is one that is fought in the streets and stores, and not at the front!"

"Sure! Rebellion! Peasant right! War in the streets against the masters! All that is Jewish nonsense! Shut up!"

That was Platoon Sergeant Benčina, an old warrior. Twice mortally wounded and decorated, his raincoat drilled through with seven machine-gun bullets, which he showed off as a trophy with great pride. He never commanded "Shoulder arms!" but changed the last part affectedly to "huck!" to make it "Shoulder huck!"

Benčina sensed that Gebeš was crossing the line of order and discipline, and for that reason intervened as a non-com, telling him he had best shut his trap and quit yapping mindless and senseless gibberish.

"That's all lies and it's all made up by Jews!" He had read in a newspaper that those are Russian Jews, who will ruin all of Russia and sell it for golden coins to foreigners and millionaires.

Gebeš refused to be impressed by the platoon sergeant's intervention. He instinctively sensed that such non-com intervention threatened not only his personal dignity as a Guardsman, but also the prestige of that concept, which he called "soldierly liberty and equality."

Non-coms won't be fixing our heads for us any longer...

Gebeš wanted to demonstrate to us all that he had mastered the Russian apprenticeship: it wasn't the Russian Jews who sold anyone anything, it's only the stupid newspapers Benčina reads that write that; Jews write that stuff out of fear that soldiers might plunder their warehouses!

And with a practiced and persuasive method Gebeš strove to explain to Benčina how miserable his life is, how he has been flung at the front five times already, how his raincoat is stitched with twenty-three machine-gun rounds, how he has been turned into a scarecrow with nine wounds, and how now despite everything (and fitted with a mismatched gutta-percha jaw) they are driving him off to the front like a dog...

"Standing on that barrel, Lenin said clearly and loudly that the front is foolishness, and that every man who goes to the front is a fool!"

The quarrel grew more and more heedless and sharp, Benčina leapt up from his bed blazing with rage and it came to within a hairbreadth of ending in a fistfight, a beating, and Gebeš getting arrested by the guard. I myself no longer know whether it was due to that insolent aggressiveness of the glorious Gebeš, whether to my own rotten mood (which disgusted even me), or whether I sensed within Benčina's rudely superior non-com's obscenities the creaking of spiked boots of our wartime Zagorje-style Vendée; at any rate for the sake of our entire sickroom I did not at any cost want Gebeš to give up his position, and so I transferred the quarrel's center of gravity onto my own person, and drew the platoon sergeant's wrath onto myself.

After prolonged clarification the matter ended in bribery and corruption, and so over a second bottle of absinthe we forgot that Gebeš had wanted to incite the sickroom to mutiny and to raise a revolution in the interest of Russian muzhiks. I don't know whence or how, but Benčina began to whistle the well-known aria from Albini's *Baron Trenk*: "Tiger now, and soon a lamb . . ."

One night the following autumn, a soldier suddenly stopped me. I was already a civilian, and the soldier caught up with me from behind, touching my sleeve like a shadow. It was raining. My freedom of movement hindered by an open umbrella in one hand and books in the other, I started with instinctive helplessness at that touch of an unknown shadow. It was Benčina.

"Oh, that is you, 'Benchins'! Hello! How are you?"

"I was at the Italian front! No end to heavy artillery and gas down there! And how are you?"

"Well fine, thank you! I'm a civilian!"

"And do you remember, sir, that crazy Gebeš, who got us into a fight one evening in the sickroom? They shot him on the Italian front!"

"Oh don't tell me! Poor man! Didn't he know to take care of himself?"

"Well, he didn't fall at the front, they shot him! They sentenced him to death at a court-martial and shot him. He hit an officer over the head with a gas mask! We later poured lime over him in a lime-pit. I can still see his knee, sticking up out of the lime! There was no putting up with him! I always nicely told him: You'll quit that Jew foolery of yours on the gallows! And now, I ask you, didn't they sing a requiem for him? What's he got out of it now?"

A month later the mercenary condottieri of the National Assembly shot Platoon Sergeant Benčina too. For him too they sang a requiem.

FINALE: ATTEMPT AT A FIVE-THOUSAND-YEAR SYNTHESIS

Humanity's position in Cosmos, at elevation 313. Ordinary scenic cross-section of a rampart, with trenches, palisades, and cannons. The setting simultaneously suggests Wallenstein's siege of some fortress during the Thirty Years War and an emplacement on any Russo-Japanese front around Liaoyang or Port Arthur in 1904–1905, or during the first imperialist war of 1914–1918. Above elevation 313 rises the celestial dome: a zodiac and a starry sky dissolving amid nighttime July horizons, with bright summer planets strewn across the great expanse between Orion and Sirius. The play of light is broken by a flickering alternation of sunny days and dark nights, accompanied by storms and ominous whistling of winds. The lighting for day and night changes with great speed so that the entire position around elevation 313 appears to rotate within a glass globe illuminated for a moment by the sun's searchlight or enveloped by night's shroud.

A trench at the front. Soldiers in all uniforms of many centuries. Presenting a picturesque potpourri of colors, from a Roman cavalry legionnaire with a horse's red tail on his helmet to a sixteenth-century Hungarian hussar and musketeer in a lace collar, all lie intermingled in a trench and wage war. Standing in the trench are various exotic deities, from a bronze Buddha to a wooden Christ, and in front of these Mohammedan arabesques, tricolored and red flags and Bushman gods, kneel Japanese in khaki uniforms and Central African blacks in their smooth dark nakedness, Croatian National

Guardsmen and Italian Carabinieri—all of them praying and bowing and kindling lights in front of statues. There is a pause amid the battles, so that only a solitary shot announces itself from time to time. Flags of all warring nationalities wave and flutter in the mistral: the Venetian Republic's lion mingling with American equatorial symbols, the blue-white Hellenic flag with that of Great Britain, in a senseless polychromatic patchwork—black-yellow-red-white-green—like during Olympic Games or soccer matches.

A soldier is praying to the Roman goddess and bowing devoutly: Hail Mary, full of grace, our Lord is with thee, blessed art thou among women, pray for us sinners now and at the hour of our death, amen!

Other worshipers follow him in a chorus of various languages from all continents: Ave Maria, gratiae plena!

Voice of the first soldier, like that of a priest in a church at vespers: Hail Mary, full of grace, our Lord is with thee, blessed art thou among women, pray for us sinners now and at the hour of our death, amen!

CHORUS: Ave Maria, gratiae plena, Dominus tecum.

This continues endlessly and tediously, in a deranged and completely senseless monotony.

To the left, in a shelter constructed of woven-branch palisades, sit intoxicated soldiers wearing helmets belonging to modern assault columns and visors of Spanish harquebusiers. They are drinking, gambling, playing cards, and kissing women camp-followers.

Nervous and impassioned voices of card-players and gamblers: Ace of clubs! Ace of diamonds! Queen of hearts! Bank! Queen of hearts! Diamonds! Ace of spades! Clubs, bank! That's not clubs, that's spades! Not seven, it's five! Bank! No bank! I give, I don't give! Blackjack! Go!

VOICE OF A PROFLIGATE: Lord God, grant us this: lots of women, lots of bliss—death to wars, long live whores!

VOICE OF A WORSHIPER: And deliver us from evil . . .

One of the worshipers falls dead.

SUBTERRANEAN VOICE OF A TELEPHONIST: Hallo! Elevation three-one-three here! Position unchanged! One dead, two wounded!

Medical corpsmen arrive, with large red crosses on white sashes, solicitously put the wounded on stretchers, and carry them off.

The previous WORSHIPER, *with dreadful monotony:* Hail Mary, full of grace, our Lord is with thee, blessed art thou among women, pray for us sinners now and at the hour of our death, amen!

A chorus of voices, card-players and roués are shouting, drinking, smashing glasses, singing. In the distance, cannons quietly thunder. Several warriors collapse, bleed, and moan. Tempo is quietly growing.

SUBTERRANEAN VOICE OF INVISIBLE TELEPHONIST: Hallo! Elevation three-one-three here! Position unchanged! Three dead, seven wounded! Send us a maximum amount of propaganda material! Morale is falling! Doubts are cropping up concerning the purpose of this slaughter! Send us five detective novels!

Medical corps arrives with red crosses and carries off the dead and wounded on stretchers.

The WORSHIPER prays, others respond in a chorus, card-players drink, cannons boom in the distance, and this process continues without a break from day to day, day and night, always the same and changeless. The sun rises and sets, the moon shines, stars and illumination flares fall, leaves fall and blackberry bushes turn green again, butterflies flit by and rains fall, storms thunder, and clouds fly through, yet these people lie in a temporary grave, praying to God and drinking and playing cards and telephoning and dying in the unvarying light of day and night, night and day. One year, another year, a hundred years, seven thousand years, night and day, day and night, always one and the same.

SUBTERRANEAN VOICE OF TELEPHONIST: Hallo! Elevation three-one-three here! Position unchanged! Seven dead, seven wounded! We have lost orientation in space and in time! Inform us: where are we, what are our prospects? What are the chances for a victory of reason? Shall we go on doing this for another seven thousand years? Complete apathy has taken over! Requesting fresh narcotics! Running out of rum and prayer books! Most urgent!

VOICE OF A WORSHIPER: Hail Mary, full of grace, our Lord is with

Finale: Attempt at a Five-Thousand-Year Synthesis

thee, blessed art thou among women, pray for us sinners now and at the hour of our death, amen!

VOICES OF CARD-PLAYERS: Ace of diamonds! Ace of clubs!

Cannons boom. Medical corpsmen. Day and night, night and day. Autumn, winter, spring, summer, autumn, winter, snow, howling blizzards, song of spring waters, birds.

A MAN who has been reading a book in the foreground and has grown thoughtful observing the goings-on nervously tosses the book over the coils of barbed wire that stretch in front of the emplacement.

MAN, *in an internal monologue:* A human being nowadays no longer walks on all fours, but is a biped who has stood up on hind legs and has been using forelegs for ten thousand years to build houses and make fire and write books. I cannot for the life of me comprehend why I have to lie in this muddy hole where at any moment I could get a round through my head. That I simply cannot comprehend.

CHORUS OF WORSHIPERS: Hail Mary, full of grace, pray for us sinners now and at the hour of our death, amen!

VOICES OF CARD-PLAYERS: Ace of diamonds! Ace of clubs! Ace of diamonds! Ace of clubs!

VOICE OF TELEPHONIST: Hallo! Elevation three-one-three here! Position unchanged! Two dead, two wounded!

Cannons. Medical corpsmen. Day and night. Night and day. Autumn.

MAN: Now it's autumn! Now a gentle breeze flutters over forests, and strands of gossamer waft through the air. Now it would be so good to stroll across ploughed fields in this warm afternoon sunshine, and to listen to the rustling of corn leaves. Why am I rotting here, what is the point of all this?

SECOND MAN, *who is lying next to him, wearing a uniform like all the others, in a quiet, resigned voice*: It is not good to think aloud about these things! That can destroy a man! These are corrosive thoughts, they eat away at everything that is called epiphenomenal superstructure. One must stubbornly believe in life, as in an unusually clever social game, whose only purpose is to go on. A social game, like all other social games, is a prolonged affair and even somewhat boring, like chess, mahjong, or bridge, for example. Social games should be played without thinking!

FIRST MAN: On the contrary! The only sound thing to do is to think aloud precisely about all this! That gives one the strength not to go insane! Because, believe me, at moments it seems to me that I have gone insane somewhere long ago and that they've buried me deeply at the bottom of some muddiest stupidity, and that all this is happening somewhere underground, in a grave! And when I look at these people who are praying in this pit to mute wooden statues and lighting candles to something that doesn't exist, and when I listen to these card-players, well, then I ask myself: why am I lying here like a dead object and why do I not move? I need to move, I am a normal person! In the name of human dignity, we need to move. We are not dead objects. Humanity today has been reduced to an idiotic formula of self-destruction. This unnatural stupidity will in the end cost us our heads!

SECOND MAN: I do not understand you! You're a pessimist: your view of everything is too black! It makes no sense to take such a black view of everything! I can't comprehend such Faustian characters! It makes no sense to smash your head against the wall! The wall is undoubtedly of harder matter than the head! Why, life itself—if one considers it philosophically—is nothing else than a sort of accommodation! One needs to know how to accommodate, that's all! Behaviorism is a contemporary scientific formula. Human beings have never invented a cleverer formula than that of adjusting to reality. Of course, humans have thought up some completely insignificant correctives here and there to machinery that moves, according to natural laws, within a total vacuum, but nothing more.

FIRST MAN: And what are you, if I may ask, by occupation?

SECOND MAN: I am a citizen, in the sense of being a householder, not a Jacobin! I'm a property owner with a quite modest rent. I own a modest two-story house with a solid prewar price of 36,000 gold crowns. That is to say, I have a two-story house in the outskirts and one in the center. The one in the center is much more profitable. I'm only waiting for this comedy to end so I can return to my balcony. In fact, you know, I have a balcony and a red umbrella on the balcony. In front of my balcony, a little water fountain babbles day in and day out! Sparrows bathe there, in that fountain; they are devilish rascals.

FIRST MAN: And you think you'll return to your balcony? Oh, you are a simple soul! We're all going to croak here, do you understand? And that is why it would be necessary in your own interest that something is done, immediately, right away, now, at this very moment, in any case still today!

SECOND MAN: No, no, please: *Quieta non movere,* that is my motto! Never start trouble. My home is my castle, my front, my little life here and now, without great pretensions, within the framework of real possibilities. I do as much as I can or as much as I may. And in general, as much as we can . . . Look, I've planted some onions and lettuce here, I'm cultivating my little garden, and to the extent that it's obtainable in the given circumstances, I'm satisfied. Every dog has its day! You take a black view of everything! Why should we leave our skins here? That's not one hundred percent certain! What's the sense of breaking one's head like Faust? There are bounds that a man must not cross. You know that beyond these Faustian bounds the devil preys on human reason! But, forgive me, may I ask you, to what calling have you devoted yourself in your civil life; that is, I mean, what is your occupation as a civilian?

FIRST MAN: I have no occupation as a civilian! As a civilian, I'm a civilian! I have no balcony, no red umbrella, no fountain in front of my own house, no little golden fishes (in my head), and no sparrows! And as far as Faustian bounds are concerned, they are stupidities, those Faustian bounds of yours! Human reason has no bounds, my dear fellow, it is boundless.

SECOND MAN: As can be seen, under certain specific circumstances human reason can hardly be said to be "boundless." These worries and troubles of ours, for example, are a case in point, I would say, and prove the opposite. But one must make peace with that too. Human pride has often misled people into fatal blunders and adventures. Faust himself is a symbol of such human weaknesses.

FIRST MAN: Why the devil are you so obsessed with your Faust? Faust is a puppet, and we are not puppets! We are soldiers! We are not literature, we are reality! We are fighting a war against our will, and moreover we don't even know why we are fighting! One thing is clear: they are killing us against our will; we are dying for alien interests.

THIRD MAN, *who has been listening to this conversation, with exaltation*: Oh, how well I understand your every word! That's right! We are not puppets on a string and we need to show our own Initiative through action! And right away too, with spontaneous enthusiasm! I shall rise, take up the white banner and cross with it to the other side, to explain to everyone what is going on, and that all this is in fact a delusion!

He leaps up, snatches a white banner, and in a flash climbs up above the barbed wire, with the white banner in hand. Several shots ring out and the very next moment the man crumples back into the hole, bleeding, and mutely dies.

VOICE OF PREVIOUS WORSHIPER: Hail Mary, full of grace, our Lord is with thee, blessed art thou among women, and blessed is the fruit of thy womb!

VOICES OF CARD-PLAYERS: Ace of diamonds! Ace of clubs! Ace of diamonds! I give, I don't give, bank, blackjack!

VOICE OF SUBTERRANEAN TELEPHONIST: Position unchanged here! One dead! Repeat request for propaganda material: prayer books, rum, and holy pictures! Doubts are arising concerning cosmic purpose. Morale is falling. Our press is worthless.

FIRST MAN *kneels next to the dead man and covers his face with the white banner*: There, you see, this is innocently spilled blood. This lamb of God has taken on all our sins and fallen for "Ideals"! Humanity's path to the stars is covered with none other than such lambs! Across the thorns to the stars!

SECOND MAN: You—personally—are guilty for this innocent blood! If you hadn't fogged up his head with some nebulous ideals about stars and humanities, he would still be alive among us! You're a Bolshevik! This innocent blood will fall on your head!

FIRST MAN: You're an idiot and a petty-bourgeois, and you understand nothing! You're a householder, devil take you!

SECOND MAN: And you're a sans-culotte and a housebreaker and a demagogue! You should be shot like a dog. Why didn't you yourself stand up on the rampart rather than send that innocent child to a certain death! You should be ashamed of yourself!

FIRST MAN: I've got nothing to be ashamed of! My conscience is clear!

SECOND MAN: You have no conscience! You don't believe in God and you're capable of doing anything! You're an atheist! As soon as the commander gets here, I'll accuse you of high treason! You wanted us to revolt! You wanted us to surrender to the enemy and to lay down our weapons! You're a coward! You ought to be hanged!

FIRST MAN, *becoming enraged, furiously*: What, me a coward? Take this from a coward!

He throws himself upon his opponent and a fistfight ensues. When the second man draws his revolver and fires several times, the first—though wounded and bleeding—strangles him in the heat of the fight. Uproar. Musketeers, Japanese, harquebusiers, hussars, Bushmen, have all gotten stirred up in the course of this row.

Voice of the COMMANDER, *in the mask of a grinning, terrifying Korean demon, with goggling eyes and sharp-edged fangs, wearing the uniform of a regular infantry colonel*: What is this? What's happened? Somebody got drunk again?

LEGIONNAIRES' VOICES: People got into a fight!

COMMANDER: What people? We're not people, we're soldiers! Who got into a fight where? What's the meaning of this? Did I tell you not to throw papers around the pit? This isn't a toilet, this is Elevation three-one-three! Whose can is this? I'm asking, whose can is this here? Did I tell you not to throw empty cans around the pit? This is not a grave, by the hundred heavenly saints, this is a front! Here every man must be in his place! What kind of salute is that? Is that a salute? Move it, everyone to his place! You call this a battle? Is this how you fight a war? Fire! Prone figures straight ahead, by the hedgerow right and left! Seven hundred meters! Rapid fire! Shoot!

The entire Internationale has scattered around the pit, and an occasional shot is heard here and there. And then faster and faster, like a machine.

COMMANDER, *to* FIRST MAN, *who is still at the same spot, staring at his opponent and not moving*: And why are you lying here like you got nothing to do? Look, a lovely prone figure by that poplar over there! That animal is sunbathing! Go get him! Fire!

FIRST MAN: A human being walks on two legs, not on four! A human is a human and ought to remain human! Humanity, humanism, humanitarianism, human!

COMMANDER: Well, what's the matter with you? Why are you staring at me like a calf? Look, a prone figure by the poplar! And another! Three more! Those swine are preparing to attack! Didn't you hear me? Do I have to repeat myself again? Shoot!

FIRST MAN: I heard, but I don't want to shoot!

COMMANDER: What? What sort of logic is this? One moment you're breaking others' heads, and the next you don't want to shoot? You are mad! Shoot!

FIRST MAN: I'm not mad, I simply don't want to shoot! I know what I'm doing! Human, humanity! Ideals! Per aspera ad astra!

COMMANDER: Wha-at? You don't want to shoot? *Draws his revolver and shoots the man.* Hey! Corporal! Hang this madman at the entrance to the pit! Write on a tablet around his neck: Be no comrade to the mad! Nicely, legibly, with penmanship! Do you understand me?

CORPORAL: Yes, sir, colonel! *Sits and writes on a tablet, nicely, calligraphically, with the thin lines up, the thicker ones down*: Be no comrade to the mad!

The man has been hanged as ordered at the entrance to the pit. The battle has paused. The card-players are playing cards, the worshipers are praying.

VOICE OF SUBTERRANEAN TELEPHONIST: Elevation three-one-three here! Position unchanged! Three dead! Three wounded! Situation so-so! Send us three cases of rum and two boxcar-loads of holy pictures! Saint Cecilia is recommended! Definitely female forms! Baroque female saints, nude Baroque female saints! And don't forget Saint Roch! He protects from wounds!

VOICES OF CARD-PLAYERS: Ace of diamonds! Ace of clubs!

VOICE OF PRAYING MAN: Hail Mary, full of grace, pray for us sinners now and at the hour of our death, amen!

Day and night. Night and day! Autumn, winter, spring, summer. Day and night. Night and day! A thousand years! A hundred thousand years! A billion years! Eternity!

DEATH OF PROSTITUTE MARIA

THIS ALL HAPPENED IN A CIVILIZATION, God forgive us, where such events are noted in the press as something barely worth a mention. On the same day when the newspapers reported that little prostitute Maria had poisoned herself in such-and-such a hotel, entire pages were covered with the arrival of His Majesty the King of Schiavonia, soccer matches, fraud at government ministries, and so the death of the little prostitute Maria did not inspire even one reporter to devote several lines to her and thus to focus for at least twenty-four hours, amid the dizzying madness of incidents, sensation, and make-believe, on all the agony that tore apart the modest existence of an innocent girl.

Maria took poison early in the morning, around four, and her groans were heard through the closed door by a hotel page come up to the fourth floor to awaken a guest in number 81 who wanted to set off by an early morning ship. At that time, when the first person heard the groans of the poisoned girl through the locked door of her room, it was most likely too late for any helpful intervention because the stomach acids had already merged with the poison and nothing could humanly be done. But several hours before that, when the unhappy and crying girl knocked on the archimandrite's door, number 74, then all the possibilities were still open, and it seems to us no exaggeration to say that the whole unhappy life of that little girl was in the archimandrite's hand, like a porcelain figurine, which that drunken bear of a man held in his paw and smashed, and then turned his buttocks to the world and started boorishly, primordially to snore, belching like a pig in front of which a rose had fallen. Yet because we do not intend to write a puritanical thesis about this event, but would like to give a report in keeping with our mission as chroniclers, we ought to present to the reader everything that happened in more or less the same order (and entirely independent of ourselves) in which this story developed.

The night was already late. The hotel was asleep, and the passengers from the last express train of the night had settled down in their rooms as in the cabins of a steamship when only the groans of the engine are heard and a light flickers on the foremast. From the depths, from the beerhall, music echoed, but as muted as under a glass bell; shaded lightbulbs glowed at the bottom of long corridors covered with soft carpets, and from time to time the elevator droned and grew silent, then after a slight pause went on droning long and monotonously.

The archimandrite, a giant in a fleece-lined fur coat, with a costly jeweled cross on a massive studded chain around his neck, was not so drunk as to forget (enclosed within the glass box of the elevator with a liveried boy) that the elevator's chain could possibly snap and send it, along with his own four hundred pounds of flesh, hurtling into the depths. He had read in a newspaper many years ago that an elevator had plummeted thus, with everyone sitting in that glass crate, and since then that unpleasant thought had not left him, so he breathed a happy sigh of relief when the liveried boy opened the glass door for him, and he felt the crossbeams and the solid concrete construction beneath his feet.

The archimandrite, then, who lived in the fourth-story room number 74, a grizzled and bearded man with oily wavy hair, like a classical figure of a Greek Orthodox priest (whom Mussorgsky sees in a gentle scherzo, and whom Demyan Bedny sings of as a spider with a blooming nose and a kalimavkion), this archimandrite shoved open his room as forcefully as a flood. Grumbling in a low voice some frivolous song a coachman might sing, he took off his fur coat and his cassock lined with red silk, and bending at the waist and belching, his digestion ravaged, removed his shoes with enormous, fat, blood-swollen butcher's hands. A heavy massive shoe dropped, first one and promptly the other. The archimandrite, illustrious preacher, who had been drinking the whole night long with three government ministers, seven embezzlers, housebreakers, and some shadowy characters who all toasted the King and the State and spoke about millions and about blood, the archimandrite, illustrious drunkard, fell into thought—should he extract sodium bicarbonate out of his suitcase, to take a teaspoonful or two and thus wash out the unpleasant taste from his mouth?—when he heard a knock on his door. The archimandrite was astonished: why was someone knocking on his door?

106 | HARBORS RICH IN SHIPS

At first he thought it was a mistake. When the knocking was repeated and continued shyly and persistently, he got up and, still in his drawers and heavy woolen socks, went to open the door.

In front of the door stood a young woman, anemic, bareheaded, dressed in silk, her face green. She was trembling as though deathly afraid.

"What is it? You've made a mistake, Miss!"

"No, I've not! I beg of you! I'm sure it's no mistake! I live here next to you, at number 73! I've wanted to come to you already before dinner! I beg of you, as I would beg before God, it's a matter of life and death for me."

"All right, fine, I understand! Keep it down, only keep it down! Why are you so upset? There's no need to be so upset! I understand! Please, come on in! Only keep it down!"

The young woman pushed her way into the room, dragged herself to a chair, and there collapsed, starting to cry aloud. Her crying was so convulsive that the archimandrite paused, half-naked in his socks, with the red-lined cassock draped over his shoulders (so that his drawers were visible and the drawstrings tied at the ankles), and simply could not decide whether these tears were true or false.

"If she's lying, she's good at it, I'll say that for her," thought the archimandrite as he surreptitiously gazed at the young woman. And when this went on and it seemed as though time had stopped, and when the young woman noticed that the archimandrite was not moving, she threw herself on the floor and crawled up to the priest on her knees. There she burst into tears again, in front of the archimandrite's legs.

The presence of a young perfumed woman, the softness of her hair, the silk through which a warm body could be felt, all this inflamed the drunkard's blood, and his voice quivered in his throat.

"Dear child! This is all unclear to me! I cannot understand any of this! Calm down! It's nighttime now! Every sound can be heard through the walls, even the parquet creaking! Is it sensible now, to be acting like this?"

The woman was very young, barely seventeen, and her crying was the crying of a child. She simply could not speak for the tears. The archimandrite caressed her face, felt on his palm the fire of her cheeks, and turned, went to the sink, poured a glass of water and brought it to the young woman to drink.

"Pull yourself together, child! Pull yourself together! What's the meaning of all this?"

"Sir! My dear sir, Father! I beg of you, I'm scared, I'm frightened, I'd like to confess, I'm afraid, I'm sick, sir!"

"You want me to confess you, child? Confess you how? Why?"

"I saw you go out tonight, and waited for you to come back. I was frightened! I would like to make peace, Father, sir, to make peace with my life! I'm frightened! I'll go insane! I'm going to die! I'm scared of God!"

The archimandrite, a womanizer and a drunkard, did not believe in God. Ever since the Büchner-Darwinian days of junior high school, the whole of that so-called transcendental superstructure had for him been definitively knocked down, and as his subsequent life tossed him hither and thither, all of that remained within him in ruins, and he lived on in a priest's cassock as an unbeliever and a cynic. His profession had led him to keep watch over the consecrated wine of legendary saints and emperors, and when he got drunk, he mocked these skeletons, spit at icons, broke bottles over crucifixes, vomited on holy treasures, and lied in church. And now, long after midnight, a prostitute comes to him, a drunk woman smelling of cognac and brandy, and here she is crying at his feet and wanting to confess. The archimandrite wanted to laugh, to laugh so loudly in his healthy and deep bass that all the guests and travelers would run out of the cabins as though there were a shipwreck and the hotel were sinking. Because this young and unknown woman was kneeling before him with her head bent, he lowered himself down to her and began, with the routine movements of an old Father guardian of souls to caress her hair, her coiffure, the top of her head, the back of her head, and below that a small downy groove, and her vertebrae, her shoulders, her neck, her back; this little bird, poor little thing, unhappy girl, who is crying, who is afraid of God, who is confessing.

The young woman cried, thrusting her head into the red-lined cassock, and spoke of some banal everyday history: about a father getting drunk, a mother rattling whole nights long on a sewing machine, a war breaking out and about herself roaming hungry through metropolises, and how she now could no longer go on. She absolutely could no longer go on like this, and a fear before some indescribable architectonic weight of an existing metaphysical superstructure, a certain superterrestrial order that she could find no way of describing and most unintelligently kept on calling "divine judgment," a fear thus before some ultimate anti-Büchnerian world order, all of this had flung her here before the archimandrite's feet, to confess, to unburden herself, to die clean. It is probable that parallel with this a strong and ineradicable impetus of a deep and healthy vitality, a frustrated thirst for life, appeared in her seventeen-year-old child's organism, and that her action, when she knocked at night on the door of a neighbor, was the gesture of a drowning person who desperately stretches out a hand to be rescued, as a final helpless signal.

And indeed, for a moment it seemed as though the archimandrite would after all comprehend what was happening and actively intervene in this drowning to pull out the morally floundering woman. But first of all the desperate artificiality of her story, that wretched naked banality of a life of one unknown little metropolitan prostitute, the presence of the young woman herself, and also that potent wine combined with a night without sleep, it all looked to the archimandrite profoundly false, and a drunk, callous rhinoceros of sensuality and instinct arose beneath his skin, so he lifted that weeping little girl onto his lap, like a wounded and bandaged body. And so he caressed that desperately unhappy child, stroked her with his hand, spoke to her of God, who by all indications seems to be good and eternal, and who has already heard thousands upon thousands of such cases, and about how there are no sinful and sinless people but all people are equally sinful before God, and God commands one to live, only to live, and to live is not sinful but holy, this is the only holiness, the only wisdom, the only road to salvation. Thus spoke the archimandrite about God, feeling under his gigantic butcher's hands female calves, thighs, hips, garters (those damned modern garters, that are tied under the waist), he sipped the girl's tears, fondled her, hushed her, and at last the room became silent.

It was still very early, and the first bluish light of day was breaking through the curtains, when the archimandrite started out of a heavy leaden sleep. People were shouting in the corridor and voices rang loud, so the archimandrite sat up in bed for an instant and reached out into the darkness to touch the woman next to him.

"She's not here. Wonder if she's robbed me!"

Worn out, dazed, half-asleep, he stretched his arm to the nightstand, and feeling under his fingers his chain and the costly diamond cross, and the golden watch in its deerskin bag, and his wallet, he turned from the left side to the right and continued loudly to snore, as though all of these movements had been somnambulistic and unconscious.

Outside in the corridor the commotion rumbled on, because of the girl who had poisoned herself in the nearby room. Someone was hissing at the servants not to shout.

"Shush! Quiet! Guests are sleeping."

Death of Prostitute Maria | 109

THE GLEMBAYS

A Drama in Three Acts

DRAMATIS PERSONAE

NACI (IGNAT JACQUES) GLEMBAY, banker, chief of the firm Glembay Ltd., privy councilor (age: 69)

BARONESS CASTELLI-GLEMBAY, his second legitimate wife (45)

Dr. phil. LEONE GLEMBAY, son of Ignat and his first wife, born Basilides-Danielli (38)

SISTER ANGELIKA GLEMBAY, Dominican nun, widow of Glembay's oldest son, Ivan, born Baroness Beatrix Zygmuntowicz (29)

TITUS ANDRONICUS FABRICZY-GLEMBAY, banker Glembay's cousin, grand rector, retired (69)

Dr. iuris PUBA FABRICZY-GLEMBAY, his son, lawyer, legal advisor to Glembay Ltd. (28)

Dr. med. PAUL ALTMANN, physician (51)

Dr. theol. et phil. ALOIS SILBERBRANDT, Baroness's confessor and instructor to her son (39)

OLIVER GLEMBAY, son of Baroness Castelli and banker Glembay (17)

CAVALRY LIEUTENANT VON BALLOCSANSZKY (24)

CHAMBERLAIN, CHAMBERMAIDS, GUESTS

The action takes place in the course of a late summer night, one year before the outbreak of the 1914–1918 war. First Act: between one and two thirty a.m. Second Act: between two thirty and three thirty a.m. Third Act: around five a.m.

ACT ONE

A red salon furnished in yellow brocade of the 1860s. In the background are double-wing doors, open, with a view of several spacious illuminated rooms. To the left a terrace, separated from the scene by sliding glass doors. On the terrace: cactuses, palms, straw furniture, two rocking chairs, and stone steps descending into a garden. To the right, a door leads into the dining room. Along the walls of the red salon, there are about sixteen portraits of the Glembay family members. The styles are Maria Theresa, Empire, and Biedermeier. Two or three heads copied from photographs. Several modernistic figures painted outdoors. The entire residence is richly lit. It is late. Guests are leaving the dining room on the right, passing through rooms seen in the background, and exiting left. Just as the curtain rises, an Austrian field marshal is crossing the stage with his wife. A rheumatic matron follows supporting herself with a cane, her back bent from sciatica. Next, an infantry colonel with his spouse and a dragoon major without a lady. Animated, banal, and loud parting conversation, out of which only sporadic shouts, incoherent words and laughter can be made out, peppered with German and Zagreb expressions.

VOICES: Küss die Hand, your illustrious highness! I kiss your hand! Servus! Good-bye, excellency! Auf Wiederseh'n, God bless! Adieu! Your humble servant, Illustrissime! My deepest bow, good night! Servus, God bless!

Following a brief pause, a white-haired lady with a marabou necklace emerges in the company of Illustrissimus Glembayer-Agramer and his fourteen-year-old granddaughter who is accompanied by two youths. Baroness Castelli-Glembay, the banker's wife, is seeing off an unknown gentleman and his lady. Students and young girls are laughing on the terrace, and as the Agramer-Ballocsanszky family leaves, an eighteen-year-old girl in white runs across to the terrace to reach her brother. On the terrace, among others, are Oliver Castelli-Glembay and cavalry lieutenant von Ballocsanszky. They all exit noisily, crossing the stage in a group. An old chamberlain and two chambermaids keep going out and coming in hurriedly with scarves, forgotten handbags, and mink and marabou tails. Johann Strauss's waltz "Tales from the Vienna Woods" has been playing on the piano in the background since the outset, but it suddenly stops. Most gentlemen guests are wearing frock coats; ladies are in gala evening dresses. Here and there a bank counselor's black salon coat. Officers are all in Waffenrock jackets, lacquer, and narrow trousers. One of the last to exit is a bishop, short-sighted, with golden spectacles, supporting himself with an ivory-handled cane, wearing a lustrine cassock, a dazzling cross, red cap and red gloves, accompanied by his personal secretary who follows a polite two steps behind carrying the bishop's felt hat and silk cape. The bishop is accompanied only by the host, Ignat Glembay. In the wake of this commotion, guests' clamor, music and laughter, there remains one Dominican nun, Sister Angelika (widow Glembay, born Baroness Beatrix Zygmuntowicz, 29), who is observing the portraits along the wall. She is slender, refined, and attractive, without a drop of blood in her cheeks, with beautiful lily-colored transparent hands which she coquettishly conceals within the rich folds of her sleeves. Beside her is Leone Glembay. He is a decadent figure, balding and graying, with an almost completely white thin Swedish beard, without a moustache. He wears a frock coat, and has an English pipe in his mouth. The play of his hands and nerves around that pipe is abnormally intense.

LEONE: It's all obscure within us, my dear good Beatrice, unbelievably obscure. "There are two strains of human knowledge which perhaps stem from a single, though to us unknown, root: sensuality and reason. We take things in with the one and imagine them with the other!" Sensuality and reason: Kant himself could not have identified more clearly all that is obscure within us! Indeed, apropos of Kant! On a bookcase in my room tonight I found a good 1848 edition of Euler's *Mechanics*! That Euler with his differential certainly saw much more clearly than Kant! And please note, forty years earlier! Euler's *Mechanics* was published for the first time in Saint Petersburg in 1736! And the *Critique*, if I'm not mistaken, came out somewhere around 1789! (That's the fall of the Bastille! A strange game of nature: Lagrange was born the same year as Euler's *Mechanics*, in '36!) Indeed! What was I about to say? Ah, yes! The Absolute, the mathematically crystal-clear—was clearer to Euler forty years before Kant, and Euler is more logical and consequential: he expressed the entire Unknown with a formula! This is essential: mathematics, symbolically speaking, is closer to the Unknown than are either language or image. A mathematic formula can say clearly what neither speech nor painting can, not even music, which is relatively the most mathematical! To use language and to express oneself through language is a technical mastery, this is already a problem of art, yet Kant wrote incredibly amateurishly, "on the wings of ideas"! He could not find an adequate—a precise—substance for his expression; and in that, exactly in that, Euler was more coherent and greater! I too, the more I paint, the more convinced I become that da Vinci was quite right: a thing can be precisely determined only through abstract mathematical coordination. And so that is my inner contradiction: instead of being a mathematician, I paint. With such a rift within oneself, what can one achieve beyond dilettantism?

ANGELIKA: I don't know, Leone, I beg you not to feel offended, I would not want to upset you, but after our conversation last night I could not free myself from the thought (I was thinking about you almost the whole night), I could not free myself from the impression that you greatly exaggerate with words! All this, I am afraid, is just pleasant chatter! You are an unusually entertaining raconteur, and you are capable of destroying all your efforts of many years for the sake of a single witticism! I, on the other hand, have kept silent a great deal during these seven years, and for me to think for the sake of being witty is uncommonly foreign. "The difference between a clear idea and an unclear one is only in logic, not in content!" Genuine truth can only be penetrated with the heart, Leone, only with the heart: with logic or witty words, never! All logic is only apparent logic, a mirage!

LEONE: So then we are left with the Dominican "hidden quality," *qualitas occulta*?

ANGELIKA: Yes, qualitas occulta, I am not afraid of that term! For as long as I've lived, I have looked at life in images: our being contains an outside and an inside. What exists between them? Something, as you say, dark and obscure: nerves, brain, flesh, something which is called our being. A certain sad void in our so-called being. And all of that develops in time and in something unknown, transcendental. And if you think that your painting is a logical plunge into that transcendental something outside of our Self, you are mistaken, Leone! Reason is of no use here! Today this is called intuition, but once upon a time it was called qualitas occulta! I am not afraid of that term!

LEONE: All that smells of Dominican sulfur, Beatrice! I concede: it is easy to live in this sort of weltanschauung. These are the prescribed views of a thousand years; that is your Dominican hierarchy costumed and armored: you as an ecclesiastical weltanschauung, you are a diluvial mastodon in armor; you live in a churchly fortress, inside a shell of a verbal lie: qualitas occulta! And the idea that I should not be a materialist in my paintings—that I resolutely reject! My handling of forms is Euclidian, Hellenic! And today, in a time of the impressionistic palette, to speak of ultimate things on one's knees, in a Dominican costume, with bowed head and a rosary in hand, that is downright Gothic! Today, in a time of godless symbolism, of the infinitesimal—Beatrice, this could truly be called pseudo-intelligent . . .

Angelika, while looking at the paintings along the wall, is gently and imperceptibly yet rather decisively drawing away from Leone, and through her silence, from his words. Leone stands beside her, speaking softly, very warmly and intimately:

LEONE: Beatrice, the only thing in which I believe in this Glembay household is your lofty and sincere intelligence! Even so, everything within us is not as simple as the weltanschauung of a maidservant! For an illiterate maidservant the question of God and ultimate things is as simple a coordination as are the decorations of a Catholic Easter celebration. Easter morning, colored eggs and Gugelhupf cake on a white tablecloth, Easter bells and solemn sung high Mass!

ANGELIKA: We all swarm about in life like worms in cheese. And none of us sees beyond the events that envelop us, Leone! Insofar as we live, we live only by submitting to a certain quiet, invisible set of laws; within us and around us everything is as dark as in a termites' nest. I think that your Romantic ascent beyond the frames of life's possibility is sterile, and even somewhat old-fashioned. It's purest 1848 Romanticism! And if you think that there cannot be more harmony in the weltanschauung of an illiterate maidservant than in your godless symbolism, you are deceiving yourself! What I am saying may be "pseudo-intelligent Gothic," but what you are saying, that is chaos, it is turmoil.

LEONE: I have been watching you continuously this evening, Beatrice, and, I don't know, maybe it is indiscreet, but I would most intensely like to know whether you are truly as calm as you seem, or whether I am only imagining it in my turmoil—perhaps I am only dreaming of this conception?

ANGELIKA: Every day I feel less and less agitated.

LEONE: Seven years have passed since Ivan's death, Beatrice, and if for these seven years you have truly felt less and less agitated every day, by now you must already be incredibly tranquil. Do you never hurt?

ANGELIKA: I do hurt! But then I—as you say—concentrate once more, and I feel better!

LEONE: Already, for the second day, I am watching you, dear child, and watching that concentration of yours, and I simply cannot understand: Where is that tranquility within you? Where is that point within you against which you brace yourself?

ANGELIKA: (*Resolutely rejecting him*) I don't know, Leone!

Thus breaking off the conversation, she moves toward her portrait which shows her in a yellow brocade evening dress with a deep décolletage and a huge fan of peacock feathers; here she stops and gazes for a long time into her own past. At that moment a piano announces itself offstage with the "Moonlight Sonata," which continues beyond the first movement, up to the arrival of Baroness Castelli-Glembay. After a pause Angelika sinks into an armchair, folds her hands as if in prayer, and remains in silent contemplation.

LEONE: (*Observing her, quietly and elatedly*) Your face reminds me of one by Holbein, I think I saw it in Basel. An oval face, the face of a fragile geisha, childlike, laughing, a milky color with a transparent pastel tint! Holbein eyes, intelligent, bright, with, somewhere deeply in a transcendental nuance, a barely perceptible phosphorescent glow of the erotic.

ANGELIKA: Leone, please.

LEONE: I am talking about Holbein, dear Sister Angelika! About an old Holbein from Basel, about which I have been thinking for seven years! There was so much laughter in that face that its dimples formed two tiny discrete circular hollows, like two symmetrical shadows above the flawless lip of a Diana. Hands the color of lily white, fragrant, fingers English, longish delicate Holbein fingers, a beautiful blue-blooded hand, such as only a Holbein was capable of seeing!

Angelika has wordlessly risen and started toward the terrace, concealing her hands within her sleeves. Leone follows her.

LEONE: For seven years now I have been entertaining the idea of your portrait! At first I saw you in black, but now I see you in this Dominican costume; it becomes you beautifully, like a courtly lady of the Trecento! You are a feudal gentlewoman, and in you I don't see a Dominican nun, but a feudal gentlewoman of the Trecento—that is how you should be painted! How quickly time passes, and how incredibly quickly costumes change in our performances! In this same Dominican costume of yours, ladies watched tournaments, listened to knightly minstrels, and I would not wish to offend you, Beatrice, but the idea that in seven hundred years women's ecclesiastic orders might be wearing Second Empire costumes, that idea suggests that everything in the world is truly relative and transitory: our costumes as well as our Dominican concentrations! In seven hundred years Second Empire costumes could become just as conservative as feudal costumes are today. And all of Impressionism was born in the shadow of those ornate ultrafashionable Second Empire costumes: the latest crinolines, toques "à la Eugénie," and Lilliputian silk parasols in brilliant colors.

This quiet flirting strikes Angelika as alien and remote, and at the same time agreeable. She listens with unconcealed interest to the warm words of a man who is congenial to her, whom she has not seen for a full seven years, and thus she scrutinizes her portrait, a picture of her youth.

Enters Illustrissimus Fabriczy accompanied by Dr. Silberbrandt. The illustrious Titus Andronicus Fabriczy, a retired grand rector, is an old bon vivant, each precious hair of whose coiffure is masterfully combed over a bald skull; he sports a thick Hungarian cavalry moustache, visibly dyed jet-black. His figure is still erect and irreproachably elegant, with a monocle on an old-fashioned string, a rosette of a high order in his buttonhole, foppishly ironed trousers, dentures, elegant and well-tended noble hands with a golden bracelet and a huge signet ring—all of this geriatrically neat and pedantically clean. He is an old, experienced epicurean who jealously watches over each minute of his sixty-ninth year. On his left cheek he has a scar from a cut by a saber. Aloysius Silberbrandt, Doctor Theologiae et Philosophiae, ex-Jesuit, now religious instructor to Oliver Glembay, the banker's only child, is around forty. A lean, tubercular figure with a pale unindividuated face, as if made from rubber; there is something eunuch-like, disagreeable, and servile about him. In his black lustrine cassock he appears slender.

FABRICZY: You are looking at your past, Baroness? How time passes, mein lieber Gott! Nine years since your portrait was painted, and how many evenings have we talked about you here under this painting, still at the time when you were, if I am not mistaken, in Shanghai.

ANGELIKA: In Hong Kong, Your Reverence, I worked in an epidemic hospital for two years. We had lepers there and much typhus. That was long ago and it seems to me as if I dreamed it. This March it was eight full years since this picture was painted. I wore this dress at the Red Cross ball in Vienna, and this may have been around the middle of February. At that same ball Ivan arranged with Ferenczy for this portrait of mine! For eight hundred and eighteen pounds, I believe. In March I sat for Ferenczy, and in June Ivan died. In June of the following year I was already in Hong Kong! To look at this portrait of myself is quite a strange experience: like seeing oneself in a magic mirror. Is it possible that this was truly me? Is it possible that there are distances in life from which one cannot recognize her own self?

FABRICZY: Jawohl, this is a typical Ferenczy! From that same Ferenczy comes the famous portrait of the English royal couple that was exhibited last year in Salon d'Automne. This Ferenczy is now painting in London—"the upper ten thousand." He is said to be enormously rich! He has recently gone to India for a holiday, with his own yacht! A splendid work! A dazzling fireworks display! And you, Herr Doktor, what do you say about this masterpiece?

SILBERBRANDT: "Pulchrum autem dicatur id, cuius ipsa apprehensio

The Glembays | 119

placet," as Saint Thomas said, Your Reverence! "Let that be called beauty, the very apprehension of which pleases." If I might add my own of course entirely inexpert and modest opinion, I cannot help finding that this portrait seems to me, by a single nuance perhaps, but still: a little too ultrafashionable. But the thing in itself is of course brilliant!

FABRICZY: Each period has its own art, I think! If an age is ultrafashionable, paintings too ought to be ultrafashionable! The work of art is determined by the totality of the general state of the spiritual and moral values that surround it: "L'oeuvre d'art est déterminée par un ensemble qui est l'état général de l'esprit et des moeurs environnantes!" That's what I think! However, I don't understand much about it! The longer I look at that painting, and I have been looking at it for over seven years now, the more beautiful I find it: Ich kann mir nicht helfen—I cannot help myself! However, I'm only a layman! But here is Leone: he is a painter himself, his paintings are winning gold medals, he will be better able to formulate it for us: well then, Leone, what do you think about the Baroness's portrait?

LEONE: I don't think anything about that portrait, dear Fabriczy! That is no portrait at all, is what I think! And it is quite understandable to me that Beatrix cannot recognize herself in it: that's the sort of portrait it is!

FABRICZY: No ja, natürlich, you with your überspannten high-strung opinions! No ja, ganz natürlich: of course the English court and the Salon d'Automne have no idea that one László Ferenczy isn't worth dreck!

LEONE: To me, it is completely irrelevant what the English court thinks about some nameless Ferenzcy or about painting!

SILBERBRANDT: "Omnis ars naturae imitatio est!" All art is an imitation of nature! There is no doubt that this picture shows the Baroness very faithfully, as the Baroness was ten years ago, of course! That Sister Angelika does not recognize herself is not the fault of the portrait, but rather of the fact that she of today is no longer she of ten years ago! True! But paintings ought to be judged quite independently of those faces which are depicted on canvas, so at least aesthetics teaches us! And by an objective aesthetic criterion, all the conditions for harmonious beauty are present. Therefore, Herr Doktor, forgive me but I definitely could not agree with you in your judgment...

FABRICZY: Na also, immer schöner und schöner! This is getting better and better! For you a László Ferenczy is nameless? And for whom is Ferenczy nameless? *L'Illustration* and *The Graphic* consider it a special honor if they can reproduce a "nameless" Ferenczy! Indeed!

LEONE: *L'Illustration, The Graphic,* and Saint Thomas with his "imitatio naturae"...

SILBERBRANDT: Pardon, but that is Seneca, Herr Doktor.

LEONE: It doesn't matter: Seneca or Saint Thomas or *The Graphic*! You ought to know that the topic of contemporary painting is two thousand years removed from Seneca and from *The Graphic*! Yes! And this: that you clip some quotations from old church books and paste them like stamps, where they do or do not belong, that may be patristic philately, but it has nothing to do with aesthetics or the culture of painting!

SILBERBRANDT: You are at times overly authoritative in your theses, Herr Doktor! I concede that I do not understand painting as you do, because you were in Florence for three years, and at the Academy in Paris, if I am not mistaken, and after all you yourself paint, true, but after all to have one's own opinion is a matter of conscience: I understand beauty as a higher harmony in an aesthetic-religious sense, as laid down by Biedermann in his study on Christian dogmas, *Uber die christlichen Dogmen*: "Erhebung des Menschen, als unendlichen Geistes, aus der eigenen endlichen Naturbedingtheit zur Freiheit über sie in einer unendlichen Abhängigkeit." The ascent of man as an infinite spirit from his own finite dependence on nature and into a freedom beyond it in infinite dependence.

LEONE: What? How was that, for heaven's sake? "Die eigene endliche Naturbedingtheit und Freiheit über die endliche in einer unendlichen"—I've not understood a word of all this! What sort of Seneca and English court and Ferenczy and christliche Dogmen? What? (*Nervously*) Take the concrete example of the Baroness's hand with the fan! Can a woman's hand with a fan look like this? There's the feeling of tube of paint, of oil, everything is gummy like resin, these fingers have been left undifferentiated like marzipan! And the hairstyle? Do you have a sense of where the forehead begins, and where the hair does? This is all lacquered papier-mâché, covered up with that banal trick of a diadem. What sort of a diadem? Why a diadem here? That silk, that brocade, those ostrich feathers, all of that is gaudy as a parrot! One Ferenczy who sells his portraits to the English court can allow himself all that, but that is not painting! What sort of painting is that?

FABRIZCY: Lächerlich! Ridiculous! One László Ferenczy does not know what painting is, but one Mr. Glembay has the knowledge in his little finger! I find that this portrait resembles the Baronness completely, and it does so now this very day and after nine years! If that is not a portrait, then I do not know what a portrait is at all.

LEONE: I think that this latter is the most accurate: that you have no idea what a portrait is! First of all, the Baroness's eyes are blue, aquamarine—an ethereal aquamarine—and the eyes on this canvas are green. Beatrice's face is a face from the Trecento, Quattrocento, her gaze, her Holbeinesque oval outline, there is no trace of any of that on this English picture postcard. And Beatrice's hands? Where are those incorporeal, transcendental hands on this porcelain baby?

SILBERBRANDT: I think that Sister Angelika's own thoughts would be the most relevant of all. Sister Angelika no longer lives the material or the spiritual life of a lady of fashion, she sees this portrait of herself from—as she deigned to say—a distance of nine years, and so she would...

LEONE: The hands stay the same! I remember Beatrice's hands from that Glembay time, and today too I see them! From educational motives, Beatrice, show these gentlemen what a hand means on a model, and what on canvas, please be so kind...

Sister Angelika had been listening to this conversation about her portrait with great interest, but has discreetly withdrawn once it shifted to her personally and to her hands. She is looking at the gallery of Glembay family portraits.

ANGELIKA: Fabrizcy, pardon me! Is this that Ludwiga Glembay who drowned herself because of that Italian painter?

FABRICZY: No, dear Beatrice, that is the old lady Foringaš! We used to boil those "non plus ultra"—superlative!—Reina Claudia plums from the Foringaš orchard, and my late mama Glembay would say: what Argentine peaches? For compotes à la Melba, the best are the peaches from the Foringaš! It was those Foringaš hills over on the hot springs side, if you kindly remember, where the spirits refinery stands today and where the Château Glembay Cognac is distilled. As for Ludwiga Glembay, that is this lady in white silk and black shawl.

They stop beneath a painting of a young woman in white, who is holding a lorgnette and wearing a heavy, costly, massive pearl necklace. A Biedermeier period work from the 1840s.

FABRICZY: This is a portrait by maestro Bartolomeo from Tuscany, that fantastic person! The unfortunate child from an adventure with this Italian painter disappeared around 1880 in Vienna. It was said that he married some servant girl there, a Styrian! In short: the unfortunate soul, after becoming completely degenerate, threw himself into the water just as his late mother had done! They say that the purported son from this misalliance is living somewhere in Vienna to this day! Yes, yes, that is the unhappy Ludwiga! As one can see, she must have been dazzlingly beautiful! Diese Büste, diese Augen—what breasts, what eyes! And this young man, that's the younger brother of this same Ludwiga! The unfortunate Felix Glembay. He joined Count Wrbna's cavalry squadron, which under Count Nugent in late autumn of 1848 was on the right wing of Viceroy Jelačić's expedition. Some time around the end of November of 1848 Kossuth's bandits captured him near Fünfkirhen and roasted him alive!

ANGELIKA: I know why this one is carrying a church! This is Franz; he built a church in Remetinec. But why is this one holding a locomotive in his hand, Farbriczy?

FABRICZY: That is Franz Ferdinand Glembay! He built the railway line Petau—Csakathurn, Csakathurn—Nagykanizsa! As the general vice director of the Southern Railway, and as vice president of Vienna Gentlemen's Club, he could have easily become a baron, had he only wanted to. And when they came to him with that proposal, the old man most courteously turned them down: "No, thank you! My father's century-old charter is much dearer to me than your two-month-old diploma! Danke schön!"

LEONE: I was still a child and I remember Aunt Marietta telling us that this one could cheat at poker so well that he was known als Falschspieler von Laibach bis Esseg—a swindler from Ljubljana to Osijek!

FABRICZY: Spare me, I implore you, these high-strung jokes of yours!

LEONE: On my word, it is not a joke! That's what I heard from Aunt Marietta!

FABRICZY: (*Passes over the remark in silence*) I don't know whether you remember this picture of your father-in-law? It was painted twenty-five years ago in Vienna, when this same firm, Glembay Company Limited, celebrated its fiftieth anniversary! The work comes from the Makart School, from the academic painter Professor Janeček. Strict in form, mild in color! At that time Ignat was still sporting his famous Napoleon goatee! Perhaps this painting too is not worth dreck, eh, Leone?

Leone has risen and stands in front of a worn-out old-fashioned Guild painting in a Baroque frame.

LEONE: And what do you think, Your Reverence, why is this Glembay holding a pair of scales in his hand?

FABRICZY: Why that's a symbol of the Guild, the scales. He weighed and traded all his life!

LEONE: Yes, he weighed all his life! That always interested me already as a boy, that he is holding a pair of scales where one side outweighs the other! And later it dawned on me: that is the first Glembay who weighed crookedly!

FABRICZY: Your ironic attitude toward everything is sometimes really out of place: back during the Directoire he was considered the richest man between Maribor and Čakovec! At the time of the Congress he'd already bought himself a palace in the Herrengasse! What need did he have to weigh crookedly? Ridiculous!

LEONE: No one yet has ever had one side of the scales outweigh the other all by itself, Your Reverence!

FABRICZY: When common people talk like that, it's still understandable! But common people cannot understand such things! Yes, paupers from off the street think that way, das ist noch verständlich! But you, a Glembay-Danielli—merkwürdig! Extraordinary!

SILBERBRANDT: (*Who has been moving like a shadow during this perusal of family portraits now speaks quietly and persuasively, in fact fawningly*) Precisely for us, for our poor illiterate nation, which lacks its national economic class, for us it is important to maintain what little is economically ours: nationally ours. And that is why some sort of modern, liberal newfangled theories, which ruin and destroy everything, are for us doubly dangerous! I humbly think, at least I have read so in the almanac der Oesterreichischen Handelsgeschichte, Austrian trade history, that in the time of Maria Theresa this Glembay already operated ships in Trieste and had branch offices in Graz and Vienna.

FABRICZY: That is correct! One must bow one's head and acknowledge things, one must regard them positively, and not just smear and disparage everything! Natura non facit saltus! Nothing can be built in twenty-four hours! All these Glembays worked and procured in circumstances much more difficult than those of today, and it is a long way, my dear friend, from that Glembay with scales in his hand to your honorable father, the Privy Councilor, who, as we heard this morning at the celebratory meeting of the chamber of commerce, employs and feeds more than ten thousand bodies! Yes, dearest fellow, that is how it is!

LEONE: Your head is still full of those toasts from the banquet! Go to the Chamber of Commerce celebration tomorrow and recite your toasts there! What are you chanting them to me for? I am neither an honoree nor a banker! I am only a transient in this house; to me these paintings tell things much darker than some toasts! To you this

Glembay holds a church in his hand; to me he holds a bloody knife! To each his own! What did I say? Did I actually say something? I said what I heard, that this Glembay cheated at cards, and that that one weighed crookedly! That is what I said! Not a word more!

FABRICZY: Jawohl, das ist die Barbózcy-Legende: Die Glembays sind Mörder und Falschspieler—the Glembays are swindlers and murderers, and all the Glembays are damned! That's an old hag's tale!

LEONE: So, all that is a Barbózcy legend? Wonderful! Consider only the events since 1848, if you would! You yourself said that this Ludwiga drowned herself, on her own initiative, and her son too plunged into the water on his own initiative. You said it yourself! The brother of this railwayman, this Eisenbahner (who married the Hochbauer woman from Vienna) died in a madhouse! His oldest son shot himself. General Warronigg's wife twice threw herself into the water. Her daughter Laura, Baroness Lenbach, is a prime candidate for suicide! Here is my late mother! All right! She is not a Glembay, but she poisoned herself within the Glembay compound! Can you perhaps deny that? Alice—and Alice, did she not drown herself? The late Ivan, did he not fall from the third story?

FABRICZY: That was purest coincidence!

LEONE: All right, and what about all the Glembays of the third and fourth lineage? All the Agramers, the Ballocsanszkys, and after all, you Fabriczys: Is das alles nicht verflucht und degeneriert? Is not all this cursed and degenerated? Is it really completely normal that Beatrice stands here in her Dominican habit? Isn't the Baroness Zygmuntowicz a widow of a Glembay suicide? And you call all this a Barbózcy legend? My dear Reverence!

FABRICZY: Yes, and so what are you trying to say?

LEONE: Oh please, really! The whole thing is too stupid!

He walks off nervously to the terrace, sits down on a rocking chair and rocks nervously, emitting puffs of cigarette smoke.

FABRICZY: Ein ungemütlicher Sonderling! What an unpleasant eccentric! For the first time in eleven years he comes to the home of his own parents and acts so überspannt, so high-strung, so rampantly nervous, it's downright contagious! (*Ridding himself of this unpleasant theme*) And you, dear Baroness, how are you spending your days? Two or three years ago one of your students told me much about you: Countess Vyeniyavski-Drohobeczka! When she returned from the English Ladies in Pressburg, she was simply charmed by your, as she herself said, "spiritually transformed harmony"!

ANGELIKA: I am no longer with the English Ladies, Your Reverence. I am with the Sovereign Court's Service in the chancellery of His Eminence Cardinal Gaspari-Montenuovo!

FABRICZY: Yes, yes, we know that too, we have the honor of knowing that too! And speaking of that, I have wanted to ask you *ex privata* for a favor: to take a message to His Eminence the Cardinal! We were together with His Eminence in Germanicum (at that time I was still in the Imperial Austrian legation in Rome!) and were then very close to His Eminence. Reverendissimus Provost Doctor Klokochki from Ladanje asked me to intervene through His Eminence Count Montenuovo for an audience with the Eminent Nuncio (to be a game of Préférence, I hear). It's a question of a certain Croatian Vice-Regal Carmelite cloister. Eine Kleinigkeit—a minor matter! Some agrarian complication or something similar. A trifle, Baroness, which would mean so much to those poor sisters!

ANGELIKA: Very gladly, Your Reverence, I will gladly do my best.

Continuing to converse, they exit slowly by a door in the rear, and Dr. Silberbrandt slowly follows them, like a lackey's shadow. A pause, during which the second movement of the "Moonlight Sonata" is heard, while Leone returns to the room and nervously paces and smokes, observing the paintings.

    Enter an annoyed Dr. Puba Farbriczy; a nervous blond individual wearing a tailcoat, a monocle over his eye, and a Havana cigar in his mouth. He limps due to rickets, and wears an iron brace on his deformed left leg, which he drags after him with its considerable and visible burden of an orthopedic shoe. He supports himself with an elegant, black-lacquered cane, and pronounces the letter "r" in an affected, artificial manner. He is uncongenial and very sharp-witted.

PUBA: This is a madhouse, in which a person simply wears out his nerves for nothing! It is late, and I do not purloin my time; tomorrow a whole basketful of work is waiting for me! So stupid for a man to be always tormenting and bothering himself.

LEONE: And who is keeping you here, dear soul? Go, and God bless you, good night!

PUBA: You are always wonderfully witty! There is an important matter I must resolve with Aunt Charlotte, and I simply cannot meet up with her. This is a madhouse, and the people here are playing with fire!

LEONE: Baroness Castelli-Glembay is playing her "Moonlight Sonata," and I think it would be best to let her finish playing her blessed "Moonlight Sonata," because it seems that she could not fall asleep without that sonata of hers "quasi una fantasia"! Go home and good night! Why do you bother yourself here? Especially if you're so above it all, and understand that all this is a madhouse!

PUBA: It's easy for you to talk from your superior olympischen Perspektive! If I had your rent, my dear, I too would not be getting excited! Do you have any idea what this is about? Do you know that the socialist press has announced a new campaign concerning the case of Rupert-Canjeg? Do you know that those gentlemen are threatening with new documents? Do you know that yesterday there was rioting and turmoil at the funeral of that madwoman, and that the police had to intervene? The mob was shouting against unpunished murderers! There they are demonstrating, there the press is preparing a new campaign, and here they are swilling champagne and playing the "Moonlight Sonata"! Don't be so nonchalant, for God's sake!

LEONE: What is that to me? I am completely uninterested in this affair! I could not care less! Let them demonstrate, let them howl, let them write what they like! What's it all to me?

PUBA: Of course it's nothing to you, it's nothing to Charlotte, it's nothing to the old man; all of you are uninterested, but when scandals blaze up once again, then, of course, who will be responsible? Of course, the attorney, Mr. Fabrizcy! Then of course I alone will be exclusively responsible!

Glembay has entered, accompanied by Dr. Altmann, and has overheard Puba's last words. The Excellency Ignat Glembay, head of the firm Glembay Company Limited, banker, major industrialist and financial magnate, the oldest representative of a distinguished patrician family, a resilient gentleman, unusually well preserved for his sixty-nine years. He is wearing a flawlessly tailored tailcoat, has thick, curly, completely silver hair, a prominent nose, a face that is hard, shaven, and decisive, with eagle eyebrows. A strong, somewhat jutting lower jaw and unusually muscular mandibles: his nervous grinding of teeth is audible at intervals. His monocle stays in place quite naturally, as though not there. Dr. Altmann, a gentleman of around fifty, blackly pomaded, with pitch-black, exuberant and well-kept hair and a strong moustache, he contains a dash of an Armenian Gypsy prelate. He is very lopsided, almost hunchbacked, with an impeccable corset under his coat, which impedes his movements. His spectacles are golden. He stores rolled cigarettes in a silver case, and his fingers are yellow from smoke like those of a typical nicotine addict. He smokes incessantly, one cigarette after another.

GLEMBAY: So what is it, my dear Puba, why are you getting upset again? What has happened now?

PUBA: I simply cannot understand any of you, Uncle Naci! I've been flying around from one person to another like some soccer ball! I have told you that I need new directives for the Rupert-Canjeg case. I wanted to speak with Aunt Charlotte: she sends me to you, you politely throw me out, and I wander around here like a moron. There have been new developments in this matter! The socialists have launched a new campaign: they are insisting that the case be reopened on the basis of some letters. This thing is definitely very unpleasant, and I warn you: to try to prevail through some ordinary trickery is risky! This is what I think: from the juridical point of view it would be best to publish a counterstatement. Here in front of outsiders I could not speak, but my position is this: either give me freedom of action as your legal representative or leave me alone! But without any directive, without any decided course of action, not knowing what to do or how to proceed, I neither can nor want to go on. And so, I wash my hands of all this!

GLEMBAY: You then propose a counterstatement in the papers? Hmm!

Hmm! (*Pause. He thinks and grinds his teeth. Then, decisively*) No, nothing doing! Of course, this sort of public controversy involving the Glembay Bank—that would be a juicy morsel for the rabble! I'd rather not! No newspapers at any cost! I'm resolutely opposed to that!

PUBA: This is typical Glembay close-mindedness! Why not? After all, I think I do not exaggerate if I say that this affair has been hashed out in public so many times that, I believe, one logical legal statement—of course, dignified and respectable—cannot do any harm. Excuse my expression, gentlemen, but I think that it is necessary to muzzle that rabble's snout once and for all! It's a preventative measure! And you, doctor, what do you think?

DR. ALTMANN: It is rather difficult to give any advice in this matter, Herr Doktor! I am not completely au courant in this whole story and to me it seems that, on the one hand, Herr Privy Councilor is quite right: The newspapers, my God, are not really an appropriate means; how should I say, the newspapers are, so to say, not a suitable soil for such delicate complications. And on the other hand, as far as I can tell, it seems to me that Herr Doktor Fabriczy might be quite right: something should definitely be done in this ticklish affair . . .

The piano-playing in the background had stopped during Puba's last words. Enter Charlotte, Baroness Castelli-Glembay, accompanied by Cavalry Lieutenant Agramer-Ballocsanszky and by her seventeen-year-old son Oliver Glembay. Baroness Castelli-Glembay is a lady of forty-five, whose body and movements are so fresh that no one would take her for more than thirty-five. Her hair is almost completely silver, and its contrast with her youthful bright eyes and fresh cheeks makes it look like a white, powdered wig. Madame Castelli, a remarkable and witty lady, pronounces her sentences precisely and very logically, and uses her lorgnon more out of affectation than far-sightedness.

She is dressed in a bright lacy champagne-silk dress with opulent jewelry and an unusually deep décolletage, and a costly ermine wrap almost a meter wide. Several seconds after the Baroness, His Reverence Fabriczy enters through a door in the background.

PUBA: (*Very nervously*) I do not understand you—to lose time philosophizing like this, that I really don't understand! What sort of brains do you have, gentlemen? You must give me a directive, or please kindly take my statement without any ill will. In this matter I have absolutely no hidden agenda, but please, I do not wish for even a minute longer to bear exclusive legal responsibility in this matter! This is my final word!

BARONESS CASTELLI: You are being bothersome again, Puba, with these stupidities! Oh, I am of course only a woman and don't understand much about this jurisprudence of yours, but gentlemen, please explain to me once and for all, does the court have authority in this matter or no? Did the court hand down a definitive decision or did it not? Then why are you being bothersome again with these stupidities? It only spoils the mood and gets on one's nerves!

GLEMBAY: Charlotte, you are needlessly upsetting yourself! The court, of course, has the final word, but Puba too is right; after all, there have been new developments! If that unfortunate hysteric had not killed herself, the matter would have died down long ago. The matter, as we know, had already been completely liquidated, but, good Lord, it is true, that person did kill herself in our house, and we, thank God, know what journalists are. But taking the newspapers into account, Charlotte, the newspapers—we should still . . .

BARONESS CASTELLI: (*Exasperated, close to tears*) Well good, then print the court's decision, because I cannot go on like this! To be constantly distressed, constantly in doubt, to be publicly spit upon—that would ruin even stronger nerves than mine, gentlemen! Ich halt' das nicht mehr aus! I cannot take this anymore! Either some energetic, definitive measures will be taken, or I'm going away! Please know that I cannot go on like this! Kindly take a look: I have turned as white as a wig! It seems to me as if all of you have agreed amongst yourselves to destroy me! (*She sinks into an armchair and remains still*)

GLEMBAY: Now you're talking in anger . . .

BARONESS CASTELLI: I refuse to be destroyed! What can I do if that person killed herself? I did everything I could! Did I throw that madwoman from the third floor?

The Glembays | 131

FABRICZY: Why, none of us claimed that you did! Charlotte dear, there is reality, and there is appearance! Don't you think so? She wrote her farewell letter, and the papers printed that letter of hers! Suicides' letters are read in the papers every day: that's nothing special! Of course none of us, personally, thinks there is anything extraordinary in that letter. A letter of one overexcited woman two minutes before her death, of course there is nothing sensational about that for anyone. But let us make a clear distinction: silly females in slum districts out there read that letter in their penny-press papers from a completely different viewpoint—the psychology of the periphery is not the psychology of our weltanschauung! The psychology of the street is overexcited.

BARONESS CASTELLI: Overexcited or not overexcited, what is that to me? Who gave that person the right to put the blame on me? What did I do to her? The day before yesterday, when she was here, I told her nicely, "Madamoiselle, here are fifty crowns for you, and now please leave me in peace!" And what can I do if she jumped from the third floor?

FABRICZY: But all this was already in a state of high excitement, and her coming to you was already in a state of high excitement.

PUBA: (*Very nervously*) O, this nebulous sophistry, I will go insane from these phrases of yours! Please, your lordships, make it concrete, authorize me to print a statement, to make a complaint.

GLEMBAY: I still think it would be the most advisable to pass over everything in superior, aristocratic silence! In my opinion, newspapers last no longer than mayflies. The garbage gets read and then just as quickly gets forgotten. And if we now enter into a public controversy, we'll just drag out the whole thing and bring it back to life!

PUBA: Permit me, dear Uncle, to state that I'm very surprised that none of you are considering this thing from a juridical point of view. Of course the so-called public opinion is not worth crap! But gentlemen, do you not remember that the entire Rupert lawsuit was conducted on a razor's edge? The public opinion is of course always on the side of those who are in the wrong! There is no appeal against that! That is a fact! But you are simply not facing the facts: a woman jumped out of an attic window and remained lying bloody in the street. That fact needs to be faced. That is, of course, a demagogic trick: to jump from the third floor, and with a child in her arms at that—à la Madonna—but gentlemen, demagogy rules the crowd! Please consider: I, as representative of Baroness Glembay, think that it would be in the interest of my client that we now do not pretend to be ostriches! To try to smuggle yourselves through this by some sort of circling of family wagons, is risky and makes no real sense! Tonight I definitely need a directive, or with all due respect I lay down my juridical function. Let me finish, dear Papa, nur einen Moment, bitte schön: I think that it would be most concrete to allow me to read the article in question, because you do not actually know what is going on, and that would be…

FABRICZY: That's just what I wanted to say.

PUBA: … and that would be the only concrete thing to do.

GLEMBAY: Shall we perhaps postpone this until tomorrow? Why bother with such stupidities now? (*He is only objecting as a formality and more for Charlotte's sake than his own. In fact, it can be seen that he is—personally—very interested, and that his disquiet is growing.*)

PUBA: Tomorrow I want to know what I am to do, Uncle Naci! These "stupidities" are being read about throughout the city and are the only topic of conversation everywhere!

FABRICZY: And I think, dear Ignat, that it would do no harm to hear the other side too—et alteram partem! That is an old, proven, and practical legal recipe!

SILBERBRANDT: (*Who has returned to the salon and has been listening discreetly in the background*) I would forbid on principle the reading of this Red press! There is no Lysol which could cleanse a man of that atheistic stench!

DR. ALTMANN: His Reverence Fabriczy is right. Before deciding, we should acquaint ourselves with the data.

GLEMBAY: I am personally opposed to wasting time on something that, in my opinion, is completely worthless. But as far as I'm concerned, please go ahead! And you, Charlotte, what do you think?

BARONESS CASTELLI: O, Gott, I can barely see from my migraine! My nerves are stretched to the absolute limit! To me, this is all so terribly boring and annoying! I'd like some black coffee, please!

GLEMBAY: (*As everyone gathers for the reading of the article, rings a bell, and a chamberlain enters*) Bitte, Franz, Whisky und einen Schwarzen! Aber schnell! Well then, if you really want to, I don't mind! Puba, go ahead!

PUBA: Well then, "Epilogue to a Tragedy . . . Yesterday evening around nine, as the doorways of city houses were already closing for the night, a 23-year-old, garment-worker, Fanika Canjeg threw herself from the third story of the banking house Glembay Ltd. and died on the spot. The name of this unfortunate woman will be familiar to the readers of our paper in connection with the Glembay-Rupert affair which terminated so unjustly before the court. Our readers will recall that the millionaire Baroness Castelli-Glembay, wife of the banker and industrialist mogul Glembay, ran over the 73-year-old workingwoman Rupert in the street with her horses and, smashing her head and breaking all her ribs, killed her on the spot. The police, of course, did not arrest this gracious baroness and banker's wife who had taken the life of an impoverished workingwoman. That lady, of course, remained free, defended herself, and defended herself successfully. The poor old workingwoman Rupert, on her way home from work, perished under the wheels of a lordly coach-and-four, but she was—and this deserves special emphasis—neither the first nor the last victim of this fine lady Baroness Glembay-Castelli. Without going into details of the baroness's personality, our editorial office today emphasizes only this, that through a conjunction of circumstances we have come into possession of most interesting material which completely illuminates the very painful and puzzling suicide of one Anton Skomrak, a day-wage worker who was employed at that same Philanthropic Office whose honorary president is this selfsame Baroness Castelli. We alert our readers to the fact that Baroness Castelli is the mother of that young little baron who, seven months ago, under heavy suspicion that he took part in the robbery and murder of the night-watchman of the construction firm Ganymede . . . (*Here the lawyer becomes confused and skips several lines. His confusion is visible, and he keeps stuttering inarticulately until he recovers. There is a stirring in the group around the Baroness.*) The late Franika Canjeg was a common-law wife of Josip Rupert, old lady Rupert's only son, who as a tinsmith's assistant fell to his death from a newly constructed building leaving behind a pregnant wife entitled to no benefits at all from the city administration. After the catastrophic death of her mother-in-law Rupert, the late Fanika Canjeg in the interest of her child filed a lawsuit for damages against the killer, Baroness Castelli, but the court rejected her claim for damages as unfounded. A workingwoman whose husband and child's father died at the bloody front of labor was treated by the court as a common mistress with no right even to damages. This injustice affected Fanika so gravely that in extremity of despair she took her young life, leaping into the abyss from the third story together with her seven-month-old child. Interesting and most characteristic of this bloody event is the fact that several minutes before her death the late Fanika Canjeg rang at the gate of the lordly millionaires, but they threw her out onto the street like a dog. Thus die the poor under the hooves of the masters' coach-and-fours . . ."

GLEMBAY: (*Gets up and passes nervously through the salon*) That will probably do, thank you . . .

BARONESS CASTELLI: (*Sits motionless, gazing ahead and quietly wiping her eyes with a small handkerchief*) It's downright perverse to sit here so helplessly and allow them to throw dirt at you day after day! I've turned gray—my nerves, my mind, everything, everything—it's awful . . . (*All sit in gloom. Silence. Pause. Leone sits on the left, isolated from the rest. He is smoking his pipe and—it is clear—listening intently. The chamberlain has entered and is serving whisky and coffee. Glembay and Fabriczy each drink two whiskies. All are smoking heavily. Clouds of smoke.*)

PUBA: (*Who feels he has finally gotten their attention*) There is no need to take this thing sentimentally as some sad case: a seven-month-old child at the breast, the leap of a young and unfortunate woman into the depths, the poor before the gates of the capitalists! We know those journalistic props very well! These are syrupy social-democratic ballads, gentlemen, for which we should not fall! The thing should be judged with juridical clarity and confidence: come what might!

The Glembays | 135

I am one hundred and fifty percent in favor of dragging those Jacobin journalist gentlemen to court, and unconditionally challenging them. Let us see that dossier of theirs! Let us formally and concretely examine those documents of theirs and let us ruthlessly put them behind bars! Ridiculous! These swindlers are tossing around libels and insults—what do they care! I am in favor of printing a counterstatement and announcing in that very counterstatement that we have launched a lawsuit charging libel and defamation of character! And that within twenty-four hours! This gutter can only be blocked with energetic intervention.

GLEMBAY: (*Momentarily pauses in his walk and stands in front of Puba*) All right, and what direct result can come out of your energetic intervention? A new trial? Until that new trial gets underway, that rabble can torment you for a whole year! We know from experience what crimes the law lets the press get away with!

PUBA: Precisely because the campaign has been transferred to the terrain of the press, and just because they're trying to hammer a juridical problem into rabble-rousing, demagogic capital, just because, Uncle, this whole affair has been transferred into demagogic dimensions, for that very reason I think it is unconditionally necessary to take up that battle! I find that here, in this concrete case, all aristocratic "isolation" is dangerous and delusional! A single hour's delay can here be of fatal significance.

DR. ALTMANN: That is true, what Herr Doktor Fabriczy says! It is in fact very true! We must by all means separate the reality from the appearance. At first sight, in the absence of thoroughly objective calm, in the eyes of the wide strata that are under the spell of that stinking press, the thing can really appear in an unsympathetic light! These demagogic tribunes always inflame the masses' darkest instincts, and if we observe this from the viewpoint of the passion of the streets, Herr Councilor, in the light of their biases (and those elements must be counted on as a given), I find that a certain passivity on our part could be wrongly interpreted!

FABRICZY: Yes, well, we see once again, gentlemen, how everything in life is relative! Everything in life seethes with imponderables, and, well, experience teaches us that everything can be explained as both right and left, conservative and liberal, false and true! Of course, if you look at the matter through bloody, Red, so-called class-conscious eyes, under a proletarian's magnifying glass, well, even our dear and charming Charlotte can be shown as a criminal beast that tramples and kills people and lives.

BARONESS CASTELLI: These are all just words! Words, words! And I do find this wit of yours presently quite out of place! Downright tasteless! One might almost say, senile!

FABRICZY: I was thinking in earnest! Pardon me, I was not trying to be witty—really not, Charlotte!

BARONESS CASTELLI: (*Irritated*) Oliver, please leave us! It is late! Staying up like this is not for you! You have an early Mass tomorrow! Enough for today, child!

OLIVER: But, Mommy, look, I would really like so much …

BARONESS CASTELLI: Not another word! Good night! Herr Doktor Silberbrandt will be kind enough to accompany you. Good night, child!

Oliver submits. After exchanging kisses with his father, he bows courteously to everyone and, with sure movements, follows Silberbrandt.

GLEMBAY: Well then, we're back to the same thing: what's to be done?

PUBA: A statement should be published and the editorial office should be charged with libel and defamation of character! In the statement two totally independent events should be separated: the death of the old Rupert woman is one thing, and the death of this Canjeg woman is another. It should be resolutely emphasized once again that there is absolutely no connection between these two deaths. First of all, the death of the old Rupert woman has been juridically liquidated! All the facts that were established by the court should be cited. First of all she was not a workingwoman at all but a beggar, hence a passive member of society, a kind of parasite! It should be emphasized, and doubly underlined, that it was demonstrated through witnesses at court that the old pauper regularly drank at barrooms and that even several minutes before her death she drank up her obligatory deciliter! Yes, I know, this is boring, but it should be explained to the females in the outskirts, we know it but—unfortunately, don't you think—those bitches in the outskirts, they are the public opinion, and not we! Indeed! And it should be printed that making the turn, the coachman properly, as prescribed by traffic regulations, twice shouted "Hop, hop," and that the baroness was not driving over the speed limit. (*He began fairly quietly, as though only dictating a draft of the statement for the papers, but later his words gain tempo, and he masterfully and urgently reiterates the entire string of familiar arguments, from lawyerly heights, "from above."*) The old drunken pauper was not run over by the coach-and-four but was downed by a mudguard, and this through her own fault, for please recall: the old woman was not knocked down in the street but fell on the sidewalk, which in the opinion of experts was shown to be a technical impossibility, for someone who is run over in the street to fall on the sidewalk! The old woman, therefore, did not die by being run over, but merely fainted, and a physician who arrived at the scene of the accident only seven minutes after the event noted that her heart was beating very clearly seven minutes later. If you ask me, I think it would be very good to append a notarized medical report to that counterstatement, and to publish the official autopsy results from which even a blind man can see clearly that the cause of death is not any coach-and-four but instead highly advanced arteriosclerosis, plus a degenerated, hypertrophied heart in a terminal phase of infirmity, plus seventy-three years, plus alcohol, logically adding up to: death! A totally ordinary case, a fatal stroke which at seventy-three years of age is an everyday occurrence, and not any murder! One has to die from something after all—lächerlich! In this context, therefore, the very thought that this is a matter of Paragraph 355 of the Penal Code is ridiculous, because, as it has been formally established by the court, and as the court logically agreed with the defense, here there was no, and there could not have been any act of commission or omission that would increase or cause danger to life, and for that very reason, because in the worst-case scenario this was all a completely ordinary traffic violation, and in no way an offense under Paragraph 355 of the Penal Code, that is why those dilettante scribbler gentlemen should be charged with libel and defamation of character! That is one thing. The death of the old Rupert woman, therefore, is one thing! I know, this is boring for you, you are, so to speak, in a celebratory mood, but you too, my dears, to whom all these facts are minutely clear, you too are losing yourselves in confusion and contradiction, and how much worse will it look to the broad strata to whom all this is served heated up on a socialist stove! The following facts, therefore, are crucial. First, the death, according to the physician's report, could have actually taken place of its own accord. Second, that Rupert woman was a pauper, who did not live in the same household as Canjeg, that concubine of her son, who himself lived separately from his mother for a full thirty-two years. Third, that drunken old woman was given a proper citizen's burial of the second grade and in her memory, under her name, a bed was founded in the Sisters Hospital and a place in the city orphanage, and in addition, in the name of that Rupert, a sum of five thousand was deposited at the Philanthropic Office as her endowment, and that endowment was registered with the Bank Glembay Ltd. at the exceptionally high interest rate of eight percent! This interest is covered by the bank's special private reserve fund, which makes for at least an additional seven hundred and fifty crowns per year, which in two or three decades will constitute the principal of quite a considerable property! This interest, this reserve fund, those regular interest rates of four percent, the place in the orphanage, the bed in the hospital plus the burial, all this amounts to over thirty thousand.

GLEMBAY: (*Interrupts him nervously*) All this should be confidential—in camera caritatis—this is delicate and anyhow all of it has already been publicized!

PUBA: Yes, of course, in camera caritatis, but those biddies in the outskirts with their penny-press rags do not read confidential reports. It is just such things that should be thrust before the noses of the street! It should be logically emphasized that the sheer chance that the old beggar was felled by a stroke just as the baroness's coach-and-four was passing by, will only bring benefit to society: in exchange for one sclerotic old woman, there is one hospital bed, one spot in the orphanage, one endowment of eight percent for philanthropic purposes. But all this is only the Rupert case! And everything that took place after the death of the old Rupert woman is one hundred percent totally irrelevant; it is all ranting and whining of the lowest sort; it is simply blackmail! That this female person, this Canjeg, happened to be the concubine of old Rupert's out-of-wedlock son, that he had not been living with his mother for a full thirty-two years—what does that have to do with Aunt Charlotte, or with any of us? An accident at one of the busiest corners of the city can happen anytime and to anyone, but that entitles no one in the world to any sort of rights, especially not toward persons who have proved through philanthropic deeds that they are not only willing but ready to liquidate their personal bad luck decently and humanely! There, the second part of the statement should be based on that! Here we should become somewhat aggressive! That this half-mad person, this Canjeg, again became pregnant, once more as someone's concubine; that she scrounged for alms here at our gate; and that being always and oftentimes generously rewarded, she got the idea of creating a permanent source of income for herself—this after all goes beyond the realm of our responsibilities; it is her own private matter! Who told this Canjeg woman to jump from a window? All patience, no matter how highly cultivated and well intentioned, ought to have its logical and unfaltering limits! All in all, it is my strong juridical opinion that a statement should be drawn up on this set of counterarguments, and that this matter should thus be energetically and definitively liquidated! Those journalists should be blown to smithereens with a counterclaim; I hold that this is in the interest of both the Glembay name and of Aunt Charlotte as my client! Dixi—I've had my say!

Silence. Everyone is thinking about these arguments. A short pause.

DR. ALTMANN: This is all very clear and logical. I believe, dear Herr Privy Councilor, that such an argumentation in this sense could not by any means be harmful!

BARONESS CASTELLI: For me, all this jurisprudence is one quid pro quo, and in fact I don't understand a thing about it! I think that all this is clever, only let something finally happen, um Gottes Christi Willen! How can I be responsible for the suicide of a person I do not know? What does my own child have to do with this? How does it come about that a person is publicly insulted and cursed in such a horrid manner? I must obtain my satisfaction! The court has acknowledged that I am innocent: we have to stress that the court itself has recognized this! And you, Ballocsanszky, what do you think about this?

LIEUTENANT VON BALLOCSANSZKY: (*With a light cavalierly bow and a click of his decorative spurs*) I certainly agree with you, gracious Baroness! I don't understand, however, why we should spend so many words on this thing! I certainly think that this lout—this newspaperman—ought to be struck across the muzzle! Heavy cavalry sabers are a perfect means for accomplishing that!

LEONE: (*Laughs loudly and sharply. Quite spontaneously and from the heart.*)

BARONESS CASTELLI: Why are you laughing, Leo?

LEONE: (*As if startled out of his thoughts into reality*) I? Did I laugh? No, not at all! Absolutely not!

Doctor Silberbrandt returns and listens to the conversation intently.

FABRICZY: I think that Puba is right. His reasons are irrefutable! Let him publish the statement as above and let him sue! That is good!

GLEMBAY: My experience makes me strongly mistrust the press, the public, and the court! What sort of satisfaction could we still obtain? We have already obtained the greatest satisfaction possible: the court has absolved us of guilt! I don't know that there is any possibility of some further satisfaction? I think that the very tone of those scribblers and pamphleteers indicates that they will spare no one! Let them write what they want! I think it would be most intelligent to wipe it with a sponge and—ad acta! And you, Leone, what do you think about all this? You have been conspicuously silent tonight, no?

LEONE: (*Calmly, quite nonchalantly, as though fully engrossed in filling his pipe and as though not uttering severe words, quite inoffensively and good-naturedly*) I think that all your arguments and counterarguments put together will not bring those dead women back to life! She jumped from the window and for her it's over!

BARONESS CASTELLI: (*Irritated*) You could really stop it for once with your high-strung views! This is all again too überspannt!

LEONE: (*Calmly and very sincerely*) Überspannt or no, that woman is dead. And her child is dead! And the old Rupert woman is dead! All are dead!

BARONESS CASTELLI: You are not possibly saying that I am in some way guilty in regard to those women?

LEONE: (*Passes over her question as if he had not heard it*) Yes, those women are dead! And if you want to know what I think about it, then please listen. But no, to me it is all the same! And so, my dear and esteemed father, what I think about this affair is that it is all irreparable! What Puba recited, that is *ius*: the law. Or better yet, that is how excellent students see the law, and Puba was always an excellent student! Puba knows it all by heart: both the arguments and the counterarguments. However, there are things which even the most excellent student cannot learn; there are things which are not written down in the penal code nor in traffic regulations. Moreover, such things cannot be solved even by cavalry methods, with heavy cavalry sabers, as we heard from that knight in a military jacket! I think, in a word, that all your words have no connection at all with the event itself!

FABRICZY: With what event? What else has happened here?

LEONE: What has happened here, is that a woman with her child has jumped from a third-story window and that both are dead. That is what has happened. That is all that has happened! And five minutes before that she rang at the Glembay gate and was thrown out into the street!

PUBA: (*Taking umbrage*) You are an artist! It is a known fact that artistes paranoidly marvel at everything! Paranoids see in everything some sort of "event"!

LEONE: So you consider art to be something paranoid that marvels at everything! And to your lawyerly brain everything that is not penal code and traffic regulations, all that is artistry! Wonderful! A woman was thrown out into the street, and to note that is paranoid! I was present at that event!

FABRICZY: Well, if you thought that it is unjust, that they throw that woman into the street, why then did you not prevent it?

LEONE: I am in this house as a passing visitor, and it does not lie within my authority to change the rules of the house. It is true that the woman was at this gate and that she was crying here for more than half an hour. But such are the rules of the house: no one who does not have a calling card can be admitted to see the madam.

BARONESS CASTELLI: Not true! The servants are not allowed to admit anyone into my presence without announcing them!

LEONE: Yes, the woman was not admitted! That's a quote from the article: "She was not admitted." She wanted the baroness to buy her a Singer machine. She is a trained seamstress, and as such she was convinced that she has a right to a Singer machine!

GLEMBAY: Well, all right, why did you not intervene, when you discovered that it's a question of such a trifle?

LEONE: She decisively declared that if she does not get this sewing machine, she would kill herself! Although she did say that she would drown herself, but according to the house rules, without a calling card . . .

DR. ALTMANN: I do not understand you! You are speaking as perversely as a cocaine addict! How can such things be spoken about so—by God—paranoidly? If you were actually present at the scene, why didn't you intervene? Herr Privy Councilor is right!

LEONE: I told that woman not to humiliate herself anymore, and not to come anymore! Because she told me that she had been here seven times in the last two days! She kept assuring me that if she had her own sewing machine everything would turn out well, but that otherwise she would drown herself! And I told her not to come anymore, because, as far as I know, they will not let her into the baroness's presence without a calling card!

Baroness Glembay-Castelli has become so upset by Leone's tone and manner that she is visibly furious and can no longer control herself. She rises energetically and goes wordlessly to the service bell. A servant enters and she explains something to him.

GLEMBAY: So you were present at that affair? And you told no one a word about it?

LEONE: No one!

GLEMBAY: Incomprehensible!

LEONE: I think that at this moment it makes no difference at all why I told no one anything about it! First of all, I had no idea about the old woman who had been run over. No one told me a word about it! And you asked me what I think about your juridical conference. Here you have it: I am expressing my thoughts! What did I know about all this? I see a woman in an advanced state of pregnancy, with a child at her breast, in tears, and they are not letting her see the baroness because she doesn't have a calling card! This woman is talking about some murders, about some lawsuit, about a Singer machine as her greatest happiness! I went to the store and bought her a Singer machine and had it sent to her address (*He reads from a small piece of paper*), F. Canjeg, Flower Street 163 A.

PUBA: Why, that is brilliant! That is beautiful! And can they confirm for you that the machine was paid for before she killed herself?

LEONE: What do you mean? I don't understand.

PUBA: Why, this is actually an uncommonly precious fact: that machine was paid for before the woman's suicide! Don't you understand? On this can be constructed a new juridical reversal of things: thanks to that paid-for machine her death obtains a totally new legal light! Her farewell letter is thereby completely nullified!

LEONE: Pardon me, but I hope you don't think I bought that machine for the sake of your lawyerly tricks! That machine is my "paranoid" machine and has nothing to do with your juridical jokes! That I was late with that Singer machine is my own "paranoid" responsibility!

A servant has returned earlier with a beautiful white Russian greyhound, and Baroness Castelli-Glembay is pointedly playing with the dog while Leone speaks.

BARONESS CASTELLI: Enough of that, gentlemen! It is up to Glembay to decide! I have no understanding of such überspannt subtleties! It's better to look a faithful dog into the eyes than to churn out such nonsense! I won't let anyone torment me! Gentlemen! There's lightning in the distance! The air outside is so lovely! Let us rescue ourselves from this smoke! Please go on, gentlemen! Come, Igor, come, you beautiful, intelligent fellow! Come, dear, dear Igor!

Stepping out onto the terrace she caresses the dog and slowly descends the stairs into the garden. Lieutenant von Ballocsanszky, Dr. Altmann, and Puba Fabriczy follow her.
 Pause.
 Dr. Silberbrandt has been wordlessly listening to Leone all this time with greatest interest. Old Ignat Glembay paces the salon agitatedly, goes to the terrace, returns, smokes his Havana, sips an occasional whisky, gazes into the darkness, and comes back. Rings for the servant. The chamberlain enters.

GLEMBAY: Franz, bring some more black coffee, would you? And ice please!

Continues to pace nervously, puffs out smoke, pauses momentarily and listens to conversation, and once again becomes engrossed in his thoughts. Fabriczy is smoking a Havana and sipping a cognac. In the distance there is thunder, which is slowly coming closer.
 Leone has sat down on a sofa under the portraits, taken out some papers and letters from his pocket, and is leafing through them, completely concentrated on his reading.

SILBERBRANDT: (*Steps up to Leone very humbly and subserviently*) Herr Doktor, pardon me, I think that a while ago you were overly sharp and one could almost say unjust toward the Baroness!

LEONE: (*Fully absorbed in reading those letters, makes himself sound absentminded, but is in fact aloof*) What? I beg your pardon?

SILBERBRANDT: I think that you, Herr Doktor, were overly one-sided in your formulation of the unfortunate incident.

LEONE: What incident? I don't understand, what are you trying to say by that?

SILBERBRANDT: I think that you had no right at all to speak about the death of that unfortunate woman so neutrally, as if the matter did not concern you!

LEONE: Well, if you want to know, that matter really does not concern me!

SILBERBRANDT: Herr Doktor, pardon me, I don't mean to speak of it as an indiscretion, it happened completely accidentally, without my will, quite accidentally.

LEONE: What happened accidentally? This is all becoming more and more puzzling to me!

SILBERBRANDT: I was present last night during your conversation with that unfortunate woman! I was on the balcony when you were talking with her in the hall, I was on my way back from the library and so, completely accidentally, without my will, quite accidentally...

LEONE: Yes—and? And then? What? Do you want to apologize for eavesdropping?

SILBERBRANDT: My conscience is quite clear, Herr Doktor, please be sure of that! I was on the balcony by complete accident and I heard every word you spoke to that woman! I heard how she wept, that she cannot go on like this with one child at the breast and another on the way, and you responded by telling her to "jump through the window"! "I beg you like before God," that is how she wept in front of you, "I beg you like before God." I heard that, Herr Doktor!

LEONE: Exactly. She begged me "like before God" to help her to reach the baroness without a calling card, and I responded to this by telling her that she would be better off jumping right through a window! Exactly! But since you were already playing the role of a detective in that affair then you should have eavesdropped better, my dear Reverend Sir! I begged that woman to be sensible and most of all not to humiliate herself in vain! I told her that the baroness is president of the Philanthropic Office, and to write a petition to that Philanthropic Office, to list all her reasons, and that way she can get her sewing machine. She replied to me that she had already submitted four such petitions, and I wrote down the numbers of her petitions, and if it interests you I can you quote you those numbers! Here you are: numbers 13707, 14222, 14477, 14893.

SILBERBRANDT: It is a question of the way in which you rejected that woman! It is precisely your brutal manner which—in my most honest opinion—does not give you any right to condemn those around you for much lesser nominal oversights!

LEONE: (*Nervously*) Please, Silberbrandt, spare me your babbling! When she gave me the numbers for the sewing machine last night I did not yet know about the incident of the old woman who had been run over—her mother-in-law! I only heard about that incident this morning. Please take it into consideration that I am no lawyer and that today I do not think that the Rupert-Canjeg incidents are not connected. Last night I had no idea about any of this! And when she talked to me about her petitions, which have been lying around the Philanthropic Office for more than half a year already, and that a single solitary word could save her, I thought I was talking with a poor woman who is seeking the baroness as a benefactor! That is why I told her: benefactors who are approached through calling cards—avoid such benefactors in your own interest! And if you expect salvation from such benefactors, then you would be better off jumping straight off through a window! That is what I told the woman and I don't deny it! And I don't understand—what is the purpose of this interrogation?

Old Fabriczy and Glembay listen with great interest.

SILBERBRANDT: Permit me only a single observation, Herr Doktor. The word was about the story in that atheistic rag of a newspaper, that this woman was thrown out from a millionaire's house last night when she came to appeal for help in her final extremity! But her ladyship the Baroness had no idea about any of this! And insofar as I know the Baroness, I think that she is a person of a very noble and gentle heart!

LEONE: Please . . .

SILBERBRANDT: Yes, Herr Doktor, I am convinced of this! And that which you earlier ironically called house rules, that unannounced people are not allowed into the baroness's presence, that is an everyday phenomenon, not even a nominal omission! I assure you that if the Baroness had had only an inkling of what was at stake, that today the woman would not be dead, and that we all would have been spared from this horrible event! As Her Excellency's personal assistant I have had the opportunity to observe her at work in the Philanthropic Office for two full years and so—I can confidently tell you—it is not a question of a momentary impression but of a judgment reached after years of experience. Her Excellency is a good person, very sensitive to the suffering of those around her, and I have known very few people in my life in whom that Platonic idea of goodness, that supreme and most lofty knowledge of goodness, is as developed as in Her Excellency!

LEONE: As her confessor, Reverend, you will surely know more about that than we laymen.

SILBERBRANDT: Yes, regardless of your irony, that is how it is, Herr Doktor, just as I say! And in this particular Canjeg case, Her Excellency's standpoint should be appreciated and understood! The Canjeg woman did not have any sort of juridical or formal connection with the old Rupert woman: she was, as Herr Doktor Puba correctly formulated it, a de facto concubine of a man who—nota bene—lived as an out-of-wedlock child separated from his mother for more than thirty years. And this woman, this Canjeg, under a delusion that she is the legal heir of a person unknown and alien to her (who happened to be felled by a stroke in the street) demanded through the court and through the press a fantastic sum! On the one hand to appeal to the court, to call on the cold letter of the law, and on the other, having lost at court, to appeal to compassion—no, that is not any sort of Christian conduct! Her Excellency the Baroness was laid up in a sanatorium with nervous shock, her hair turned white before our eyes within twenty-four hours, so to speak, while those same people around the Canjeg woman were stirring up such scandalous rumors about her and about her earlier life, and then for that person to show her face one day here at the Baroness's gate in the role of the humblest beggar as though nothing had happened. To be an arsonist on one hand, Sir, and to call for mercy on the other, what sort of hypocrisy is that? Is that the Christian way?

LEONE: Then you too are against any sort of a pardon? In that case I was right to tell that Canjeg woman that she would be better off jumping through a window than hoping for any sort of help from Her Excellency, especially without a calling card!

SILBERBRANDT: That is dialectics, Herr Doktor!

LEONE: And the fact that the baroness is an honorary president of the Philanthropic Office, that is not dialectics? On the one hand we trample people, and on the other we do them good—that is surely some sort of a moral equilibrium!

FABRICZY: Leone, I have always been enamored of paradoxical weltanschauungs, no doubt about that, but I maintain that it is factually überspannt to attribute that accident at the street corner to the Baroness! That was an unfortunate incident, and I can tell you—of this I am deeply convinced—that the Baroness's coach-and-four is neither the first nor the last to leave old hags lying in its wake. Jawohl, unfortunately that's how it is!

SILBERBRANDT: And I think, Your Reverence, that to trample people in a given case bodily, physically, is not nearly as sinful as to trample a person morally, spiritually, ideally!

LEONE: I literally know in advance what you are going to say! A priest's pulpit is like some attorney's office!

SILBERBRANDT: All people live with a great surge of life within them, up to a certain psychological line, and once they cross that final demonic black line, then they are ripe for a godless death! Every indi-

The Glembays | 149

vidual carries within himself a fundament of that Augustinian divine goodness: that is the basic vital principle of all phenomena. Deus est in omnibus rebus, as Saint Thomas wrote. God is in all things. Not fear but admiration and gratitude created gods—non timor sed admiratio et gratitudo deos fecit—those are admittedly the pagan words of Cicero, but they are applicable even today. People are full of that divine admiration and that supernatural gratitude and all people believe in some higher otherworldly meaning of their subjective lives and Fichte's "moral world order" is more or less sealed in all souls. People carry within themselves a moral faith in that Ens Realissimum, most real being, being itself, in God, in divine authority and in social hierarchy—in fact, in a strictly disciplined system in a material sense. With these and similar images within themselves people can cling to the surface in life's crises. That is the biblical lamp within us. Lux in tenebris: light in darkness. But when a subject thinks he has perceived that there is nothing above him: neither moral authority, nor idea of God, nor goodness, nor even social hierarchy, then the feeling of an infernal vacuum swallows such a man. And you, my dear Herr Doktor, threw that woman into such a moral vacuum! You killed the idea of goodness within her, the idea of God and of all hope!

LEONE: And you think that she jumped from the window because I killed the idea of goodness within her!

SILBERBRANDT: Not only because of that! But certainly, so long as she could still write petitions, knock on strangers' doors, beg for pity from her neighbors, she must have had faith both in moral authority and in social hierarchy! She still believed in the idea of goodness, because if she had not, she would not even have come here! And you resolutely declared to her that none of that exists: neither goodness, nor pity, nor God! What was left to that woman after this? What? And, you see, according to moral classification that act of yours weighs more heavily than if someone accidentally runs over a sclerotic old woman, or if house rules somewhere demand that visitors are announced with calling cards!

LEONE: That she jumped through a window—that she had to jump through a window—is mathematically clear! That is pure mathematics! This afternoon I visited her apartment and I assure you, Silberbrandt, if you lived in that room, you too would jump through a window together with your moral authorities and quotations!

FABRICZY: And you seem as though you are perversely satisfied that she jumped through a window?

LEONE: That is mathematics. That is as clear as two times two. That is the inner logic of the thing itself! That has its deeper reasons!

FABRICZY: I find your logic more puzzling every day!

LEONE: That is pure Glembay logic! I think I have discovered the causality of that event, and maintain that the whole secret is rather clear to me. One reason among numerous others is that it's in the Glembays' interest that as many people as possible die. That is the Glembays' business!

FABRICZY: This is becoming more and more unclear and puzzling!

Old Glembay has paused in his nervous pacing and is intently listening.

LEONE: Capital invested in funeral enterprises brings in about sixty percent profit. As far as I know, Bank Glembay Ltd (among its other honorable business projects) finances almost the entire funeral trade in the city and in the province!

GLEMBAY: Sooner or later you will end up in a madhouse!

Indignantly, Glembay goes to the terrace and descends the stairs into darkness. Distant laughter is heard from the garden. Thunder is coming closer.

SILBERBRANDT: I do not understand that nihilism of yours! The point in question is not about the banking business but about the fact that you have made a concrete accusation, and are not able to prove your assertion! You are wantonly toying with all sanctities, Herr Doktor . . .

LEONE: The point in question is not about anything! The point in question is about the fact that you have been lecturing me and pestering me for half an hour already! What sanctities? Do you think that your benevolent parades under the protectorate of Baroness Castelli are one such sanctity, in which people should believe as in metaphysical authority and social hierarchy? To die under the hooves of the Baroness's coach-and-four with a faith in metaphysical authority and social hierarchy! Or, instead, to approach such a creature and to tell her: "Remember, woman, that you are the equal of the one before whom you are humiliating yourself, and do not humiliate yourself! Walk erect, do not cry before others' gates, because there is no one for you behind those gates, spit and slap, but do not humiliate yourself!" According to you, that amounts to morally trampling someone! Anyway! It is unintelligent of me even to be talking with you. I hope you are not trying to turn me into some sort of a convert!

Breaks off the conversation, waves his arm, walks across the salon, looks at the paintings along the wall, and then collects himself nervously around his pipe.

SILBERBRANDT: (*With Jesuitical mendacity, obsequious sorrow, and a confessor's monotone*) You are uninformed, Herr Doktor, because if you were informed of the charitable work of Her Gracious Highness the Baroness you could not call those beautiful Christian results a parade! Please permit me: the numbers speak for themselves. Only in the course of the current year, under the Baroness's presidency, the following were given out... (*With a ready and practiced gesture he extracts a prayer book from his cassock and reads from a small piece of paper*) Here you are, Herr Doktor, given out were: one hundred and fifty seven pairs of shoes, three hundred sets of children's clothing, eight hundred and fifty-three children were given winter meals, twenty-eight thousand crowns was given in relief, and three hundred and eighteen legal interventions were undertaken free of charge! I leave it to your conscience, Herr Doktor, to call such beautiful and Christian results a parade. And if you really want to know, this year's survey concerning the material and moral status of our clients, conducted at the initiative of Her Highness the Baroness herself...

LEONE: (*Stands before Silberbrandt challengingly and ironically*) Listen, Silberbrandt, none of your numbers will convince me that the Baroness is a benefactor! I have my own personal opinion about all that! Did you know Skomrak, the day-wage clerk at the Philanthropic Office?

SILBERBRANDT: Do you mean that paranoid young man who hanged himself less than a month ago?

LEONE: Yes, none other than that "paranoid" young man, who hanged himself a month ago! He left his correspondence behind, and from that correspondence it can be clearly seen that your gracious president Baroness Castelli-Glembay had an intimate relationship with that twenty-year-old Skomrak!

SILBERBRANDT: Herr Doktor! How can you speak like that about your stepmother? About a lady, Herr Doktor, by the merciful God!

LEONE: Very easily! I have the Baroness's letter here in my pocket—from which it follows…

SILBERBRANDT: Pardon me, Herr Doktor, but this does not interest me in the least!

LEONE: I am surprised! That means that your friendship with the Baroness is no longer so intimate…

SILBERBRANDT: (*His nerves very tense*) How do you mean?

LEONE: When someone sleeps with a woman for whole nights on end, he surely ought to be interested in whom the woman in question is corresponding with.

SILBERBRANDT: (*Pale and agitated, trembling*) I don't understand a word of any of this, Herr Doktor!

LEONE: No? Really? I only ask of you, since you are already receiving the Baroness's nightly visits, to be at least a shade more discreet about it! At least for as long as there are extraneous guests in the house! Anyway! Good night, gentlemen!

He leaves hurriedly, and with a contemptuous gesture. Silberbrandt gazes after him astonished, without a word.

FABRICZY: (*After a pause*) An unpleasant, eccentric creature, I say!

Glembay stands on the terrace, white as a sheet, devoid of a drop of blood. He had been standing there unnoticed for some time. Silberbrandt had seen him but had been unable to communicate this to Leone. Slowly, brokenly, Glembay approaches the table and slumps into a chair. He pours himself a whisky, and drinks it up. He pours another and drains it. In the distance it is thundering.

GLEMBAY: Do you hear it, Fabriczy? Es donnert! Thunder! Do you hear it? That was my lower back this morning. Es donnert! I felt it, that something was going to happen!

He walks over to the open terrace and listens to the thunder.

[CURTAIN]

ACT TWO

Takes place twenty to thirty minutes after Act One. The scene shows a Biedermeier-style guestroom in the Glembay house, clean, simple, and modest. Two lacquered rocking chairs, two armchairs of flower-pattern cretonne, Dutch seascapes in golden frames. On top of a fairly large lacquered table, a silver candleholder with seven candles. This is the only illumination. Curtains on the window to the right and on the door are dark-red, Bordeaux color. On the right, a door to the adjacent room. A wardrobe in front of the door. Leone is packing: there are two enormous suitcases and several smaller ones, made of leather. Painting equipment, rolls of canvas, palettes and frames. On the armchairs, scrolls of paper and sketches. Outside, wind and thunder are growing. In a rocking chair, Silberbrandt is in visible distress. He has lost all traces of his mask, pose, and priestly superiority, and is showing an overall lack of pride. He is futilely chattering and nagging.

SILBERBRANDT: All the same, dear Herr Doktor, I think that it was not in best form to speak that way in front of an outsider! True, His Reverence Fabriczy is a cousin of Herr Privy Councilor, but he is still outside the immediate family! Fine, fine, Herr Doktor: considering your nervous indisposition I could understand it if you allowed yourself to make such an undeniably brutal joke directed at my humble self when we two are alone! Though I could not understand it even then, I could certainly overlook it! But in such a way, Herr Doktor, so brutally, so wrongly—in front of an outsider . . .

LEONE: I have asked you three times already, Silberbrandt, not to bother me! Why the devil are you bothering me? You see that I'm busy! I cannot round up my words and bring them back like sparrows. I thought it and said it—it's done! Besides, remember once and for all: There are no roses without thorns! Il n'y a point des roses sans épines! And now I beg you once again to leave me in peace! It bores me to talk about all that, and, believe me, you would be doing me the greatest favor if you left me alone!

SILBERBRANDT: (*Desperate and lost, remains silent. After a pause, tearfully and with a boyish lack of dignity*) Herr Doktor, you must understand my position! Why, I am the Glembay family's philanthropic assistant and confessor to Her Highness the Baroness, and instructor to her son! And believe me, I would not be making this into any sort of a problem if it were not for that fatal conjuncture of circumstances: this role of family instructor with an especially delicate mission with respect to little Oliver. Herr Doktor, please, you must understand! Herr Doktor, if only His Reverence alone had heard this! But your honorable father, His Excellency the Privy Councilor, heard every single word! You could not see him, he was behind the doors of the terrace, Herr Doktor! Those words of yours were so formidable, dear Herr Doktor, and none of your speculations has any basis in reality. I hope that you will be a gentleman...

LEONE: (*Very untidily and nervously, he is tossing clothing and suits, books and various nearby objects into suitcases. He tightens plaid capes with belts, and seems to be absentmindedly looking for something.*) What can I do, Silberbrandt? That statement of mine has not been printed in newspapers, and even if it were it would surely be in some "atheistic rag"! Anyway, somewhat weightier statements have been printed in the newspapers, yet you have been able to analyze away the false elements in a gentlemanly manner! There is no negative truth which cannot be justified in a gentlemanly manner! That Canjeg woman threw herself through the window with her own child, yet you in a gentlemanly manner succeeded in proving that I killed the God within her, and that she was a harlot and a criminal! As for some "paranoid" type saying that you are a lover of some Glembay woman—who will believe that? Assume, my Reverend Herr Doktor, that I did not say it, or that I made it all up merely to compromise you! Well and good! I did not say it! I expressed myself wrongly! You are not the Baroness's lover! Glory to Lord God! Good night!

SILBERBRANDT: First of all, Herr Doktor, I never, nowhere, and on no occasion considered you paranoid or abnormal. To the contrary, Herr Doktor, so far as I can remember, I have always been a sincere admirer of your talent (which, between ourselves, has not been a most profitable role within this household). When you, Herr Doktor, exhibited your painting *Charon Ferries His Victims Across the Lethe* in Munich two years ago, I excerpted all the favorable reviews of the German critics and published them in *Saint Cecilia's Herald*. And

I sent you a copy by mail, and, if I am not mistaken, you were then in Aix-les-Bains and, I don't know, perhaps that paper never reached you, Herr Doktor. But you see, Herr Doktor, your honorable father, Herr Privy Councilor, he heard every word of yours . . .

LEONE: And you think that, because you once printed some reviews in *Saint Cecilia's Herald*, that I should retract my words before my father?

SILBERBRANDT: Yes, well, but what will your honorable father, His Excellency Herr Privy Councilor, think?

LEONE: His excellency my honorable father has had twenty years to think about all this as much as he likes, but it seems he has not come up with anything particularly intelligent!

SILBERBRANDT: Herr Doktor, please pardon me, I truly have no intention to bore and molest you, but my whole career lies in your hand! My position depends on one single word from you, you can explain all that as nervousness, as unthinking verbal nervousness . . .

LEONE: (*Packing and wordlessly ignoring Silberbrandt. Pause. A green reflection of distant flashes of lightning, thunder, and wind. Pause.*)

SILBERBRANDT: Herr Doktor, don't be so stubborn. Please, dear Herr Doktor . . .

LEONE: (*Nervously and loudly*) By god, you are feebleminded, Silberbrandt! None of it is as important as it appears to you! You see that I am busy! It would be very civil and discreet of you to leave me in peace. I still have two or three letters to write and I beg you not to get on my nerves but to go to sleep! What sort of manners is it to disturb someone so tirelessly? Excuse, me but that is a total lack of tact! (*Knocking. Repeated, louder knocking. Leone has broken off his work. Pause. Repeated knocking. Strong wind and claps of thunder.*)

LEONE: Come in!

Old Glembay enters, wearing a smoking jacket of dark-orange silk. His pale, elderly, tormented appearance forms a complete contrast with the figure in the salon of half an hour ago. His powdered and shaven mask has transformed into the face of a sick person with dark circles under his eyes, whose movements are uncertain, while his lower jaw is abnormally suspended, as though his lips were hanging on their own and grinding the air. The face is flabby and bloodless; this man is in the grip of depression. He looks like someone who has risen to fight his last battle. This is why in the first part of the dialogue he is quiet, almost pathetically solemn, and only gradually will the sinews of those jaws grow tense again, those teeth bestially grind again, and that fist rise of its own accord to bloody this monster who confronts him—his own son.

GLEMBAY: (*Quiet, amiable, conciliatory, and discreet*) Pardon, am I in the way?

LEONE: (*Nervously, controlling his confusion*) Oh please, not in the least! Please come in, we were just talking about you!

Silberbrandt was struck speechless by the knocking, and when Glembay appeared at the door, he shuddered and froze, then rose from his chair as if hypnotized. He makes a deep, subservient, Jesuitical bow to Glembay, without a single word. Glembay directs a barely perceptible, cold and very dark nod at this priestly figure who stands mutely like a wax doll in a cassock. After closing the door very quietly and with seeming caution, Glembay approaches Leone. He is visibly surprised by the candlelight and the open suitcases. Glembay observes all of this disorder and mutely marvels with his eyes.

LEONE: The noble Monsignor and I were just talking about you! Monsignor said that it seems to him that you drink too much! And I too was surprised tonight by your whisky!

GLEMBAY: I see!

Pause. Leone, who had been standing erect over a suitcase, has bent forward and his head has vanished behind the open suitcase.

LEONE: (*From the suitcase*) Well please, take a seat, go ahead, sit down!

Glembay stands motionless and silent.

LEONE: (*Straightening up*) Won't you sit down? Please, go ahead! (*He goes over to an armchair and removes palettes, frames, and other painting equipment from it.*) Here you are, please!

Silberbrandt has remained standing in place, motionless and with overdone courtesy. Glembay acts as though this person were not present at all. He has sat down in the proffered chair and is silent. Pause.

GLEMBAY: What sort of lighting is this?

LEONE: I don't know. It seems to me that a wire burned out somewhere in the wing! A short circuit!

GLEMBAY: And why hasn't it been repaired?

LEONE: I don't know!

GLEMBAY: And this here?

LEONE: These are suitcases! I'm packing!

GLEMBAY: You're packing?

LEONE: Yes!

GLEMBAY: You're going away?

LEONE: Yes!

Pause. This dialogue is severe, but very courteous, as though two completely deaf men were conversing in the equality of their own organismic limitation. Thunder is much louder and growing. From time to time, flashes of lightning cast green reflections. The gap between flashes and explosions is from five to seven seconds. Wind and rain beat against windowpanes.

GLEMBAY: May I light up? The smoke won't bother you?

LEONE: Please feel free to! I myself am continuously smoking my Dunhills! (*He lights his father's cigar. Pause.*)

LEONE: What number is this one tonight?

GLEMBAY: Tonight? The seventh tonight!

LEONE: And what does Paul Altmann say about your heart?

GLEMBAY: Nothing! What can he say? Nothing! Medicine knows nothing anyway!

Pause. Thunder. Leone keeps on working. He has opened the wardrobe and is packing his tailcoat and chapeau claque.

GLEMBAY: (*Gazes at the frames and canvases, blankly. It is clear that he finds the presence of Silberbrandt unbearable.*) Is there among these paintings the one that won the golden medal in Paris?

LEONE: It is not here! It got left behind in Aix-les-Bains!

Pause. Thunder. With the powerful detonation Silberbrandt has seized his first opportunity to leave.

SILBERBRANDT: Well then, Herr Doktor, I certainly hope that we will meet again at tea. I think it is time for me to go to bed. I am tired, and tomorrow I'm celebrating an early morning mass. It is already rather late. My compliments, Herr Privy Councilor! Good night, Herr Doktor, please accept a bow from your humble servant!

LEONE: Farewell! Good night!

As Silberbrandt opens the door to depart, a strong gust of wind blows through the room, and the Bordeaux-red curtains at the window and door start to wave like banners. The curtains continue to undulate as though the entire room were sailing in a storm. Wind, downpour, thunderclaps.

GLEMBAY: It would be good to close the window!

LEONE: I like thunder! But if it bothers you, yes of course! (*Moves to shut the window*)

GLEMBAY: It is not necessary on my account. Thank you!

Pause. Flashes of lightning. Wind. Pause.
Glembay, emitting thick and very nervous puffs of smoke, has gotten up and moved toward a bundle of rolled-up canvas paintings, of which there are about twelve. He has unwrapped one of the bundles and is mutely gazing at the paintings. It is plainly visible that to him this is totally useless material: canvas daubed with oil paints. Without indignation but certainly with an indifferent gesture, he tosses the canvas, not rolling it up, back to its previous place. Pause. He then goes to the table and gazes with interest at a costly travel case with silver fittings.

GLEMBAY: Where did you buy that *nécessaire*?

LEONE: In Calcutta!

GLEMBAY: Expensive?

LEONE: I don't remember. If I'm not mistaken, five hundred and fifty dollars!

GLEMBAY: I too used to have one like it. A companion of mine, general director of Messageries Maritimes in Marseilles, brought it to me from India as a present. You were three years old then! This is antelope! This is very finely cured antelope! (*He opens a crystal bottle and smells the contents.*) And what sort of water is this?

LEONE: That is some Tibetan grass! That grass grows on the eastern side of Mount Everest! Around Phari Dzong!

Pause. Thunder is booming, and wind. Leone has stopped packing. Apparently tired and enervated he sits in a rocking chair and starts to rock. All his nerves are visibly vibrating. He is toying with his pipe and smoking. The old man is picking through neckties and sketches on the table, nervously and mutely. Then he crosses the room. After pausing for thought:

GLEMBAY: So you are going away?

LEONE: Yes!

GLEMBAY: But didn't you actually come to take part in the Glembay Bank Jubilee, Leone? Such a jubilee is not celebrated every other year. That means you will not attend tomorrow's ceremonial session of the Chamber?

LEONE: Yes, I've come to be at this Jubilee. I have finally seen you, we have seen each other! This morning I attended the bank's session, and tomorrow's event is more or less a gala performance! I think it's best for me to go. I've been absent for eleven years and, you see, I no longer feel—how to put it—at home here. People are creatures of habit! And you yourself will concede, that to feel a stranger, a sort of transient, at such an intimate celebration, in the house of one's parents, is not a most pleasant feeling!

GLEMBAY: That depends on who feels what! I think that those feelings of yours are completely unfounded. You're high-strung—überspannt—that's all.

LEONE: (*Stands up nervously, as though stung. He has reacted nervously to that word.*) In your whole vocabulary could you not find a word other than just "überspannt"? You've been telling me this since I was five years old! Anyhow! (*He has controlled himself. Soberly and calmly with a somewhat malicious ironic tone*) Please excuse me, but let me ask you, to what good fortune do I owe this late visit?

GLEMBAY: (*Rises, hurt. Internally he is seething. His depression is growing into violence. Gazing long at his son, he nods his head.*) Yes, you had already been just this arrogant toward me at nine years of age! This is that Venetian blood of yours! (*He grinds his teeth, smokes, and walks up and down the room. He halts sternly and resolutely.*) Well then, let us not waste time! I was on the terrace, when you were talking with Dr. Silberbrandt, and I heard every word you said.

Pause. Father and son gaze long into each other's eyes. After that pause, Leone raises both arms with a shrug, and then helplessly lowers them.

GLEMBAY: Well! And?

LEONE: Nothing! Then you heard every word I said.

GLEMBAY: Well? And? (*Pause*) And?

LEONE: And what? Silberbrandt told me a while ago that you overheard it! Forgive me! I was deeply convinced that you were somewhere in the garden! I did not have any bad intention!

GLEMBAY: It is not a question now of what sort of intention you had, but rather, is it true?

Pause.

LEONE: I think it is superfluous for the two of us to say even a single word about it here! I did not say it to you, but to Silberbrandt!

GLEMBAY: Is that so? And what would you do with a man who declared in front of two witnesses that your own wife sleeps all night with her lover?

LEONE: I don't know!

GLEMBAY: Is that so? You don't know?

LEONE: Of course I don't know! First of all I don't have a wife, and second, I'm not sixty-nine years old! I therefore don't know what I would do in your place!

GLEMBAY: Well, all right, fine, let's assume that is so. All right! You don't know! All right! Fine! All right! (*He crosses the room and then stops.*) Can you speak with me for two minutes as a friend?

LEONE: No!

This is an excessively abrupt and sharp response to a question that contained a shade of warmth. Sensing that the word was too strong, he attempts, after an uncomfortable pause, to dilute it with commentary.

In fact, I—In fact I think that people either are friends or they are

The Glembays | 163

not! One cannot be a friend for two minutes. And perhaps the two of us do not even know each other: we have spoken hardly once in these eleven years, that is, ever since that morning when Mother was found dead! And, you see, I wouldn't want to be insincere; since Mother's death I have not even once felt the need to speak with you as a friend! Yes! I would be lying if I told you that I can speak with you as a friend, be it even for only two minutes! You see: I've packed, I'm leaving! I think that my arrival in this Glembay household was a kind of final sentimental blunder. You invited me in writing, a Jubilee, parental considerations and all that goes along with such a celebration, but this is all stronger than my nerves! I am, as you say: überspannt! They consider me "paranoid"! A "paranoid" should not be taken to task. But please accept my strongest assurance that everything I said to Silberbrandt was not directed at you! I give you my word of honor that I had no idea that you were listening on the terrace!

GLEMBAY: Well, all right, if you will not as a friend, then purely as a human being you must tell me what is going on. You must tell me that! Do you understand me?

LEONE: I don't have to do anything—I have never had to do anything! But if you insist, all right! Nothing special is going on. What is going on is that the noble vicar, or whatever he is, Monsignor, Herr Doktor Silberbrandt, confessor of your wife and instructor of your son, is the Baroness's lover. That is what is going on, if you really want to know! Nota bene: that gentleman is your candidate for an honorary canon and is your protégé in every respect.

GLEMBAY: (*As if he does not yet understand, and as though he is feeling ill*) Well, all right! And are you aware of all the consequences of this declaration of yours?

LEONE: I have nothing to do with that! Ask your wife about that! What do I care about that?

GLEMBAY: Well, all right! And can it be that all this is not true? Can it be that it is all invented? What then? Who is responsible for it then?

LEONE: If it is not true, and it is all invented, then there is no responsibility either!

GLEMBAY: (*Moves toward his son in agony, frailly, like an old man*) I beg of you, never in my life have I begged you for anything, but now I beg of you: Leo, don't torture me! Tell me, what is going on?

LEONE: Look, I don't have any juridical proofs in hand! I didn't study law! I'm not a doctor of law like Puba Fabriczy! There exist no juridical proofs against the Baroness! The Baroness ran over the old Rupert woman, but has been juridically acquitted of guilt! Autopsy results have documented that the old woman's heart had a diameter of two hundred and twenty millimeters! And the Canjeg woman jumped from a window, but there is no proof! I as a "paranoid type" killed the "God" within her, and that is why she jumped from a window! How can I know what is going on when the matter at hand is of a completely delicate, intimate nature! Other than the Baroness and Silberbrandt, no one can know that! And if one of them swears an oath that it is a lie, where is the truth then?

GLEMBAY: (*Still sunk in gloomy thoughts, as though unable to understand*) Well, all right, then how could you so categorically claim something about which you are in no way sure?

LEONE: I don't know. On the one hand I see clearly that all this is stupid, what I'm saying now, but on the other hand, I don't know if you can understand it. I would not want you to take me for a neurasthenic, betrayer, or slanderer! I have slept for five nights under your roof, out of which the Baroness spent two nights in Silberbrandt's room! Maybe he was confessing the Baroness. But that she was in his room I have had the honor to ascertain through personal experience. We are neighbors—adjoining rooms.

GLEMBAY: Parlez plus bas, parce que les murs ont des oreilles! (*Looks at the door that leads to the adjacent room and which is blocked by the wardrobe. Goes to it and returns.*)

LEONE: Please, once again, what I said I did not say for you, you heard it accidentally! I am admittedly überspannt, but I do not wish for the sake of form to appear in your eyes as a slanderer, and especially not on account of a—to me—completely indifferent woman!

The Glembays | 165

GLEMBAY: And you cannot conceive that this is not a matter of some "indifferent woman"?

LEONE: For me that woman is completely indifferent, not to say something much more negative!

GLEMBAY: (*Gazes at him at length without a word. Silence. Thunder, but weaker. Wind. Then, bitterly*) Yes, that is you! A true Danielli!

LEONE: Personally I am glad that I am not a Glembay.

GLEMBAY: (*Thoughtfully and with resignation*) Yes, yes, it's always been like that! Whenever I approached one of you, in regard to anything, with whatever request or intention, the same thing always happened. Yes, always: this Danielli grimace of yours always appeared before me, with its lofty contempt for everything other than yourselves! Lords! Lords Danielli, Venetian grandees! And I, who am I? Some provincial parvenu from Međimurje. How dare I entertain the idea that to me a certain woman is not indifferent, when to you—to Sir Danielli—she is something much more negative! Yes, of course, what do you care about my wife? The very idea of holding you, a Danielli, responsible, when you deign to break your walking stick over someone's head!

LEONE: I am convinced that this whole conversation of ours is completely superfluous! I'm leaving! I am about to go, I will probably never return, and I think it is wisest to part in peace! Because, look, our points of view are diametrically opposite in everything, including this matter. I know you would like to salvage the formal, "juridical" aspect of the question. In your view that could be done if I declared I lacked sufficient "juridical" reasons to think that way about the Baroness and that priest. And in my view, I think it would be the most advisable if you pretended that you did not hear anything! Then all the possible "juridical" consequences would be superfluous, including our own conversation! Therefore, please, forgive me! I said all that in a mood of nervous annoyance with that Jesuitical creature! That whole hypocritical legal manner was getting on my nerves. That impossible Puba, those corpses—three corpses under the table. That lieutenant with his heavy cavalry saber, I am überspannt, therefore I said more than I ought to have said—and you were not supposed to hear it...

GLEMBAY: So then it is not true after all?

LEONE: (*Stays silent and gazes at his father*)

GLEMBAY: Then it is not true?

LEONE: (*Stays persistently silent. Pause.*)

GLEMBAY: You see, in this too you are a Danielli! Not to speak the truth—of that you Daniellis are always capable. But to admit it? No! Never! To spit at someone in the face the Venetian way, to humiliate and smear him, that, yes, yes, that's in your blood. But when it comes to consequences, then silence. That's exactly how your mother was too!

LEONE: And what would you get out of it even if I were to give you a "juridical" declaration that the thing is not true? Would anything in the status of material facts change by even a single millimeter? I think that after all every word about it is superfluous between us! Is there anything else you would like from me? I actually still have two or three letters to write!

Thunder is slowly disappearing. Flashes of lightning are reflected in the phosphoric lighting of the room, and detonations are slowly falling behind. Wind and the murmur of rain. Leone's agitation is growing and he is visibly barely controlling himself.

GLEMBAY: So then you would like me to leave? That means you are politely showing me the door!

LEONE: I'm not politely showing you the door, I'm only asking you! I think it would be best for us to part in peace. I am not a lawyer, I do not think juridically, nor am I a stockbroker! So what sort of a deal could the two of us possibly come up with?

GLEMBAY: To be arrogant toward one's father, that is most elegant! That is grandeur! Yes! That is the Danielliesque Greek manner: to look into the eyes and think what you will! But you have launched one incredibly muddy story, you have sullied my family's purity! Tonight you have debased the status of my family to some sort of promiscuity, as though life at the Glembays were lived in the bohemian manner! But you need to comprehend that we Glembays are not bohemians! We are solid conservative citizens and we shoulder full formal gentlemanly responsibility for every word we utter! What gave you the right to express yourself in that—I won't say what—manner in front of Silberbrandt and in front of Fabriczy, concerning my wife?

He has spoken the last two sentences in a staccato and with his chest thrust out: violence continues to grow.

LEONE: (*Still quietly*) Please allow me merely to repeat certain things! I have come at your personal invitation, and please understand that I consider myself a guest in your house! I thought that after all I have no right not to participate as an extra in this commemorative decorative performance, when you have already assumed the role of a director! And I have to confess something else: after these eleven years, I was burning with a small nostalgia for all this. Traveling this way, I was feeling innocently happy, that I would see Mother's grave, and Beatrice, and these old paintings of ours, and you. Yes! And you! But in this Glembayesque atmosphere of blood, murders, suicides, in this unhealthy atmosphere of lies and intrigues and hysteria, my old migraine appeared right away. My head began to ache from all that. Allow me also to observe this: you do not understand that someone can get a headache in this Glembayism! We are, as you yourself said, two races: Glembays and Daniellis! We are—according to you—Greek liars and Venetians! You have never loved me, because after all within your weltanschauung you had no reason to! And for that very reason, that we two are two races, you have from the beginning, as far as I remember, not only been indifferent toward me but quite the opposite: you could not endure me! Ivan, yes, him, yes! He was a rising star on the Vienna and the Amsterdam Stock Exchange! Ivan was for you a full-blooded Glembay! And I know that you would have been much happier if I had died instead of him! About Ivan you always said that he would become an Austrian Rockefeller! And me you sent to sanatoria! Yes! Why are you looking at me with such disgust? (I remember still when as a boy I sat on your knee how that same look of yours was sharp and cold behind the glass monocle.) And lo and behold, I did not become a stockbroker and operator for the firm Glembay Ltd. I spread paint over some totally worthless canvases: paintings that are totally alien and puzzling to you! I am a bohemian, and you are a banker! I live in promiscuity and you in a strictly conservative citizen's model of matrimony! I lie, I'm a neuropath, half-mad and unpleasant, "a high-strung eccentric," as old Fabriczy puts it, and so what, I ask you, is the point of the two of us squabbling here? The fact that one *minderwertig*, worthless character such as I am declared or did not declare something, how can that be so important to you? Why? I therefore maintain that it would be the most advisable to pass over that with contempt and—good night! I am leaving anyway, and you ought not to have heard it, and we're quits! I don't see why it would be necessary that I, for formal-juridical reasons, declare that I've lied. I did not lie, but I don't have legal proofs in hand!

GLEMBAY: Well, all right, but what gave you the right to speak so ignominiously with nothing concrete in hand?

LEONE: Some things can exist in the head even if not in hand! So you would like at any price to prove me to be a slanderer and a liar?

GLEMBAY: Either you have concrete proofs, or you should not have spoken like that in front of two outsiders! What gave you the right to express yourself so shamelessly in front of two outsiders? Don't you think that you have thereby spit in my face? Don't you think that you have thereby sullied my honor?

LEONE: If anyone's honor is at stake, it is exclusively the honor of your wife!

GLEMBAY: No one's honor can be at stake so long as there is no proof for it!

LEONE: If it is not enough for you to tell you that your wife slept for a whole night in the room of an instructor, then it is ultimately all the same to me! In law there exist not only proofs but also indications; I am not a lawyer, but I know that much about law! There were no legal proofs with Alice's death either, but all the facts suggested that she did not drown herself because of proofs but because of indications.

GLEMBAY: What sort of indications?

LEONE: Alice drowned herself in the Kupa at Gorjanski, at Aunt Zygmuntowic's place! In the boat they found her sketchbook, her straw hat, her parasol, therefore she jumped into the water fully dressed, and had not been swimming as you later misreported through your paid press! Alice was a first-class swimmer! Why did she drown? By sheer accident? The boat did not capsize. Alice drowned because of indications!

GLEMBAY: I don't understand a word!

LEONE: Please! Eleven years have passed since we buried Alice! That was the last time I was at home. In eleven years did it never occur to you to ask yourself: "Why did my twenty-year-old daughter jump into the water"?

GLEMBAY: This was all in her outlandish Danielli blood. Your mother too attempted her first suicide when she was seventeen! I am sure it happened without any real reason!

LEONE: Outlandish Danielli blood! It happened, my dear, because Alice found out that young Zygmuntowic was sleeping at your lady the Baroness's! Alice was innocently in love with the young Zygmuntowic! She drowned herself innocently and naively without any juridical proof: simply because of indications!

GLEMBAY: (*As though driving phantoms away from himself*) These are all fantasies!

LEONE: The old lady Zygmuntowic found among Alice's papers a draft of her farewell letter; that little paper, written in pencil and without a date, I have somewhere in Aix-les-Bains. In that letter there is nothing—juridically—concrete. The night before, she happened to see young Zygmuntowic go into the Baroness's room.

Pause. Distant thunder. Last flashes of lightning. Wind. The storm is slowly vanishing.

GLEMBAY: And why did you not tell me this then?

LEONE: It would not have made any sense to tell you, just as it doesn't today. That woman exercises such miraculous influence over you, that every word is superfluous! Pardon me, I don't feel called upon to give you advice, but I think that that woman is your doom!

GLEMBAY: (*Solemnly, with the pathos of recalling a golden past*) The happiest day of my life was when I met that woman!

LEONE: (*Absently, as though talking to himself*) I met her on that winter morning when Mother poisoned herself! Mother was lying dead, and this woman came in with a big bouquet of Parma violets and with her Maltese Pinscher, Fifi. What refinement! To come, with a Maltese on your arm, to see your dead rival! Apropos of Mother's death! What do you think? Did Mother poison herself because of proofs or because of indications?

GLEMBAY: What do you mean?

LEONE: Did Mother have some sort of legal proof in hand, that you are living with that woman, or did she conclude this exclusively from indications?

GLEMBAY: (*Stands up heavily, like an old man, and goes to the window where he drums on the pane and gazes into the darkness for two or three seconds, and then returns wearily.*) You are horrible!

LEONE: I am horrible, and the lady Baroness is for you a symbol of pure sublime happiness! I remember it as if it were today: how she stood over Mother's body with her Fifi. She was reciting the Lord's Prayer. She did not even reach "and lead us not into temptation" when she absentmindedly crossed herself, turned and went over into our old salon! There she stopped over that Persian Kerman, bent down and tried out its quality! Do you remember that Kerman carpet? As a child I always played "Thousand and One Nights" on it! (I called that powdery aquamarine tint it had snow!) She had that "Thousand and One Nights" of mine, our old Kerman, transferred to her villa, Above the Linden, that same day. Amid the mass of those expensive Tabrizes and Khorasans (which you used to scatter all around) she had no other concern than to transfer that Persian carpet to her place that very same day. What a noble philosophy of life!

GLEMBAY: These are all fantasies! Sooner or later you will end up in a madhouse!

LEONE: I've been hearing that for years, that I am überspannt and that I will end up in a madhouse! That I will go to a madhouse has nothing at all to do with Mother's death! My mother poisoned herself in the era of scandals with that adventuress, and seven years later, at Alice's funeral, I found a dog's quilt made from mother's fur wrap. That lady's dog covered itself with my mother's fur!

GLEMBAY: Leave me alone, please, with these stupidities of yours! All you Daniellis are psychopaths, building accusations in the air from your crazy and bizarre observations! All that is fog and cobwebs! Please! All your proofs and indications have nothing to do with anything! Your mother first raised her hand against herself when she was seventeen! She had not even met me yet! She spent three years in Swiss nerve clinics, a fact which of course the Lords Danielli cunningly, in their Greek and Venetian ways, hid from me! This was a woman who abnormally feared the smell of roses, or a dark room. I can't even remember if there exists anything in the world she did not fear! She squealed with horror if someone somewhere forgot to shut the door! One time she wanted to jump out of a speeding express train, while she was still pregnant with you, and where was Baroness Castelli then! Quit talking nonsense! All this that you are raving about is a sickness of the brain! Das alles sind Hirngespinste nur! In fact, it is arrogant and cruel, toward your own father! You're a capricious neuropath, like your mother was! And please! Wait, let me too tell you the truth: those twenty years I lived with your mother were so difficult that I heaved a sigh of relief over her deathbed, like after a nightmare! There, now you have all your proofs and indications.

Violently turns to leave. Leone excitedly follows him. Stops him directly in front of the door.

LEONE: Excuse me, repeat that! What did you say?

GLEMBAY: (*Breaks away from his son irritatedly*) Leave me alone! Damned be the day when the Daniellis crossed my path! I've been tormented in these Danielli fogs for twenty years! What else do you want? Aren't you satisfied yet?

LEONE: Please, just a moment, let us clarify! This may be the last time! Are you convinced that Mother did not poison herself because of the Baroness?

GLEMBAY: The municipal doctor formally determined that she took an excessively large dose of veronal. She had not been able to fall asleep without veronal ever since Alice's birth. That is what the municipal doctor determined, and that is what was written in the police report.

LEONE: Fine! But it was an open secret throughout the city that the Baroness was your mistress! You bought the villa Above the Linden for her. I remember that I was always afraid of the Baroness's equipage in the street, that she may be driving you in her carriage again!

GLEMBAY: (*Thoughtful, introspectively*) I broke off with your mother that year we sent you to Cambridge. But because of you we did not formally divorce! (Children!) Ivan was just finishing up in Berlin! Alice was still with her governess.

LEONE: Well, fine, fine! But two years before that villa Above the Linden you had already bought the Baroness a three-story house in Vienna near the Carmelite church!

GLEMBAY: How do you know that?

LEONE: Why, everyone knew that: the servants and the governesses. The whole staff!

GLEMBAY: (*Uncertainly, like an old man, and wearily*) Everyone knew that? And I thought that no one knew it! Well all right! If they all knew it, the whole staff, they could not know that that woman was worth more than seventy-seven thousand other women! I bought her the three-story house in Vienna, yes, I bought it, so what if I bought her a three-story house and if the whole staff knew it? Yes, for that heart, for that élan vital, for that culture, for that youth, my dear—a three-story house? What is one three-story house for all that?

LEONE: (*Gazes long at his father. Quietly and sadly*) It's always been like that between us, from the outset! Everything of yours, from the first day that I remember, was foreign to me: your soaps, your English eau de cologne, your tobacco, your smells! When you caressed my hair, I was always afraid of your nails, that they didn't scratch me! Everything physically yours stood between us like a wall! You terrified me as a child with your monocle, and I simply could not understand why you wear that little glass disc over your eye! It's just because of that monocle that I could never believe you in anything! It is all a performance. You are playing banker Glembay, who is seeking formal juridical capacity to wash away a slander from his mistress! What heart? What élan vital? That woman washes herself daily with twenty-seven pomades and creams; she smears herself with lilies and honey and doesn't do anything for days on end but bathe in lemon juice and milk! Her fifty-three suitcases and three greyhounds—that is her culture! If one added up all the pounds thrown away annually for her brassieres, corsets, and cosmetics, one could feed all the paupers of her charitable Philanthropic Office. What am I saying? With that money, the whole country could feed itself till it bursts! That benefactress tramples people with her coach-and-four, and you are dreaming about her heart! How miserable all this is. Oh, man! That woman tramples lives with such charming criminality, that it boggles a normal person's mind! And this old gentleman sits here with a monocle on his eye and sings a song about her heart! What an infernal image! And how can people say that there is nothing to paint today! There are no painters, but motifs are teeming in hell! One should paint you! This irrational lofty smile on your lips when you speak about her—that should be preserved! "Who is she?" "Does anyone have any idea who she is?" "And such an überspannt neurasthenic like your lost son at that?"

GLEMBAY: (*Rises without a word and sits down again in an armchair, on top of Leone's boxes, paintings, and sketches. He is inwardly crooning some associations while engrossed in meditation about her.*)
That woman taught me to live! After that mass of women, she was the first who taught me what it means to live and to be happy! One should have seen her in her shantung-silk with golden embroidery! You see, she could combine the most extravagant colors, on her it was all always chic and inventive! Her snakeskin shoes, her Chinese umbrella, her orchids, all of that was brightness and golden color! And what do you want from me? To tear out of myself everything that for me has been the maximum—and why? Why? You have set yourself up before me like some inquisitor and you want my head, on the basis

of some fictions! All of what you're saying here is empty air! For seven years I carried your mother with these arms of mine without getting one single millimeter closer to her! That woman remained isolated from me with her seven isolations and I never knew who she was or what she thought. She had been buried, I think three or four years, when I found a whole series of letters in a secret drawer from some Marquis Cesare Kristoforo Balbi! Yes! That was when she was pregnant with Alice! Jawohl! Her travel to the Dolomites, her mysterious annual visits to Lake Como, yes, that was your lady mother!

LEONE: Pardon!

GLEMBAY: (*Refuses to be interrupted*) Kindly let me finish! I bought Charlotte a three-story house—you accuse me of that! And do you think that your mother was not expensive? Can a man ever own something in this world that he hasn't paid for? Charlotte elevated my entire household by three ranks! Charlotte finally placed me in the center of my own home! She bought all those Kermans, Khorasans, and Tabrizes because of me, because Persian rugs are my passion! That Lothringen tapestry, the Dutch dining room—all that she arranged for my sake. And for my personal comfort! Who was the first to think of binding my books? Who paid any attention to me in my own house? And what's the meaning of this tone of yours toward the lady who is my wife? What sort of manners are these? This is nothing other than your Danielliesque envy that I can be happy! It is those Danielli teeth of yours sunk in me! Your superficial upbringing is the best proof of what your lady mother actually was.

LEONE: Pardon, excuse me, but you are sitting on my papers, my sketches! Allow me . . . (*Pulls out several rolls of sketches and rather crumpled boxes from under him*)

GLEMBAY: (*He has risen and is looking at these papers with indignation, ill-temperedly.*) What sketches? (*He picks up one or two sheets of art paper, looks them over, and tosses them away contemptuously.*) Well, this is worth nothing! A waste of time! You are just playing with these paints, und die Zeit vergeht—time flies! You have never seriously taken a single thing into your hands! Pointless backtalk and slander, that you can do, yes—that's the only thing you can do! You haven't earned a single penny . . .

LEONE: You talk that way because I allowed you to operate with the Danielli capital for eight years at four percent?

GLEMBAY: What?

LEONE: Until Alice's death the entire Danielli capital was in your hands. Did I ever even once ask you for a settlement of accounts? You paid me four percent, and let's say that you operated at a minimum of twelve percent (which is still little), how much was left to you after all that? Why are you insulting me? True, I have not earned money, but I've never in my life weighed the Glembay way; I have never short-weighted anyone! And as far as my paintings are concerned, I myself know that I have no talent, but you are the least qualified to talk about my paintings! You understand others' interest rates, that is your Glembayesque talent. As for anything else, please forget it!

GLEMBAY: (*Wearily but with total superiority*) You are completely confused, my child! You are ill, and by God it would be best if you settled down in some sanatorium! You are sleepwalking on rooftops, my dear, along with your talent! Where is that talent of yours? What is all this, for God's sake? All this isn't worth crap! Look at yourself! You roam around the world like some chimpanzee with this shaggy beard of yours! Like some ghost! You are old, you have no roof over your head! You have not even established a family and you are roaming around studios like some circus performer with suitcases! What interest rates? What do you know about interest rates? Danielli capital? Where is that Danielli capital?

LEONE: Yes, and Mother's money, was that not Danielli capital? Società di Navigazione Danielli, International Cognac Danielli, DDSC shares, Crédit Marocain, British Steel Corporation—what was all that, if not Danielli? In the Blue Star Line alone there was, if I'm not mistaken, seven hundred thousand francs! Did I ever exercise control over that? I wandered around watching glaciers on fire at sunrise!

GLEMBAY: (*With a superior smile*) Yes, yes, the Blue Star Line, International Cognac Danielli! Stop your nonsense, please! You are gaping at clouds! You sit on a terrace of some fashionable first-class alpine hotel somewhere, and enjoy alpenglow! As though your alpine daydreaming could even exist if we did not bleed! I mean, we: all of us who work and take risks! You think the world is a velvet box with gentian and edelweiss! And you see, looking at you like this as you babble childish gibberish, my heart tightens in my throat! I feel like I've drunk a deciliter of iodine! You are my son? My only son? I wanted to put everything of mine into your hands, like Corneille's Don Diego: "This sword that my arm can no longer wield, I give up to thine, to avenge and punish!" Et ce fer que mon bras ne peut plus soutenir, Je le remets au tien pour venger et punir! And what has become of my hopes?

LEONE: I knew it, that your Corneille would turn up at some point! They taught you that Corneille of yours at the commercial school in Marseille, and that is the only stanza you know! Your concept of beauty: a velvet box with alpine flowers! Your favorite color: gold! I remember still as a child: all your Tauchnitz novels on your nightstand had their pages uncut! Please tell me: in these eleven years that we haven't met, did you ever hold a book in your hand?

GLEMBAY: You are walking on rooftops, my child! And please take note that I will not be able to leave you very much! I have my own financial obligations, and I also have an underage child who is not provided for! So much for your personal information! I cannot tell you more! If you were trained in business, some transaction could possibly be found, but to put a business into your hands would mean to throw it out the window! Just two nights ago I had a conference in Fiume concerning modern petroleum refineries, good Dutch capital: twenty-three percent guaranteed. But what would you do with that?

LEONE: Thank you! I do not need any petroleum refineries! I am satisfied with my Danielliesque material situation! The Blue Star Line is paying me my pounds; for me that is enough.

GLEMBAY: Where do you have those nine hundred and thirty thousand that I took out of Allgemeine Hamburger Kredit A.G. two years ago?

LEONE: Congo Belge seven percent.

GLEMBAY: Unsound and weak. Business involving Negroes is unsound!

The Glembays | 177

LEONE: But not as unsound as the Glembays Ltd.

GLEMBAY: The Glembays have earned on their own everything they have! And please know that I find your continuous casting of insinuations insolent and ungentlemanly! What is unsound about the business of the Glembays Ltd.? What is that supposed to mean? Please, state it concretely. Please list one single Glembay transaction that is not solid! To me this has now crossed all limits! What sort of brazen behavior is this?

LEONE: As far as I know, collecting trash is not especially solid! At least to my taste! And besides, Castelli is rather interested in Budapest's explosives factory Baron Schwartz A.G.!

GLEMBAY: What trash?

LEONE: Well, the Rag and Bone Central, isn't that financed by your bank? The famous Glembay trash cartel?

GLEMBAY: That's just a subsidiary of the paper factory. The parent company has no sort of connection with it. Waste products are used in England too. Jede Arbeit ist ehrlich! All work is honest! And that is not solid to you? What's not solid about it?

LEONE: So, killing people—to you, that is solid!

GLEMBAY: In the current state of technical sciences, explosives are (so far as I know) absolutely necessary!

LEONE: Of course. Shrapnel and shells at twenty-three percent profit! Very useful products for human society!

GLEMBAY: That is legal business like every other business! And only people with a rotten brain, such as yours, see in it something dishonest! Business is business! Les affaires sont les affaires! M'avez-vous compris?

LEONE: So according to you it is permissible to kill people only when it is legal? This is why at the other end you immediately bury them, is it? What counts is that there are traffic laws that permit running people over! And then it's just a Bárbóczy legend: "Die Glembays sind Mörder"—the Glembays are murderers. Last night a woman killed herself in the Glembay house with her child, and that Glembays kill people was of course invented by old Bárbóczy! To finance Pompes Funèbres, to manufacture shells and dynamite, to collect trash, to put off paying bonds, to pay out four percent instead of eighteen percent, that is all fair! That is all solid!

GLEMBAY: Who is burying people? You are completely mad!

LEONE: So, operating the Pompes Funèbres trade is a desperate measure! And it looks like the Glembay Bank is not doing so brilliantly, when it's dealing in corpses and trash! All sorts of things are being said in town, my dear!

GLEMBAY: (*Nervously and no longer confidently*) And what is being in said in town?

LEONE: What do I know! I haven't taken much interest in it; in any case it is known that your Viennese bonds stand extended for two years already!

GLEMBAY: The bond business? You're an idiot! I'm a man who has been dealing with bonds for fifty years, and it's not been heard once in fifty years that even a single Glembay bond was late by a second! What does it mean that my bonds stand extended for two years?

LEONE: What do I know? That's just what I heard! But of course I'm not up to the weltanschauung: les affaires sont les affaires?

GLEMBAY: Not another word, do you understand? That woman killed herself here last night because you perfidiously drove her to her death! And while Charlotte's hair has turned white from that disaster over the old hag, you grin here like some chimpanzee! You're a monster of a man!

LEONE: Castelli's hair turned white? She stopped coloring her hair! To her that's chic: to change her wig after such a disaster! Please! That woman held her Maltese Pinscher while praying over my dead mother!

GLEMBAY: You're a madman! You don't have any conception about the meaning of your words! Do you have any idea what you are yapping about?

LEONE: I do not like your tone!

GLEMBAY: I am your father and I have a right to it!

LEONE: Don't shout! Who are you shouting at? Shout at your bankers and brokers, my dear, and not at me! You've grown accustomed to having people stand before you with bowed heads, but you won't overpower me with that brutal voice of yours! Shouting others down belongs in a tavern! I think that there's been enough of all this. Allow me, please, to go to bed! I'm tired and I'm leaving! My train leaves around eight-thirty! Now it's past two! I haven't even finished packing yet, and I've letters to write! Therefore, please: finissons! And good night!

GLEMBAY: Is that so? You think that it's all finished: you'll write your letters, sit down in a Pullman, and finissons! Bon voyage! Oh no, my dear, we won't liquidate things that way! You will first properly settle your accounts. We are not children, to babble lies and then get out of it through some paranoid jokes! Oh no, my dear, it won't finish that way, you are bitterly mistaken, sir! You think that it's allowed in polite society to sling such heavy slanders, and to pass over it, as though nothing had been said? Maybe that's how they think in your bohemian circles, but here with us there's a different custom! Please explain how you dared say publicly in front of two outsiders all that which you said?

LEONE: (*Wearily, as though bored by starting over again*) O my god, how tiresome it all is...

GLEMBAY: All that you babbled in the salon tonight without any material foundation, all of that is moral insanity!

LEONE: And what would happen if I did have a material foundation? Moral insanity according to you has to be established juridically?

GLEMBAY: Without a material foundation all of that is a mirage in the sky! And you had no right to sully my family honor this way! That was completely disrespectful toward your own father!

LEONE: (*With a feeling of disgust, more nervously than consciously, tosses onto the lacquered tabletop those two lilac-colored letters he had been reading earlier in the salon.*) Here you are! Look for yourself!

GLEMBAY: (*After a pause picks up the letters from the table, surprised and uncomprehending*) What is this?

LEONE: Those are two letters from Charlotte to Silberbrandt!

GLEMBAY: But here it's signed Mignon!

LEONE: Don't be funny! That's Charlotte's handwriting! And the very tone of the letters and the signature leave no juridical doubt that those are letters of intimate nature!

GLEMBAY: And how did you get hold of them?

LEONE: The letters were found with that day-wage employee Skomrak who worked at the Baroness's Philanthropic Office. He hanged himself, and those letters were found among his effects. How he got them, no one knows! It seems that he stole them. As a clerk of the Philanthropic Office, he used to come to the house to see the Baroness. These are the new documents about which Puba was reading tonight, and that the socialists are going to print!

GLEMBAY: This is all unclear! And how did these letters come into your hands?

LEONE: The editor of that, as you call it, "rag" gave them to me. (I helped him out of some trouble in Geneva once.) So, do you now have some legal proof in hand?

GLEMBAY: The handwriting is Charlotte's, but she never signed herself Mignon! All right! But what leads to the conclusion that this was written to Silberbrandt? This "Mister" can be Monsignor but also Monsieur.

LEONE: If not to Silberbrandt, then to someone else, that's completely irrelevant now, monsignor or monsieur! That young boy, the day-wage worker, thought that those were letters written to Monsignor—Silberbrandt! At least that's what he wrote in a poem of his! He left behind some fifteen poems—dedicated to the Baroness Glembay—and these two letters!

GLEMBAY: Those are all fantasies! These assumptions can all be wrong! This is all moral insanity! The letter is not dated and Charlotte should be asked when she wrote it and on what occasion! And then some obscure character, who steals others' letters, and then some newspapermen who utilize others' private property, and of intimate nature at that, all of that is filthy and disgusting! So this is the sort of thing you've started occupying yourself with? All your Crown witnesses are either dead or worthless! Now you're grubbing through that muck like some coprophile!

LEONE: (*Seriously, sternly, and very darkly*) Merci! So that is moral insanity! The suicide of your first wife and of your twenty-year-old daughter is moral insanity? And this, the fact that you consider this woman sublime and charming, that is not moral insanity? No one even knows that woman's name, and her birth certificate is a forgery, and you call her a Baroness? What sort of baroness is she? Is there anyone who knows what sort of baroness she is? Who is that woman? Where did she come from? Old Fabriczy found her in a Viennese hourly hotel! Ask him where he partied with her before that, before he planted her on you, the old pimp! Old Fabriczy procured that woman like merchandise for you bon vivants of Zagreb—and now I'm a coprophile? The Viennese city authorities whom you hold in such high esteem have documents concerning that woman...

GLEMBAY: Not another word, all right?

LEONE: Anyway, you're right! This is pointless! You say that the lady is charming, and that is all you know about her! The fact that she is charming is to you ultima ratio—your paramount consideration! Indeed, she has charmed you so thoroughly that you cannot even move! Like a boa constrictor, that's how she has charmed you!

GLEMBAY: It's abominable what you're saying here, do you understand? Say just another word, and I'll beat the life out of you!

LEONE: I have already told you not to shout at me! That woman has been destroying you morally and materially for years now, to my personal shame! For years I've been ashamed for you, for years I've stayed away from my parental home: you are the laughingstock and scandal of the entire city!

GLEMBAY: Quiet! If you say just one more word, I'll...

LEONE: I won't be quiet! For years I've been getting ready to tell you this! She is charming! Do you think that that silly Lieutenant Ballocsanszky comes to this house because of your bridge games, or because he too has been charmed by the lady Baroness? You've allowed yourself to be charmed by a harlot and for years we've all had to stare at the ground in shame...

GLEMBAY: (*Beside himself, shouts in the highest register, by now downright voicelessly*) Wha-a-at?

LEONE: She is a common, nameless whore, who doesn't belong...

GLEMBAY: Wha-at? You, you say that to your father? Shut up...!

Stunned, dazed with rage, he furiously falls upon Leone, and in a flash, before Leone can react, he slaps his cheek with all his might. That slap has inflamed some wild primitive rage within him, and he slaps Leone once more so that the latter, instinctively retreating two steps, snags a rocking chair, loses his balance and stumbles.

GLEMBAY: (*In the instant that Leone falls, he snorts as though beside himself.*) Here's what you wanted, take this! (*And at that moment with a practiced motion, quicker than Leone's fall—which is relatively slow—he strikes Leone a heavy and experienced boxer's blow straight to the jaw with such force that Leone topples like an inert object over the rocking chair and onto the floor.*)

LEONE: (*Not expecting such a wild eruption of rage, he jumps to his feet with predatory, Glembayesque, instinctive animality; his jaw, nose and mouth bloody, hands and face bloody; he straightens up and moves toward Glembay with much hatred as though about to hit him back. But now reason is stronger than impulse, however, so bleeding from nose and mouth he wipes himself with a handkerchief, and then, shaken, speaks quietly.)*

Thank you, sir, for that too!

(Looks at his bloody hands, touches his mouth and teeth, is bleeding over his shirt and from his nose.)

Nice, beautiful! In style! Glembayesque argumentum ad hominem!

He goes to the washbasin to rinse his nose, teeth, and face. Dips towel into some disinfectant and stanches the blood. Glembay, sunk in depression, stares ahead half-blindly like an epileptic. Then with heavy, elderly, seemingly drunken steps, he goes to an armchair and sinks into it. His heart is pounding, and like a sick man he clutches at it with his hand. He is breathing deeply and with difficulty, as though afflicted by asthma. He gasps for air with his entire chest as if about to suffocate.
   Pause.
   Leone is still rinsing his nose at the washbasin and stanching the blood with his fist, but to no effect. The blood continues to gush, while outside wind is heard and the murmur of rain.

LEONE: *(Resignedly, but firm)* I talked with you the last time after Alice's funeral. That was eleven years ago. This morning I'll leave: we shall not meet again. This is the last page of our bookkeeping. This is Glembay-style liquidation! Therefore, hear me out please, so that you know. When I returned from Cambridge a year after mother's death, I found everything here in the same state as today: your cousin Monsieur de Fabriczy, and as a knight of honor to the Baroness a certain de Radkay, lieutenant-colonel in the Imperial Cavalry. There was also a court clerk, I think he was called Holleschegg, if I'm not mistaken. A counterpart to today's Lieutenant von Ballocsanszky! All those gentlemen were charmed by the gracious lady Baroness. Her "Moonlight Sonata," her Maréchal Niel roses on silk, her conversation, and Lothringen tapestries! Among all those gentlemen, the lady Baroness succeeded that summer in charming me too! And she did it with her "Moonlight Sonata". Our sonata was indeed eine "Mondscheinsonate" almost a fantasy, up in the villa Above the Linden! And only in Cambridge, in those fogs, several months later, retrospectively, it dawned on me how things stand with that lady's charm. Only then it dawned on me what it is that we Glembays call moral insanity! Yes! You see, that is moral insanity: to be an old man's mistress, to have at the same time three other lovers, and to fear a twenty-year-old Cambridge student! That woman wrapped her legs around me to rid herself of any vestige of control!

GLEMBAY: (*Rises again, violently approaches Leone, and tears him away from the washbasin*) And you could look me in the eye?

LEONE: I was doing my doctorate then. I was twenty-one. And afterward I left and did not come here anymore. I left! I felt ashamed before my late mother! And if there is anyone who can call me to account, it is only Mother! You—never!

Glembay clutches at his heart as though it is stabbing him. He breathes in as if choking, and goes to the open window to inhale night air. He is visibly ill. He staggers to the wall as though drunk, and rings for the servant. Silence. The bell is heard somewhere far off in the corridor. Silence. No servant comes. Glembay is sick. He is feeling dizzy. He goes to the table and with a trembling hand pours water from a pitcher into a glass and drinks a few drops. Still no servant comes. He moves nervously to the wall and rings. The bell is heard echoing unpleasantly in the silence. He returns to the window with heavy steps, inhales the air again, and then staggers off to the armchair. He sits but immediately rises and starts to pace the room unsteadily, lighting a cigar. Leone is still rinsing his nose at the washbasin and stanching the blood. Chamberlain enters, very confused and still sleepy.

GLEMBAY: Please tell the gracious Frau Baroness to come here right away! Wake Madame up, but hurry!

After issuing this order to the servant, he continues to pace about amid the furniture of this small room. The cigar does not agree with him and he throws it away. He sits in the armchair and bracing his arms against his knees nervously rocks his upper body, breathes with difficulty, and shakes his head as if amazed and incredulous. His heart is aching. It is squeezing him. He heaves deep sighs.

CHAMBERLAIN: (*Enters nervously*) I'm sorry, Your Excellency, I cannot find Her Excellency anywhere. Her Excellency is not in her room! I don't know where Her Ladyship is!

GLEMBAY: What? The gracious lady's not in her room? And where is Anita? Call Anita! Have Anita come here right away! Anita here! Quick!

There is frantic running in the corridor. Voices are heard, and slamming of doors. Shouts and footsteps. Glembay rises and, exerting his final strength, goes to stand at the open door, listening and waiting. Chamberlain comes again, with Anita behind him, and at that moment Baroness Castelli also appears, wearing the same champagne-silk dress as before. Leone has turned away from the washbasin with interest and is waiting to see what will happen!

BARONESS CASTELLI: What is it? What happened? What is this commotion? Why did you call for me? What is it, Glembay? What happened? What's the matter with you? You're so terribly pale!

GLEMBAY: Where've you been?

BARONESS CASTELLI: I? In the garden. My head hurts, a migraine, the air outside is wonderful, so easy to breathe—and my migraine…

GLEMBAY: M-m-m-i-grai-n-ne? (*Mumbling this, he staggers, and falls.*)

BARONESS CASTELLI: Um Gottes Christi Willen! What's wrong, Glembay? Quick, bring ice! Eis, schnell Eis, bringen sie Eis!

[CURTAIN]

ACT THREE

Banker Glembay's bedroom: a blue room with blue plush furniture of the 1880s and lacquered chests of drawers in the style of Louis-Philippe. In the corner stands a tall white Swedish stove. There is a dark door to the left, an open window to the right, and an alcove in the back. In the alcove, on a broad Louis-Philippe bed, lies banker Glembay dressed in black. On nightstands to his left and right are silver candlesticks holding nine candles. The alcove is draped with a plush curtain that hangs in opulent folds from an old-fashioned crossbar of lacquered wood. Dominican Sister Angelika kneels in deep prayer at the feet of banker Glembay; the kneeler is overlaid with blue velvet. A globe light of milk glass burns on the table. Leone is sitting in a Biedermeier recliner beside the bed and sketching his father's death mask in charcoal. In armchairs by a round table sit the old rector Fabriczy, Silberbrandt, and Dr. Altmann. It is dawn. Halfway through the scene the morning chirping of birds commences, and gradually grows toward the end. Puba Fabriczy is seated on a stool to the left and telephoning.

PUBA: Yes, it is I! Franjo, please listen carefully! Go and very gently wake up the honorable Governor General! Tell him that I called, and tell him, but sensibly, that the honorable General Director Glembay has died! Yes! This morning, some time after three! A stroke! Yes! So tell this to the honorable Governor General and ask him to telephone me right away! What? Yes! I am here, at the Glembay Bank's private number! So make sure, Franjo—have him call me right away! It's urgently important! Good-bye!

He searches for new numbers in the telephone book.
Fabriczy stands at the entrance to the alcove and gazes from a distance at the dead man.

FABRICZY: Grim reaper, grim reaper, he works with precision! Yes, he works twenty-four hours a day! And now these paupers will come, the ones who stink of onions and sweat, and carry away His Majesty's Herr Privy Councilor like they carry all heavy things—pianos and kitchen cabinets. Still to come: those massive steps, those unpleasant heavy boots on the parquet, then down the stairs, and—now here, now gone.

DR. ALTMANN: Just as we stupidly live, so we also stupidly die! I've long been tormented by the idea that our funerals are actually barbarically primitive and tasteless! That thought has been tormenting me for a long time! Haven't you noticed a terrible thing: how our dead travel through the city alone, quite alone, from home to the morgue? In the houses there is still weeping, there people still lament, shout, sorrow sincerely; at the cemetery it's more or less a performance, but the real funeral, the dead man's last stroll through the city streets, this is that lonely stroll between the bed and the morgue. Completely abandoned and alone, people travel from their home into a place of no return!

FABRICZY: (*Returning from the alcove*) Yes, your observation is very correct, Herr Doktor! At funerals it's always cheerful! It's always a sort of theatrical performance. Speeches are held there, torches are lit, people carry umbrellas. It's strange how at funerals one always sees umbrellas! And another thing—have you noticed?—people are always witty at a funeral! People all tell jokes, they're funny! And you are right, the real funeral is this journey through the city to the morgue: on that road, man is completely alone!

SILBERBRANDT: A dead man cannot be alone, Illustrissime! That is a perfectly atheistic attitude, Your Reverence! The dead can no longer be alone following their own subjective death! In death a man conjoins the final cause of all things: as all waters return to the sea, so our soul after death flows back into God. Causa efficiens, formalis et finalis—substantial, formal, and final cause!

DR. ALTMANN: If you had dissected even a single frog in your life, you would not be so desperately annoying, dear Silberbrandt! At times you truly get on my nerves with this chaplain's manner of yours! Death is nothing other than a completely logical change in matter: from organic substances into inorganic. When a man starts transforming into carbonic acid, ammonia, and H_2O, then he's finished! He admittedly does flow into the sea, as you say, but only as H_2O!

SILBERBRANDT: A logical change of matter? As though matter were something material, as though the latest empiriocriticism (of those very Machists and social democrats, if you like) had not refuted that dogma of matter as such! As though today it were not more valid than ever to say: "Ipsa etiam materies, si quis intentus aspexerit, ex incorporeis qualitatibus copulatur"—Matter itself, carefully observed, is composed of immaterial qualities!

Telephone rings.

PUBA: Yes, it is I! Doctor Fabriczy! Your most humble servant, Herr Governor General! Pardon me, but *vis maior*—act of God! Yes, Herr Governor General! Totally unexpected: a stroke of lightning! Yes! No, no! He was in an excellent mood, he smoked, yes, and drank two glasses of champagne, but only last night as an exception! Yes! The catastrophe took place very rapidly, Herr Governor General! Yes, yes. Hallo! Yes! Dr. Altmann arrived in just a few minutes! Yes! Camphor injections. But without success. The agony was very brief, with very rapid respiration! A catastrophe! It is! No, no! He was in a room, up under the roof in the guestroom with Leone! They were talking and in the middle of conversation suddenly, without any reason! Hallo, hallo! Please! Herr Governor General, please excuse me but, as a legal attorney I have a business question for you: on the eleventh, hallo, on the eleventh that bond for seventy-two thousand dollars at Disconto Italiana is reaching maturity. Hallo! You didn't know about that? Yes! Hallo! That's right, yes, and you have an interest there! General Director Friedmann has no idea about that. He's lost his head! No! The deceased did not leave any directives! Nothing! Absolutely nothing! Chaos! Friedmann knows nothing about it! In Hamburg, Friedmann says that he's covered everything! Hallo! Yes! There are several smaller ones too, yes, but none is more than a hundred thousand. One of one thousand two hundred pounds at Wiener Bankverein! Hallo! That would be good, yes! Three days ago, Herr Governor General, I took a testament from a notary public at his own initiative. I don't know! It seems because of some changes! I know nothing! The keys to the Wertheim safe and the typewriter desk are with me. Yes. The Baroness gave them to me as soon as I arrived. Yes! I think that would be the best. I have called Friedmann and Radkay, I expect them any minute! This is very important, please! Good-bye, Herr Governor General! I'm much obliged to you!

FABRICZY: (*Has gotten up again during the telephone conversation and*

his swift and sharp movements indicate he is very nervous. He goes to the open window, drums distractedly on the glass, then enters the alcove, and returns again to his place.)
There comes a point where a man is forced to strip naked, like a recruit! A man is simply stripped! Everything's stripped from the man: tails and top hat and wig and titles and the supreme-honor award, that too! Voilà: chief of the firm Glembay Ltd, chief of Glembay et Comp., Société Anonyme, president of the Industrial Bank, financial magnate, patrician—and all that vanishes. It's all stripped from the man! Actually: terrible! "Il trionfo della morte" is actually a revolting picture! Glembay is four months younger than I! There, all evening we were talking, laughing, joking, two hours ago he was still on his feet, talking like we are, moving, walking, oh Lord, where is that same man now? Oh my Lord! A man falls and shatters as if made of porcelain! All this is not so simple. Our Silberbrandt might be right: there is something more to this thing! What can such cobwebs as your materialistic medicine do in all this, my dear Altmann!

DR. ALTMANN: And what should medicine—according to you—be able to do, Your Reverence? To prevent death? And why can't theology prevent death?

SILBERBRANDT: Theology teaches only this, that a subjective life is only a passing phase in much vaster metaphysical complexes. Complexes that are much more incomprehensible than it appears to us from our narrow anthropocentric standpoint. Our life is like a page of a book which is in God's hands.

DR. ALTMANN: And medicine teaches only this, that a subjective life is only a passing phase in the organic development of certain complexes, whose functions can be precisely determined. Medical case Glembay is very simple and determinate. The medical case Glembay arose from a disruption in the functioning of the heart, and once due to certain reasons that functioning ceased, Glembay ceased in parallel with it. The phase of carbon and ammonia is only a chemical consequence of that medical case. A very clear and logical consequence.

SILBERBRANDT: Pardon, but one can never go through this with logic. That is the same as trying to illuminate the Amazon jungle with a single Swedish match!

DR. ALTMANN: Please, my dear, tell these provincial jokes to maidservants at a Sunday afternoon sermon! You're constantly tangling these Swedish matches into my words! Why are you constantly interrupting me? I diagnosed the medical case Glembay a full four years ago: highly advanced arteriosclerosis, an endangered heart. Therefore diet, rest, mountain air. Whereas the patient ate beefsteaks and rumpsteaks, smoked Havanas, drank whisky, got excited over business, played cards (and it seems that his erotic needs too were still rather acute), and instead of going to the Dolomites he spent two months in the Casino de Paris playing Macau. Of course his aorta burst like a tube of chalk! A completely normal and logical occurrence!

Leone gets up from old Glembay's bedside and, sketchbook in hand, joins the group around the table. Pause. Leone is pale, glum, and tired.

LEONE: (*Engrossed in thought, as if to himself*) Things dissolve in death like sugar in coffee. Death is actually very deep: it is entered like a well in summertime. Brightness and the fragrance of grass remain outside, while death is damp and dark like the bottom of a well. From a lifeless mouth reeks the icy breath of the grave. And what remains in the end is a grotesque: a black cutaway on a white canvas. And who can dematerialize that black cutaway on white canvas, dematerialize it and transfer it to paper?

PUBA: (*Takes Leone's sketchbook from his hand*) Pardon, please excuse me for just a moment!

DR. ALTMANN: (*Rises, with great interest*) Ah, did he finish it? Please show me, Puba!

LEONE: (*Devoid of will, apathetic*) It's quite poor. I'm tired. My head hurts, no good for work.

PUBA: I find this remarkable! Extraordinary!

FABRICZY: (*Has gotten up and is looking with the rest*) Yes, that is to say, this is truly colossal! Yes, indeed, I've not seen something so colossally impressive in a long, long time! This is a most original approach!

DR. ALTMANN (*Mutely nods with approval*)

LEONE: My head hurts and and I haven't worked for a long time now. I've taken too much bromide, and the charcoal feels as heavy between my fingers as a pole. It's impossible to draw that preternatural something that the dead have around the lips. All the dead, both psychopaths and philistines, all have something preternatural around the lips. The forehead is all right: hard, Glembayesque, prominent. And the hair is good! But this jaw, this bony lower jaw, that is much weaker than the upper part. It is not structurally connected: it lacks its inner proportion. Weak, very weak!

(He goes again to the dead man in the alcove and gazes at him with painterly expertise, from several angles.)

FABRICZY: In painting, I actually don't understand anything that came after Schwind. Schwind and Füger, those were painters! All this modern tomfoolery is incomprehensible to me. But if this is modern, yes, then there's certainly something here! This, by God, is stupendous!

DR. ALTMANN: This is as good as a solid Munch!

LEONE: (*Returns to the group and picks up the sketchbook*) Pardon, gentlemen!

He returns with the sketchbook to the deceased and gazes at him from the alcove entrance. Compares the sketch with the model, and then with a spontaneous gesture tears that page from the sketchbook, rips up the picture and tosses the paper into a corner.

PUBA: By God, you're often quite incomprehensibly bizarre! What kind of foolishness is this?

He bends down and collects the discarded pieces of paper, carries them to the table and reassembles them.

LEONE: Ah, please, let it go!

Goes wearily to the window and gazes long into the garden. Pause.

FABRICZY: (*Helps his son reassemble the torn sketch. Dr. Altmann has gotten up and is gathering his medical equipment and putting it into his bag.*)

LEONE: (*By the table*) It's an interesting thing! I must not dream about fish. As soon as I dream about fish—it is not good. Last night I dreamed about rotten dead fish that were swimming on the surface of some gray, muddy water. And an entire heavy past swam up to the surface like a dead fish! I'm hungry! I'd like to eat a bloody beefsteak and drink beer! I'm thirsty.

DR. ALTMANN: That's a very good symptom. The organism is doing nothing other than adjusting to substance change! So long as substance change is normal, all is well, and hunger is certainly a very positive occurrence in such circumstances. Neurasthenics like you must eat large amounts of rich food in such circumstances—I speak from experience!

LEONE: You and Silberbrandt and Puba are perfectly similar. For Silberbrandt the whole problem lies in the Seven Sacraments, for Puba in traffic order, and for you in substance change! Anamnesis, status praesens! Penal Code and Saint Thomas—all antediluvian professions! You, doctors, if you were more logical, would walk about in a cassock like priests! European lawyers in their robes have understood things correctly. Priestly mantles and your materialistic substance change? Those materialistic ideologies do not suit you at all! What kind of materialists are you? You always step quietly, open doors mysteriously like magicians. You frighten patients! Patients lie in front of you on tables like ancient sacrificial victims and you slaughter them to the deity of diagnosis, anamnesis, and substance change! I tell you, I've never believed a single word a lawyer or a doctor says!

DR. ALTMANN: We've already heard that, thank you very much, in variations from Molière onward. In the imperfect urban society of today we are just as imperfect a profession as all other urban professions are imperfect!

LEONE: Yes, exactly, but other urban professionals are not masked! Train engineers are train engineers; gravediggers are gravediggers! But you are privileged black-magic artists! Your stunts are covered with a black cloth, you are ambassadors of some higher power with the right to extraterritoriality in today's urban society! I watched you upstairs this morning when you were giving the injection! Your cassette of syringes stood on the table, your hand was completely white, and your face grew instantaneously transformed: at that moment you were no longer my friend Altmann, at that moment you were offering a sacrifice to Sacred Diagnosis! If I, an ordinary mortal, had given the old man that lethal injection, I would already have been arrested! But you are allowed to kill people, you can do it, because you are a black-magic artist!

DR. ALTMANN: You sometimes say such bizarre things one seriously begins to doubt your sanity! What lethal injection? Since when are camphor injections lethal? And please remember that physicians, if they conduct their business at all, conduct it the same way as your gravediggers and train engineers. Our business is transparent and public, much more so than your conversationalist virtuosities! If you think these things you say aren't covered with a black rag, you're obviously deceiving yourself, my dear!

Telephone rings. PUBA stops reassembling the torn sketch. LEONE has exited.

PUBA: Hello, Dr. Fabriczy here! A most respectful bow, Herr General Director! Yes! Yes! Correct! I am speaking from the home of the deceased, on a private line. Yes! I've informed the Governor General and he told me he would telephone for a conference of all the shareholders, for eleven o'clock! In the bank hall, Herr General Director! I don't know. According to Friedmann's calculations, liabilities won't exceed three and a half million. Still! Imagine! There, you see—that's how it is, Herr General Director, that's how it is—one never knows! I'll definitely be at the bank at ten. Right away? Yes, I can come right away! Certainly! Yes! Friedmann assesses the property at Wörtherseeu at two hundred thousand! I really don't know that! Of course! The son, Herr Doktor Leone Glembay has been here in Zagreb for a whole week now! He came for the Jubilee celebration! Bitte schön! Also, auf Wiedersehen, Herr Generaldirektor!—General Director Rubido has just told me that the liabilities are calculated at more than five million! Gentlemen, I'm going. I must urgently be on my way!

SILBERBRANDT: Gentlemen, I think you can dispense with me for the moment! I must get ready for the Holy Mass at the convent! I could not imagine that I would this morning be praying for the soul of Herr

Privy Councilor! He was a good and noble man, may God rest his soul! I commend myself to your kindness, gentlemen!

PUBA: Good-bye for now, Papa! Küss die Hand! You can phone me at Rubido's! The decorators from Pompes Funèbres will be arriving any minute. Be especially careful about titles when composing the obituary. Call me at Rubido's, anyway I'll be back! If Radkay comes, have him wait for me! I'll come right away! Küss die Hand! Servus, Altmann! Kiss your hands, Baroness!

SILBERBRANDT: Good-bye, gentlemen. Sister, praise to Jesus.

Exeunt.

FABRICZY: (*In a tone of completely senile gossip*) So, there you have it. Did you hear? Five million in liabilities! I sensed right away that there was something fishy about this Jubilee of the Glembay firm! I thought to myself right away: there's something hidden behind this! First of all, in business, the seventieth anniversary is not celebrated at all! And then this pathetic drumroll in the press about the supreme-honor award! And then this Spanish medal! Downright tasteless! When a man is an honorary consul of Virginia and Cuba, he doesn't receive a Spanish medal! And then those trumpet flourishes at the reception in the Chamber of Commerce! I thought to myself right away: Behind that, sir, hides some monkey business! And sure enough, five million in liabilities! So, I congratulate Friedmann and the Governor! Danke schön! And you, dear amice, what do you say to that?

DR. ALTMANN: We know nothing about it yet. If the liabilities are so high, the assets too will certainly not be any smaller.

FABRICZY: Can we be sure of that? The Glembays, my dear, have been living like the Rothschilds for two or three decades now! Danielli had her villas in Merano and Corfu! And Baroness Castelli—better not even talk about that! We know it from our daily experience, thank God!

DR. ALTMANN: But Danielli is said to have been enormously wealthy!

FABRICZY: Wealthy, what does it mean, wealthy? One trip to the Far

North, one to Egypt, one to the tropics, one palace in Vienna's Herrengasse, one given to Castelli near the Carmelite church! Nothing is bottomless! Please allow me: I know on good authority, but of course I didn't want to bring it up, but now why not? I know on good authority that two weeks ago at the Trade and Commerce Bank, construction operator Wagner signed a seventy thousand guarantee for Ignat. And did it indirectly, through a certain discreet person: Puba told me that as a business secret! Can you believe it! To take seventy thousand from the likes of Wagner! So, doctor, what was it? What happened? He was upstairs in the guestroom?

DR. ALTMANN: I don't know, Illustrissime! When I arrived, about twenty minutes had passed since the first attack, and of course the situation had changed. He probably grew excited while talking with Leone. There's nothing surprising about that: Leone and Glembay—like negative and positive for years now! Latent friction!

FABRICZY: Yes, but Janko tells me that Leone was all bathed in blood! You don't even know what happened in the salon last night? Well then, I have to tell you . . .

Leone enters, nervous, and paces up and down the room.

FABRICZY: (*Breaking off*) Yes, that's how it is, my dear Altmann! What do you think, Doctor, shall we have some tea made for us? There, that's life: tragedies take place, yet the organism demands its own! Standing next to the body of his intimate friend, a man thinks of his own stomach—strange! My seventieth year, dear doctor, wound up like some Swiss chronometer!—every single minute is allocated. And tonight, such terrible catastrophes and perturbations have occurred within my program, that I really don't know how I'll be able to adapt myself to all this. And your standpoint is that of metabolism. Therefore: a warm tea would do us good! In any case, it will do us no harm! Leone, if you need us, we'll be downstairs in the dining room.

Exeunt, except Leone.
 Leone paces the room like an agitated beast. Pause. From the outside, telephones can be heard ringing. Voices. Doors slamming in the distance. Angelika has crossed herself, stood up and quietly, word-

lessly, come up to the table. There she gazes at the torn-up portrait of old Glembay that lies on the lacquered tabletop, under the lamplight.

LEONE: Do you hear them telephoning? Panic! The ship is sinking! S.O.S. Sauve-qui-peut! Run for your lives! Seven million in debt so far. And they were saying that it's nothing but a Bárbóczy legend: "The Glembays are murderers and swindlers—Die Glembays sind Mörder und Falschspieler!" Seven million in debt. In just half an hour now, gentlemen partners in Vienna and Trieste will start clutching at their pockets. As soon as the telegrams that are still on their way arrive! And you, Beatrice, what do you say to all that?

ANGELIKA: We are all unhappy, Leone. I feel sorry for Charlotte! Poor woman! What torments await her now! If it's really come to a collapse, she'll be forced to atone for it terribly! She has her unhappy child after all!

Enter Charlotte, Baroness Castelli-Glembay. She is dressed in black. Pale and distinguished, she is carrying an enormous bouquet of white roses. Nervous and quiet, she goes to the alcove, lays the roses at the body's feet, and remains standing quietly, absorbed in thought. Then she crosses herself, nervously, and returns to the table.

BARONESS CASTELLI: (*Dignified, defeated*) Forgive me, dear Angelika, don't be offended, but I am so confused and my head hurts so much that I don't know where I am. Three times already I've forgotten what I want. Do me a favor and go upstairs, Anita is there, she is looking for a formal black tie. That black tie is nowhere to be found and this one here is dreadful! And have her bring a pair of lacquered dress shoes, please tell her that, dear Angelika, I will be very grateful to you! Please, be so kind!

ANGELIKA: Very gladly, dear Charlotte! Just a moment!

Exits.
  Baroness Castelli steps over to the deceased, makes some adjustments to the candlesticks, clips the wicks with nickel-plated scissors, and remains by the bed gazing at Glembay. Leone observes her steadily, with great interest. Baroness Castelli, with the nickel-plated scissors in her hand, returns to the table where Leone is sitting. The

The Glembays | 197

Baroness is tranquil and thoroughly dignified. Her voice is sentimentally broken.

BARONESS CASTELLI: I know that you hate me! I've felt every one of your thoughts just now. I know what you were thinking while I was standing near Glembay: seventeen years ago when your late Mother was lying there, in the same place, I came, like this morning, and you were sitting in the same place you are now!

LEONE: Yes! You brought a bouquet of Parma violets and had your Maltese Pinscher on your arm. Today you haven't got that Pinscher, that's the only difference! Then you became the legitimate Madame Glembay, and today you are the legitimate Widow Glembay. Anyone who wishes you happiness could congratulate you! You have happily liquidated the Glembays! You have secured the palace in Trieste for yourself, and the testament has happily disappeared! If anything is left over from those seven million in liabilities, it will be split up among the legal successors.

BARONESS CASTELLI: To the best of my knowledge, you occupy the first place in the testament. And, if I may say so: due to my own personal intervention. The deceased was too much of a gentleman toward me to refuse me such a favor!

LEONE: Thank you! I've never given a thought to the Glembay money, and especially not to the Glembay debts!

BARONESS CASTELLI: What debts? I don't understand!

LEONE: You haven't heard talk about seven million in liabilities?

BARONESS CASTELLI: That does not concern me at all! I've always been uninterested in business!

LEONE: That I believe! Knowing you, out of those seven million in liabilities, you have set aside for yourself at least three!

BARONESS CASTELLI: Tell me, please, why do you hate me so much?

Pause. Silence.

BARONESS CASTELLI: (*Conciliatory, beguiling, coquettish, naïve*) What have I ever done to you? Have I ever personally done you any harm? You have been treating me unjustly for years now, and this is the truth: if anyone in this Glembay household ever enjoyed my sincere and completely unselfish sympathy it has been nobody but you! And when your telegram from Aix-les-Bains arrived the other day, I was so sincerely happy. So purely and so naively! And since then you've been constantly insulting me! Why? Why?

Leone gazes at her with surprise, in silence.

BARONESS CASTELLI: (*Comes close to him, speaks intimately*) Why are you silent, Leo? (*Pause*) Why all this? That scene in the salon tonight, and in front of whom? In front of that old dissolute scoundrel Fabriczy! And in front of your father! You should have known that he could hear every single word from the terrace! All evening you were unjust toward me! And in that horrible Rupert incident, my dear God, I had terrible luck! I knocked down that poor sick woman with my horses, and I didn't mean to do it! And you, you see, up in your room just a while ago, you were much more cruel toward your father and he collapsed and never got up, because of his sclerosis. And it would never even occur to me to accuse you of murder!

LEONE: Do you mean to say that I killed my father?

BARONESS CASTELLI: Please, Leo, I overheard everything. I was in Silberbrandt's room, next to yours! I knew that something bad was about to happen, and I—I myself—sent Silberbrandt to you! That's why you didn't find me in my room, and I couldn't leave the room because of the servants! I heard everything!

LEONE: So then, you heard me kill my father?

BARONESS CASTELLI: No, no, I did not say that, Leo, you turn everything upside down! Whatever happened between Glembay and you doesn't matter to me! I would just like to tell you that I act much more peaceably toward you than you do toward me! You deny me every human quality, and yet, you see, I don't get angry at you at all! I've forgiven you everything!

The Glembays | 199

Leone has fallen silent. Pause. Baroness Castelli is nervously tapping against the table with the scissors she continues to hold in her hand. Leone has begun again to pace the room restlessly from wall to wall, skirting various objects like a jaguar.

BARONESS CASTELLI: Tell me, please, why? Say a single word!

LEONE: What am I to tell you? Below us, it's smoking on all sides like phosphorus, we're sinking, we stand here amid horror, what should I tell you? What am I to explain to you? If you've never stood on the edge of a volcano, you don't know what it's like when that phosphorus smoke is rising from the crater, when you feel like throwing up, you don't know that! You don't understand that!

BARONESS CASTELLI: Oh, I do! I climbed Vesuvius! We drank some rotten champagne up there! I saw Stromboli too. At night. From an Italian boat! It was wonderful.

LEONE: (*In nervous motion*) Yes! Yes, of course! Of course: it was wonderful! It is so right that you should stand on top of Vesuvius and drink champagne! Of course, what else would you do on top of a volcano than drink champagne? And if someone later asks you what you did on the volcano, you should reply in this Seidenbonbon sweet-candy voice of yours that it was wonderful! Of course! That is what I cannot understand: it was wonderful!

BARONESS CASTELLI: I don't understand a single word! What is the matter with you? What do you mean by that? Please, this running around is making me nervous: sit down, please, so we can have a quiet conversation for once! Um Gottes Christi Willen, why are you looking at me so oddly?

LEONE: (*He has stopped.*) I am looking at you as you are! For twenty years now you've been playing the "Moonlight Sonata," painting Maréchal Niel roses on silk, drinking champagne on top of the volcano! You stand over your dead husband just as innocently as you stood over his dead wife, and you've just come out of your confessor's room! And your reasoning is this: "Why are you looking at me as though I've killed your mother? You too have killed your father!

But I don't reproach you at all: let us reconcile!" That is your reasoning! What is left for me to tell you?

BARONESS CASTELLI: You are fantastically überspannt! I haven't said a single word of that sort! On the contrary, I said that you cannot be held responsible for your father's death! That's what I said! You are distorting everything like a funhouse mirror! It's simply morbid!

LEONE: (*Sternly and resolutely*) I was twenty-two years old when I thought that these things you say might possibly be true! Sixteen years have passed since then, my dear! If somebody brought together all the gentlemen whom you've charmed with your Seidenbonbon voice, I don't think that they would fit into this room! Alice, who was so much in love with you, who considered you the ideal of a lady, that Alice . . .

BARONESS CASTELLI: Everything you said about young Zygmuntowicz, all of that is a lie! I swear to you by my child's happiness!

LEONE: And that penciled note Alice left?

BARONESS CASTELLI: I swear to you on Oliver's head, not one word of it is true! Young Zygmuntowicz was in love with me, yes, but there was nothing ever between us—nothing concrete!

Pause.

BARONESS CASTELLI: (*Very quietly and persuasively*) Why don't you believe me? You've been doing wrong to me for years. Upstairs in the room, you stressed to your father with such pathos that I am a "whore," as though I ever concealed that organic imperfection of mine! Each one of us bears within ourselves something for which others would stone us! And I? Haven't I always been consistently sincere: at least in this respect? Please! You, you who once fantasized so much about my "erotic intelligence" (at that time you considered me "erotisch intelligent"), you of all people should not be so vulgar! If for no other reason than at least out of a feeling of solidarity, you should not have dished that out to you father! (You knew about his heart!) But leaving him aside, you behaved ungentlemanly toward me! It is simple, of course, to toss out a slogan about a woman, "Sie ist eine Dirne!—She's a whore!" And especially you, who are so brilliant and proud of your logic, you of all people should be more logical in making your distinction between a whore and an erotically intelligent lady—zwischen einer Dirne und einer erotisch intelligenten Dame! And, you see, I am not in the least angry with you—it only hurts me! It hurts me precisely because of the memory of everything that happened between you and me! I can't help myself, but whenever I think about it I become sad! For the first and last time in my life I lost myself, I began to soar, for the first time I completely forgot the ordinary, the sensual, with you at that time I experienced the immaterial—and you of all people, you! (*Melancholy, she stoops, and remains speechless. Quietly, with tears in her eyes*) See, to this day I keep a lock of your hair in this medallion!

LEONE: (*Has grown upset and is moving about the room*) I was going on twenty-two! I was writing my doctoral thesis at the time!

BARONESS CASTELLI: Yes, in that horrible letter of yours from Cambridge you did not once mention your mother! And then, when—prepared for an honest outcome—I was waiting for your decision from Cambridge, came the shock! And you never gave me the opportunity to explain! All my letters fell through, you never again answered me! And if truth be told, what harm did I do to your mother? I didn't know her at all, I was twenty-six then and a success everywhere, without me doing anything! Everybody was kneeling before me, and your mother was a refined lady, a nervous lady; she had tried several times already to take her own life; I have never done anyone any harm! Leo, you do not know how it was! For four years your father tormented me, for four years he kept annoying me, he wanted to shoot himself before my eyes, he wept on his knees, but I did not want a scandal, because of your mother I did not want him to get a divorce, and I held out honestly and loyally up to the last minute! Precisely in this respect I was completely pure! Eine Dirne! A whore! (*Quietly cries to herself. Speaks pianissimo, in a voice choked with emotion.*) It is very easy to say "eine Dirne"! Of course! Fabriczy drank with me at assignation hotels, yes, and that very Monsieur Fabriczy, the noble old gentleman grand rector and aristocrat, is such a swine, just like all the others around me! Das Körperliche in uns ist nicht schmutzig! The physical in us is not dirty! On the contrary: in us women everything is physical, and I do not deny that! I am honest! And I, you see, I have experienced a lot since I was fifteen, in front of my legs I've seen bishops, and generals, and waiters, yes, valets and clerks too, and what I always experienced over and over is this: almost all those who crawl before us, later on always spatter us with dirt so terribly loftily, which is completely incomprehensible to me! And these are men and gentlemen? I've never guarded myself against the physical in me! I am weak by nature, I've always recognized it. I don't hide it even now, but, you see, I swear to you before my mother's grave, toward you I have never been a whore! Toward you—never! And it was you of all people who humiliated me most terribly! No one but you!

Quiet tears. Leone is shuttling about the room, pacing hither and thither among the furniture. From the alcove to the window and back, continuously.

BARONESS CASTELLI: (*Calmly and sadly*) In this whole dark Glembay house, you were the only ray of light for me! I entered this house for material reasons—I admit that! You must understand that! I did not spend my childhood as you did, playing Thousand and One Nights on a Persian carpet! I ended up on the street at twelve, Leone. You don't know what it means to roam around parks in the autumn rain, hungry, in rags, and without a roof over your head! You began life with a rent income of twenty pounds per month, and I with torn shoes and an old fox around my neck! My marriage to Glembay was a financial transaction! I admit that! And, you see, I had already gone through a degenerate marriage with a sixty-year-old Baron Castelli and much else, but believe me, I speak before the dead face of this old man: considering everything I had to do in these beds and in this marriage, I was very poorly paid! I don't know, maybe there exists Something above us, but, so help me God, I paid very dearly for this Glembay transaction of mine! A bloody price! Terribly bloody! You yourself know who and what your father was! And all the charges that you totaled up against him in the room upstairs tonight, I watched all of that from behind the scenes for a full twenty years. Unscrupulous, hard, and horrible was this Glembay, and this man who was capable of stamping out a person's existence as if crushing a worm, this man became the father of my son! Oliver is his perfect duplicate! And everything that is so awfully dark in this child—that is my cross to bear! All right, the boys agreed to rob some brickyard cashier! My God, a piece of childishness that almost ended in blood. It's a question of puberty, and puberty is full of criminal impulses! But the worst crime is not that such a sixteen-year-old Glembay loads a hunting rifle to rob a cashier—that is undoubtedly horrid! The most horrible of all is that I knew it! Crime grew in that boy's blood continually and stubbornly for sixteen years, crime began the day when that child's heart began to beat within my womb! This Herr Glembay, the Privy Councilor: here lies the cause of crime and guilt! And you, Leone, you yourself know best what the Glembay blood means! And you see, in this twenty-year-long fear of mine, in my twenty years of panic before the horror of the Glembay blood, you have tonight accused me so terribly wrongly! And it hurts me, Leone, because it comes from you, just because of that! If I am guilty of something, I swear by the Holy Mother of God that I've bloodily atoned for it! (*Quietly cries to herself*)

LEONE: This is all obscure! My head aches and I'm starting to lose myself in all this. I came back here completely calm, all those stains that I felt for years because of my mother's desecrated memory had entirely evaporated, and I was completely calm! But, pardon me, all this that surrounds you here! This Oberleutnant, this confessor of yours, then the death of that pregnant woman, and that old woman trampled by horses, the whole manner in which those things were talked about in this house, you have to understand that it got on my nerves! I'd like to know how you would explain the case of that day-wage worker Skomrak?

BARONESS CASTELLI: (*With sincere sadness*) That death I did not want! He fell in love with me, my God, during sessions in the Philanthropic Office, a fantastic, high-strung soul! Poor little devil! Speaking of him, Leo, there's one favor I'd like to ask you! Tonight you spoke of some poems of his that you found on him! Could I have those poems for a minute? That would interest me!

LEONE: That would interest you? Here you are!

Extracts crumpled sheets of paper from his pocket and hands them to her. Baroness Castelli takes those crumpled sheets and leafs through them with interest. Pause. Leone observes her with great calm.

BARONESS CASTELLI: (*Leafing through the manuscript*) But this is not bad! The little one seems to have been talented! This is lovely! This is even very lovely! Listen how lovely it is! (*Reads monotonously and sadly*) "I go to my own funeral in autumn on a foggy twilight. Through the City, where people carry lies in their hearts, I carry a Blossom through the City! And that is that: I carry a Blossom through the City and that Blossom of mine glows like the phosphorus of a firefly! It is muddy, bright clouds die out in the distance. It is morning before daybreak, roosters flap their wings and cry: Everything is a shipwreck in the dark. I'm dying!" This is very lovely! Das ist sehr schön! (*She cries from aesthetic emotion, and wipes her tears. These are her first sincere tears of the morning.*) Poor little devil! He really hanged himself!

Sister Angelika enters.

ANGELIKA: Well, we have found the necktie, Charlotte. The servant will bring it! And the shoes also!

Several seconds behind Sister Angelika, enters the chamberlain carrying a pair of shoes and several neckties

CHAMBERLAIN: Herr Doktor, begging your pardon, please go to the telephone! The Trade Bank is calling you!

LEONE: Me? That must be a mistake!

CHAMBERLAIN: No, it's you they want, Herr Doktor. Trade Bank. Main office.

Leone leaves.

BARONESS CASTELLI: Merci, dear Baroness, thank you! You've done me a great favor! Johann, put the shoes on the gracious master's feet, would you? (*All three go to the alcove.*) This wide one, I think, is better! This one looks much more old-fashioned! That's it! This I'll do myself. Merci! I just want to get rid of this terrible necktie! He does look better now! (*She ties Glembay's necktie.*) Johann, look, take that scarf, over there on the armchair, and tie it around the Councilor's chin! It isn't nice to see the teeth! Over there, Johann, on the chair by the mirror.

They tie a silk scarf around Glembay's head. Baroness Castelli arranges it all with calm and dignity.

LEONE: (*Comes back even more nervous than earlier*) Baroness, the Trade Bank's general director is calling you on the phone!

BARONESS CASTELLI: Me? What is going on? Why does he need me? Tell him, please, that he cannot talk with me now! It's five o'clock in the morning!

LEONE: I don't know. It has to do with your current account at the Trade Bank.

BARONESS CASTELLI: My account at the Trade Bank? But I don't have any business relations with the Trade Bank.

LEONE: Your account at the Trade Bank is overdrawn by eight hundred and forty thousand.

BARONESS CASTELLI: (*Calmly and naively, but already on her way to the telephone*) Impossible! It is impossible! I have my account at the Viennese Disconto Italiana!

LEONE: I've no idea! Please! Go to see!

Baroness Castelli leaves, and the chamberlain follows her.

LEONE: So the old Bárbóczy woman made up that die Glembays sind Falschspieler und Mörder! And who tied that scarf around the old man?

ANGELIKA: Charlotte.

LEONE: That's awful! It looks as though he's suffering from a toothache! The most terrible thing about death is that on the one hand it's supernatural and on the other hand, comical! Death is one of the most ludicrous phenomena in civil society! Even on his deathbed a man must be shaved, manicured, trussed up. In a civil death, a man must not yawn! It's too stupid! (*Returns to his thoughts, which that sight had interrupted*) Well, then, it appears that this old gentleman forged the

Baroness's payment orders, that he signed her bills of exchange and moreover personally guaranteed those forged bills. The Trade Bank has not been able to talk with Vienna (interurban telephone interruptions) but telegraphic communication already suggests: a complete debacle! The Glembays are of course honorable men!

ANGELIKA: Leone, please don't feel offended, but that manner of yours strikes me as unusually brutal and strange. For as long as I have been in the house you have done nothing else than curse the Glembays. As though you were not a Glembay!

LEONE: From the first day I started to think, I've done nothing but fight against the Glembay within myself! That is what is most terrible about my own fate: I am a pure, genuine, hundred percent Glembay! All my hatred for the Glembays is nothing else than hatred for myself. In the Glembays I see myself as in a mirror!

ANGELIKA: (*Shyly, but with her serene firmness, penetratingly and meaningfully*) You love paradoxes, and you distort everything. I'm afraid of your jokes, but please listen: years of experience have convinced me that there is indeed a great deal of unexpressed and gentle wisdom in the maxim "love your neighbor as yourself"! And to be able to become a Christian, one must therefore first of all love oneself!

LEONE: Beatrice, pardon me, be so kind and remove that scarf! It's frightful how monstrous it looks!

ANGELIKA: That must stay in place! The jaws are still soft! (*She steps up to the corpse and feels his lower jaw with her fingers.*)

LEONE: It reminds me of one of Daumier's caricatures: Daumier's philistines always wear napkins tied in that way!

ANGELIKA: And an open mouth showing the teeth is much uglier still! (*She has removed the scarf, and is feeling the lower jaw which has already grown stiff. Outside, morning bells ring in the distance.*) He is completely cold. How quickly a man grows cold, and how shortsightedly he thinks that he will live forever! (*Reties the scarf around the corpse's head, and then washes her hands*)

LEONE: I would like to know what forces you to go about the world washing and touching corpses like this! What sort of a mania is it that compels you to love yourself in such a Christian manner?

ANGELIKA: That would be a long and sad story, Leone. Let it go! I'm sorry! And besides, I think it would be best for you to lie down! It's morning! I'll go to my room now, here everything is finished and in order! Good-bye, Leone! (*She gives him her hand, quietly and calmly*)

LEONE: (*Holding Angelika's hand in his*) Beatrice, why are you avoiding me so much all this time? I've been looking at you these five days as one looks at paintings in churches, and your eyes are closed; last night down there under your portrait was the first time I caught your eyes! Why are you avoiding me? Why do you move away from me? Do you believe me when I tell you that I would have left on the first day if I hadn't found you here amid all this! Maybe it's stupid of me to tell you all this, but it's also just as unintelligent of you to be edging away! This Dominican silhouette of yours is for me the only touch of brightness in this Glembayesque squalor! In this chlorine and morphine, among these horrible masks around us, I feel a need for you as the person you are. Beatrice, I need someone in this inferno, and you are so conventional! That is not noble of you! (*He suddenly releases her hand, and starts to pace around the room, restlessly and nervously.*) My head aches so terribly, my whole insides are rising up as if I've eaten rotten meat! I'm sweating—like ice—as if I'm getting foggy, as if I'm about to faint! (*Staggers, and loses his balance*)

ANGELIKA: It would be best for you to lie down! It's all from the nerves! Here, lie down here for two or three minutes, calm down, and then you can go to get some proper sleep! It's morning! It's dawning already!

She takes two pillows from an armchair and like an expert nurse sets them one on top of the other on a sofa, then comes up to Leone like a true Sister of Mercy and, with an infinitely gentle caress, leads him to the sofa as though he were a patient.

LEONE: (*Giving himself up to her self-sacrificing tenderness like a sick child*) I don't feel well, Beatrice! A nervous pulse, a nervous heart—here, a migraine, I can barely hold myself together. Thank you.

He lies down, barely conscious, and breathes with difficulty. First birds in the garden. Morning in the window's quadrangle. Angelika pours him a glass of water, dips a bandana in eau de cologne and places a compress on his forehead, feels his pulse. Birds are chirping.

LEONE: Your hand is as cold as camphor! Your Holbeinesque hand, Beatrice! Oh, how hard it all is!

ANGELIKA: It's best not to think about it all!

LEONE: I can't! It's all still a panic inside me! (*As though seeing living images in a delirium*) One time I fell from a horse at a gallop, my foot got caught in a stirrup and the horse dragged me behind along the road for I guess a hundred meters. Some women were desperately shouting, I heard those women's voices clearly even later in the hospital, with my clavicles broken, I felt that gallop long long afterward, that horse's black diabolic power, and listened to those women shout: the women shouted all through the nights, for a long, long time! This is all still a gallop, they're shouting still—it's an uproar! (*She gives him a glass of water and he thirstily drains it.*) I got into a life-or-death fight with that man! And what happened? After sixteen years of getting ready for that fight, I didn't know what to say to him! I talked with him as if with a stranger, nothing but vulgar stupidities! He couldn't understand a single word I said! And on top of that he hit me in the teeth with his fist and drew a liter of my blood! This was the whole result: my bloody mouth! And worst of all—in all that uproar, I am completely, thoroughly empty! I never felt how absurd it all was as I do right now! (*Heaves a nervous sigh, on the edge of a breakdown*)

ANGELIKA: (*She has taken a chair and sits down facing him, taking one of his hands in both of hers.*) Everything will be all right, Leone!

LEONE: Nothing will be all right! You know, Beatrice, I destroyed this man here! I wanted to knock down a hard, enormous Glembay, and that over there was one desperate wretch facing bankruptcy! A pitiful scarecrow! I was fighting a fiction! (*Pause. Leone, drawing short, agitated breaths, his mouth dry as in a fever, rapidly and nervously, but not loudly*) All of this is criminal! Glembay-style criminal! I was still studying irregular Greek verbs when I experienced criminality for the first time! A windstorm had blown up, pulling up trees by the roots, and we boys, on a botanical excursion, with a basket for plants and a butterfly net, took shelter inside an inn, in a forest near a quarry. And there in the darkness, in a stinking inn, by the oil lamp, some black and shabby charcoal-makers were saying that someone's blood ought to be spilled! "Ought to kill him!"—is how one of them put it. I ran off into the darkness as if in a frenzy, driven by a terrible fear, into the night, through howling wind and thunder and lightning, shouting with fear and running like mad! That was the first time I really experienced that people kill each other! In those days I roamed through the world with a butterfly net in hand and a safflower bulb! And today I'm old and stupid, today I'm sick, and I still live in a bloody inn! Oh, if I could escape from all this! (*Bells in the city. Birds. Day is growing.*) There is no way out of this. The old Bárbóczy woman was right: the Glembays are murderers! That Glembay from Varaždin, who's holding the Remetinec church in his hand, in the Vinica forest he robbed and killed a goldsmith from Kranj who was delivering gold for the Varaždin churches! I heard it from one of the coachmen who'd been serving the Glembays since the time of the late Ferdinand!

ANGELIKA: That's rumor and myth! There isn't any foundation to it!

LEONE: Oh, dear Lord God, why do you always think about some foundations! Nothing ever has a foundation! I heard it from a coachman and throughout my whole childhood this has been for me the most real reality of all to be found in this whole house! How many times I saw that man from Varaždin walking through his house with a bloody knife in hand! He usually came on winter nights, with the wind in the chimney! He'd cross the main staircase into the red salon, and once I met him in my late mother's room, but he quickly hid under the piano! He held a big kitchen knife in hand, thoroughly bloody, and then he suddenly vanished. And tonight, Beatrice, tonight he's come to this house again! He is here, he's waiting somewhere behind the wardrobe!

ANGELIKA: Dear Leone, calm down; it's your nerves! Let Dr. Altmann give you some sleeping pills—let me call him, he's downstairs drinking tea with Fabriczy.

LEONE: But it's got nothing to do with nerves! Thank you, I don't need anything. It's got nothing to do with nerves! It's good that you haven't yet called me überspannt! It's the truth! That Glembay from Varaždin built a golden Baroque altar in the Remetinec parish church for the salvation of his soul, but his soul wasn't saved! You see, look at that Glembay over there! Everybody said his lower jaw had a Velázquez-type outline, when actually it was the criminality in him: bestial criminality! That one was a dreadful predatory beast! And my incomprehensible hatred for that man, that foul hatred I felt for him from the first day when I began to think for myself, that is the Glembay, the criminal in me! That is my Glembay blood! Fine, I acknowledge, it is paranoia, it is not healthy, yet this filthy, muddy, bottomless something has been dominating me for years. I've been carrying it around with me like my own insides! I've wanted to explain rationally this terrible instinct inside me! Mama's death struck me at the time as a sufficiently reasonable motive for this subconscious hatred. From that moment I had enough reasons to hate him consciously: as my mother's murderer! But in fact I bit into him like one jackal biting another: it was the Glembay blood biting us from within!

ANGELIKA: Leone, in God's name, I beg you, Leone, be sensible . . .

LEONE: That is the way it all is, that is precisely the way it is! And there is only one solution: either to gnaw at oneself like a jackal, or . . .

ANGELIKA: Or?

LEONE: Or to kill oneself!

ANGELIKA: Leone!

LEONE: Yes, only that! You see, for years I've been dreading the criminality that broke out last night. Like a jaguar with a tail between its legs, I've been circling around this secret of mine. I did not come to this house for eleven years out of a fear of crime, and when one day I turned up here after all, I smelled the blood right away. In this fog, among these corpses, I instinctively feared something, and yet I perversely enjoyed the feeling that a convenient opportunity would present itself. And when an opportunity indeed very conveniently presented itself, instead of moving away from the abyss, I jumped around just like an unintelligent monkey until the whole thing came crashing down! Even in the last second it was clear to me that it would end badly, but passion was stronger than reason! The Glembay imperative—that is what conquered me, and I made myself filthy with my own blood. It's all chaos, my dear Beatrice! It's all so horrible! (*Without tears and without sobbing, his outburst is that of a man who thinks about himself cruelly and hopelessly.*)

ANGELIKA: (*Caresses him warmly and compassionately as though he were a sick child*) No, Leone, everything is not so black. To see and know that you lack the ability to do something against it all, that would be dreadful and hopeless. But to look at everything clearly and reasonably, that is not terrible at all. That means having power, inner, higher power, to resist all these dark urges: that means sensing the possibility of salvation. And after all, you, with your great bright talent, with your superior intelligence, Leone, you have no reason at all . . .

He is gratefully kissing her hands. He places her hands on his forehead, slowly gets up, kneels humbly and devoutly before Angelika, and remains on his knees.

LEONE: Oh, how good you are, Beatrice! The only possible light in all this would be someone's pure hand on my dark headache! Under the magnet of someone's ethical intelligence I could still wash all this away from myself, in one such imaginary otherworldly harmony I could still find my raison d'être, and my talent could clarify itself, confirm itself, I could work, create, enjoy, heal myself—to break out of this . . .

At that moment Baroness Castelli enters. Her entrance is so furious that Leone remains kneeling in front of Angelika, losing all orientation. The Baroness is utterly deranged, her hair is disheveled, her movements are abnormal, she is beside herself to such an extent that at first she gives the impression of a madwoman. She is squealing with despair and rage.

BARONESS CASTELLI: Damn the hour when I met this son of a bitch! The miserable impostor! My hard-earned money, my bloody suffering, that old impostor swine robbed me! The whole city is telephoning left and right, I've been robbed, why this is horrible, this is unbelievable, I'm about to lose my mind, this is horrendous—miserable scoundrel, Schuft, criminal . . .

LEONE: (*Has gotten up and is looking at this furious woman*) Please, behave decently! What sort of conduct is this! You're not alone in the room!

BARONESS CASTELLI: Is that so? And so somebody like you is going to tell me how to behave? That old man robbed me, and now you will insult me? Not only at the Industrial Bank but also at the Crédit Lyonnais, and at the Wiener Allgemeine, he robbed me on all sides! I've been robbed, don't you understand? This old swine has robbed me! You are swine and scum, that's what you are! Is this the behavior worthy of a nun? That's how a streetwalker behaves, not a nun! This is not a whorehouse! I will not allow a swine like you to talk to me like this!

ANGELIKA: Charlotte, for the love of God, calm down, Charlotte!

BARONESS CASTELLI: What've I still got to lose? I've been robbed and plundered. They stole my money that I sweated blood to earn! What are you playing a saint here for? As if everyone didn't know that you're having sex with Cardinal Montenuovo—get out of my sight, please!

LEONE: (*With raised voice*) Not a word more! Get out!

BARONESS CASTELLI: What? You want to throw me out? And who are you in this house? This house is my property, I'm the master here! Not only would you rob me but throw me out too? Because I won't let you, in front of this dead scoundrel, turn this corpse's room into a brothel? Please go to some hot-sheet Stundenhotel—but not here.

The word Stundenhotel opens Leone's eyes. From this moment on he sees.

LEONE: Stundenhotel, of course: obviously. For seventeen years I clearly saw you as you are, but this morning you squirted ink around yourself, you lost yourself in the dark like an octopus. You concealed your face for fear of consequences! Like a chicken before a hawk, you took refuge in your lies! A parrot, an elegant parrot! Everything you told me here this morning, those were my own words from nights past: and I believed what I myself had said. (*He moves toward her.*)

The Glembays | 213

BARONESS CASTELLI: What do you want from me? The old man robbed me, foully robbed me. He pawned all my cash . . .

LEONE: Everything you'd been stealing from him for years—he took it back! But we have other scores: a person who comes directly from a hotel that's a brothel, such a person must now keep quiet here! Do you understand me! From that Persian Kerman till today you've been continuously stealing in this house! Here, you have to keep quiet. Do you understand me?

BARONESS CASTELLI: I have to keep quiet? I caught you here red-handed with this fake saint! Here in front of your dead father, oh, lovely swine you are, all of you together! Murderers and swindlers, old Bárbóczy said it right: Mörder und Falschspieler!

LEONE: (*Moves toward her, Angelika tries to hold him back but he resolutely pushes her away. He snatches up the scissors from the table, and then everything happens very tensely and very fast.*) Not another word!

BARONESS CASTELLI: What do you want from me? Let me go! Let me go, you murderer!

Leone tries to grab her, but she shrieks and, screaming madly, runs instinctively to the door and out. Leone stiffens for a moment, then rushes insanely after her. There are sounds of doors banging, glass breaking, Charlotte screams "Hilfe! Hilfe! Help!" and then silence. After a pause, voices are heard. Once again, there is banging of doors, accompanied by an uproar. Voices. Chamberlain enters running, looks madly around as though he had lost something, and grabs Dr. Altmann's medical equipment from the table.

CHAMBERLAIN: Herr Doktor's butchered the Baroness! (*Runs out*)

Angelika stands motionless throughout like a figure in a wax museum. Birds are chirping.

[CURTAIN]

Glossary

Aber schnell!: But fast! [German]

Ad acta: Consider the matter closed. [Latin]

Aix-les-Bains: A spa town in southeastern France, on the shores of Lake Bourget.

Also, auf Wiedersehen: So, good-bye. [German]

Amice: Vocative case of amicus, friend. [Latin]

Amore, amore, amore!: Love, love, love! [Italian]

Anamnesis, status praesens: Medical case history, present condition. [Latin]

Archimandrite: Eastern Orthodox priest.

Argumentum ad hominem: Attempt to clinch an argument through a personal attack. [Latin]

Armee-Kommando: Military command of the Austro-Hungarian army, known by the acronym A.K. [German]. The initials of the Supreme Military Command (Armee-Oberkommando) were A.O.K. and were mockingly glossed as *Alle ohne köpfe*—all without heads.

Au courant: Fully informed, knowledgeable, up-to-date. [French]

Axelrode, Maximilian: A fictitious character loosely based on Count Galeazzo von Thun und Hohenstein, an Austrian nobleman who was Grand Master of the Sovereign Military Order of Malta from 1905 to 1931 (see Sovereign Order of Malta, below). His full title was "His Most Eminent Highness Fra' Galeazzo von Thun und Hohenstein,

Prince and Grand Master of the Sovereign Military Hospitaller Order of St. John of Jerusalem, of Rhodes and of Malta, Most Humble Guardian of the Poor of Jesus Christ."

Az apád istennét! Csönd!: By your father's god! Shut up! [Hungarian]

Az atya úr istennét, ennek a Ruszkinak! Ruszki!: By lord god the father, this Russky! Russky! [Hungarian]

Badalić: Hugo Badalić, a late nineteenth-century Croatian writer.

Bárbóczy: Angelika Bárbóczy, a noblewoman who married into the Glembay family and came to loathe them. Although no longer alive by the time the drama opens, her damning judgment, "Die Glembays sind Mörder und Falschspieler" (The Glembays are murderers and swindlers), constitutes both the play's leitmotif and its most famous line.

Baron Trenk: A popular 1908 operetta by Croatian composer Srećko Albini.

Beatrice: Italian form of Beatrix, Angelika's birth name. Leone's use of this name calls to mind Dante Alighieri's beloved Beatrice, and suggests that Leone is in love with his brother's widow. Following the events described in *The Glembays*, Leone will be committed to a psychiatric hospital, and Angelika will leave the Dominican Order. Once Leone is released, the two will marry.

Bedny, Demyan: Pen name of Yefim Alekseevich Pridvorov, a Soviet Ukrainian poet, Bolshevik and satirist.

B-H: Bosnia and Herzegovina.

Bitte: Please. [German]

Bon vivants: Those who indulge in luxurious living.

Brusilov: Aleksei Alekseevich Brusilov, Russian Tsarist general, initiator of a successful 1916 offensive. After the Revolution, he sided with the Red Army.

Büchner: Ludwig Büchner, nineteenth-century German philosopher, physiologist, and physician, exponent of scientific materialism.

Chapeau claque: A collapsible top hat that can be folded flat for storage. [French]

Chevalier de Justice: Knight of Justice, a title signifying admission to the highest level of membership in the Sovereign Order of Malta (see below).

Condottieri: Mercenaries [Italian, from *condotta*, "contract"].

Corneille: Pierre Corneille, seventeenth-century French playwright, author of the tragicomedy *Le Cid*.

Cvetan, Lisak, Rosy: Affectionate names given to domestic animals such as horses and cows.

Danke schön: Thank you very much. [German]

Das ist noch verständlich!: This is still understandable! [German]

Daumier: Honoré Daumier, nineteenth-century French printmaker, caricaturist, painter, and sculptor.

Die Meistersinger: *The Mastersingers of Nuremburg*, an 1867 opera by Richard Wagner.

Einz: A variation of the card game blackjack. Its name comes from German slang for "one" (eins).

Eis, schnell Eis, bringen sie Eis!: Ice, quick, ice, bring ice! [German]

Et alteram partem: Accusative case for "the other party too." [Latin]

Euler: Leonhard Euler, eighteenth-century Swiss mathematician, physicist, astronomer, logician, and engineer.

Ex privata: On one's own initiative. [Latin]

Fillér: Smallest unit of Austro-Hungarian currency, one hundredth of a crown [Hungarian]. In the Austrian portion of the Habsburg Monarchy, known as Heller. [German]

Finissons: Let us finish, let's end this. [French]

Fra' Giovanni Battista Ceschi a Santa Croce: 74th Grand Master of the Sovereign Order of Malta (see below), 1879 to 1905.

Franz Josef: Franz Joseph I of Austria, a Habsburg dynasty monarch who was emperor of Austria and king of Hungary from 1867 until 1916.

Freiherr: Baron. [German]

Galicia: A petroleum-rich rural province of Austria-Hungary, located in East Central Europe (presently southeastern Poland and western Ukraine). During the First World War a scene of prolonged and heavy fighting between the Central Powers (Austro-Hungarian Empire and Imperial Germany) and Tsarist Russia.

Garibaldi: Giuseppe Garibaldi, Italian revolutionary and nationalist, fought in the 1848 Revolution and in Italy's ultimately successful wars of independence from Austrian rule.

Général de charge: A ceremonial trumpet flourish to announce the arrival of a high-ranking general in the Austro-Hungarian army [French].

Golgotha: Calvary, "place of the skull" outside ancient Jerusalem's walls where Jesus is said to have been crucified.

Gospodi!: Lord! [Russian]

Gott: God. [German]

Gott erhalte!: God save! Opening words of the Austrian imperial hymn composed by Josef Haydn: "Gott erhalte, Gott beschütze Unsern Kaiser, unser Land!" (God save, God protect, our Emperor and our home!). (A variation on the English anthem "God Save the King"; Haydn may have derived its melody from a Croatian folksong.)

Gottfried of Bouillon: Godfrey of Bouillon, eleventh-century knight, one of the leaders of the First Crusade; he perished in Jerusalem.

Grand Priory: A central organizational unit in the Supreme Order of Malta (see below).

Green Cadre: Deserters from the wartime Austro-Hungarian army who took refuge in forests. As rebels against war and economic hardship, they enjoyed considerable sympathy from villagers who often supplied them with food and clothing. Green Cadre also lived by robbery, usually targeting the rich. By 1917 their numbers had reached around 20,000. In Croatian: Zeleni kader.

Guardsman: *Domobran* [Croatian], meaning home guard or home defender, a deceptive term designating Croatian soldiers serving in the army of the late Habsburg Empire. As members of the Imperial Royal Hungaro-Croatian Home Guard, the *Domobran* conscripts essentially belonged to a branch of the Hungarian Army, and even the name they bore was a direct translation of the Hungarian term for its military, *honvéd* (home guard).

Gubec, Matija: Croatian peasant and revolutionary, a serf who was elected leader of a large-scale Croatian and Slovenian anti-feudal revolt of 1573. The peasants' uprising, provoked by brutal living conditions that prevailed under the rule of domestic and foreign nobility, aimed at constructing an egalitarian cooperative commonwealth. After the peasants' defeat at the Battle of Stubica, Gubec was captured and taken to Zagreb, where according to legend he was publicly tortured and executed at about age thirty-five. Thousands of peasants died during the revolt, and many of the captives were subsequently hanged or maimed. Gubec's fame as Croatia's greatest national hero has lived on: a unit in the Russian Revolution, another in the Spanish Civil War, and a Partisan (anti-fascist guerrilla) brigade in the Second World War all bore his name. Numerous schools, streets, cultural societies, folk ensembles, and sports teams have also been named after him. The peasants' rebellion of 1573 has inspired novelists, poets, sculptors, painters, filmmakers, and composers—including creators of a rock opera. One of the best known artistic representations of Gubec and the uprising he led is Antun Augustinčić's powerful sculpture *Monument to the Peasants' Revolt and Matija Gubec*. This insurrection and several others are also commemorated by the Slovenian sculptor Stojan Batič.

Harambašić: August Harambašić, a late nineteenth- and early twentieth-century Croatian writer.

Herr Doktor: Doctor (literally: Gentleman Doctor). [German]

Hilfe!: Help! [German]

Holbein: Hans Holbein the Younger, German and Swiss artist and printmaker, considered one of the greatest portraitists of the sixteenth century.

Honvéd: Home Guard [Hungarian]. A national self-defense force organized by Kossuth (see below) in 1848 during his efforts to win Hungarian independence from the Austrian empire, the Honvéd remains the name of Hungary's army. A similar term—Landwehr—was used by Austria, Germany, and Switzerland.

Hum, Bosnia, Flor: Three brands of cigarettes.

Hungaro-Croatian Agreement of 1868: Also known as the Hungaro-Croatian Compromise (or Settlement), it prevented Croatia from forming a distinct political entity within the empire and compelled it to remain linked to Hungary. The people of Croatia were in effect subjected to a triple hegemony inside the imperial realm of the Croatian, Hungarian, and Austrian politicians and potentates. In Croatian: Madžarsko-hrvatska nagodba od godine 1868.

Hussites: Followers of the early fifteenthth-century Czech Catholic priest and reformer Jan Hus, who was burned at the stake for alleged heresy.

Ihre kaiserliche Hoheit denkt nach: Her Imperial Highness is thinking. [German]

Il trionfo delle morte: The triumph of death. [Italian]

Illustrated: *Ilustrovani list*, a Zagreb weekly newspaper from the First World War–era that regularly carried photographs of decorated and promoted officers. Krleža describes this opportunist tabloid as "a petty-bourgeois advertisement for death."

Illustrissime: Vocative case of illustrissimus, the illustrious one. Medieval form of address, also a feudal title denoting high nobility. [Latin]

Imprimatur: An official declaration of approval. Literally: Let it be printed. [Latin]

Irredenta: Literally, "unredeemed" [Italian]. Here pertaining to Italian Irredentism, a nationalist movement of the late nineteenth and early twentieth centuries that sought to unify all ethnically Italian peoples. It supported annexing sections of the Austro-Hungarian Empire that were inhabited by an Italian majority, but also some whose majority was in fact Slavic.

Ist das aber wirklich dumm! Ist das dumm dieses 'peri!' Was ist das, du, dieses—peri?": This is truly stupid! This "peri" is stupid. You, what is this "peri?" [German] ("Peri" is the Croatian imperative form of the verb "to wash.")

Išten: God. In Hungarian, Isten, here with Croatian pronunciation and spelling.

Jacobin: A revolutionary radical, after a political club formed in 1789 during the French Revolution, whose membership would grow to half a million or more.

Jawohl: Yes indeed, yes sir. [German]

Jelačić: Josip Jelačić, nineteenth-century Croatian viceroy whose troops, fighting for Austria, helped prevent Hungary's bid for independence.

Johannine (Johanniter): Pertaining to Saint John (see below).

Kaiserjäger: Imperial hunter [German]. Member of an elite alpine unit in the Austro-Hungarian army, recruited from mountainous regions. The Kaiserjägers' emblem was a stylized tin edelweiss worn on caps and collars.

Kalimavkion: a stiff cylindrical head covering worn by Orthodox Christian clergymen.

Kingdom of Serbs, Croats and Slovenes: Formed in 1918, the kingdom was from the outset popularly known as Yugoslavia, though it was officially so renamed only in 1929. The Yugoslav kingdom disintegrated in the course of the Second World War, and was replaced in 1945 by the Federal People's Republic of Yugoslavia (which would become the Socialist Federal Republic of Yugoslavia).

Kolo: Circle, wheel [Serbo-Croatian]. A collective folk dance often performed in a circle by a group of dancers who may be holding each other around the waist or by the hands. Traditionally popular in Croatia, Serbia, and Bosnia.

Kossuth: Lajos Kossuth, a leader of the Hungarian Revolution of 1848, who tried to win the country's independence from Habsburg rule.

Kozarac: Josip Kozarac, a late nineteenth- and early twentieth-century Croatian writer. His best known novel is *Dead Capital* (*Mrtvi kapitali*, 1890).

Küss' die Hand: I kiss your hand. [German]

"La Machicha": A lively and popular early twentieth-century song composed by Charles Borel-Clerc.

Lächerlich: Ridiculous, absurd. [German]

Lenin: Nom de guerre of Vladimir Ilyich Ulyanov, a Russian Marxist revolutionary, principal leader of the 1917 October Revolution. Strongly opposed First World War which he considered a predatory imperialist conflict of no benefit to ordinary people: "Picture to yourselves a slave-owner who owns 100 slaves warring against a slave-owner who owns 200 slaves for a more 'just' distribution of

Glossary | 223

slaves." Shortly after the Revolution, Lenin withdrew Russia from the war. Miroslav Krleža, though hostile to Stalin, retained his admiration for Lenin throughout his life.

Levorver: A mispronunciation of revolver.

Lieb' Vaterland, magst ruhig sein: Dear fatherland, put your mind at rest. Opening words of "Die Wacht am Rhein" (The Watch/Guard on the Rhine), a German patriotic anthem.

Luftgewehr: Air rifle. [German]

Luogotenente: Lieutenant. [Italian]

Mamma mia!: Mother! [Italian]

Mannlicher: A bolt-action military rifle designed by German engineer Ferdinand Ritter von Mannlicher; widely used by the Austro-Hungarian Army throughout the First World War.

M'avez-vous compris?: Have you understood me? [French]

May First: International Workers' Day, a socialist holiday that originated in the United States.

Mein lieber Gott: My dear God. [German]

Merci: Thank you. [French]

"*Mert arról én nem tehetek*": "What can I do, when I love you," a Hungarian popular song.

Micsoda: What. [Hungarian]

Minderwertig: Inferior. [German]

Molière: Stage name of Jean-Baptiste Poquelin, seventeenth-century French satirical playwright and actor.

Mondscheinsonate: German title of the "Moonlight Sonata," Beethoven's Piano Sonata No. 14 in C-sharp Minor "Quasi una fantasia."

Munch: Edvard Munch, Norwegian expressionist painter.

Mussorgsky: Modest Mussorgsky, a nineteenth-century Russian Romantic composer.

Muzhik: A Russian peasant.

Nadásdy hussars: Flamboyantly uniformed light cavalry horsemen belonging or attached to a prominent Hungarian aristocratic family.

National Guardsmen: see Guardsman.

Natura non facit saltus: Nature does not jump. [Latin]

Nécessaire: Overnight bag or case. [French]

No hát, Istenem!: Why, good lord! [Hungarian]

No ja, ganz natürlich: Well yes, quite naturally. [German]

Nota bene: Note well, take notice. [Latin and Italian]

Nu este permis a ščipi per podele!: Spitting on the floor is not allowed! [Romanian]

Nur einen Moment, bitte schön: Just one moment, please. [German]

Oberleutnant: Senior Lieutenant [German], comparable to First Lieutenant.

Olympischen Perspektive: Olympian perspective. [German]

Pannonia: Ancient province of the Roman Empire, covering present-day western Hungary and parts of Austria, Croatia, Serbia, Slovenia, Slovakia, and Bosnia and Herzegovina.

Para-bolum: A nonexistent word, the use of which attests to the platoon sergeant's ignorance. He is thinking of Parabellum, a semiautomatic pistol popularly known after its German inventor as the Luger.

Parlez plus bas, parce que les murs ont des oreilles!: Speak more quietly, because the walls have ears! [French]

Per aspera ad astra!: Through the thorns to the stars! [Latin]

Pompes funèbres: Funeral rites. [French]

Porca Madonna io parlo Italiano!: Damn it Madonna, I speak Italian! [Italian]

Préférence: East European card game. [French]

Pro Fide: For Faith. [Latin]

Quasi una fantasia: Almost a fantasy [Italian], part of the title of Beethoven's Piano Sonata No. 14, popularly known as the "Moonlight Sonata."

Quieta non movere: Do not move settled things, i.e., don't rock the boat, let well enough alone. [Latin]

Raison d'être: Reason for existence. [French]

Riz Abadie: A brand of rolling papers for cigarettes, originally from France.

Saint István: First Christian king of Hungary, ruled in early eleventh century, canonized late in the same century. Also known as Saint Stephen.

Saint John: John the Baptist, patron saint of a monastic and military order of knights who called themselves the Hospitallers of St. John of Jerusalem. See: Sovereign Order of Malta.

Salon d'Automne: Autumn Salon [French], an annual art exhibition held in Paris.

Sans-culotte: A revolutionary. Sans-cullotes (French for "without breeches") were those citizens of late eighteenth-century France who, too poor to wear fashionable silk knee-breeches, wore ordinary trousers. Many of them became radicalized and took part in the Revolution of 1789.

Santa Maria Latina: A guesthouse built in Jerusalem in the late eleventh century that later became a hospital for treating pilgrims. Associated with Hospitallers of St. John of Jerusalem. See: Sovereign Order of Malta.

Sauve-qui-peut!: Save yourself, anyone who can! [French]

Schnapps: A type of alcoholic beverage distilled from fermented fruit.

Schuft: Scoundrel, villain. [German]

Second Empire: Here the term refers to the Second French Empire, 1852–1870.

Servus: Hello, good-bye, at your service. [Latin]

Sovereign Order of Malta: A religious and military brotherhood originating in the eleventh century. Its early members—known as the Hospitallers of St. John of Jerusalem—built a hospital in Jerusalem to care for sick or injured pilgrims. Knights Hospitallers became one of the most powerful armed Christian groups in Palestine during the twelfth century. Expelled from Palestine by Muslim armies in the late thirteenth century, the knights occupied the island of Rhodes from the early fourteenth to the mid-sixteenth century. Defeated by the Turks, the surviving knights moved to the island of Malta which they held until being dispersed by Napoleon at the close of the eighteenth century. The Order of Malta, now headquartered in Rome, comprises over 12,500 Knights and Dames, and carries out medical and humanitarian missions in dozens of countries, from Afghanistan to Zimbabwe.

Stundenhotel: Hourly hotel, where rooms are rented for sexual encounters. [German]

Syrmia: A fertile region of the Pannonian Plain, shared by Croatia and Serbia. (Srijem in Croatian, Srem in Serbian.) Formerly a Roman province called Sirmium.

Szerbusz: Hallo. [Hungarian]

Šči rumunješči?: Do you speak Romanian? [Romanian]

Šenoa: August Šenoa, a renowned and still popular nineteenth-century Croatian writer. One of his novels, *Peasants' Revolt* (*Seljačka buna*, 1877), is about the 1573 rebellion led by Matija Gubec.

Te! Mi az?: You! What does that mean? [Hungarian]

Trecento: Three hundred, short for *mille trecento* (1,300), signifies the 1300s, i.e., the fourteenth century. [Italian]

Triune Kingdom: A Croatian entity within the Austro-Hungarian Empire. (In Croatian: Trojedna kraljevina). Also known as the Kingdom of Croatia, Dalmatia and Slavonia.

Ultima ratio: Conclusive argument. [Latin]

Um Gottes Willen: For God's sake [German]; similar to *Um Gottes Christi Willen*, For Christ's sake.

Umiráju, umiráju, gospodi, umiráju: I'm dying, I'm dying, Lord, I'm dying. [Russian]

Und einen Schwarzen!: And one black (coffee)! [German]

Überspannt: Hypertense, high-strung, overexcited. [German]

Velázquez: Diego Velázquez, a seventeenth-century Spanish painter.

Vendée: A province in western France whose conservative peasants revolted against the Revolutionary government in 1793.

Verdienstkreuz: Cross of Merit, Austrian decoration awarded to officers for distinguished service.

Villány: A town in southern Hungary that is famous for its wine.

Villiers de l'Isle-Adam: A French aristocratic family whose members include Philippe, a sixteenth-century Grand Master of the Sovereign Military Order of Malta, and Auguste, a great nineteenth-century Symbolist writer.

Weltanschauung: Worldview, outlook on life. [German]

Zagorje: Rural region to the north of Zagreb, Croatia, characterized by rolling hills, forests, villages and vineyards; it extends west into Slovenia. Scene of the great peasant uprising of 1573 centered on the village of Stubica and led by Matija Gubec.

Works by Krleža in English

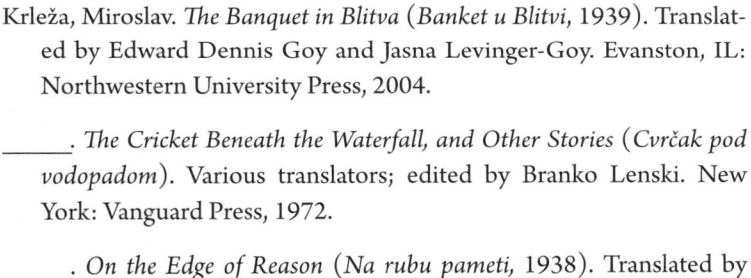

Krleža, Miroslav. *The Banquet in Blitva* (*Banket u Blitvi*, 1939). Translated by Edward Dennis Goy and Jasna Levinger-Goy. Evanston, IL: Northwestern University Press, 2004.

———. *The Cricket Beneath the Waterfall, and Other Stories* (*Cvrčak pod vodopadom*). Various translators; edited by Branko Lenski. New York: Vanguard Press, 1972.

———. *On the Edge of Reason* (*Na rubu pameti*, 1938). Translated by Zora Depolo. New York: New Directions, 1995.

———. *The Return of Philip Latinowitz* (*Povratak Filipa Latinovitza*, 1932). Translated by Zora Depolo. Evanston, IL: Northwestern University Press, 1995.